MAY 12 04			

Emotion
Inhibition
and Health

Emotion Inhibition and Health

edited by
Harald C. Traue and James W. Pennebaker

 Hogrefe & Huber Publishers
Seattle • Toronto • Göttingen • Bern

EDITORS

Harald C. Traue
Abteilung für Medizinische Psychologie
Universität Ulm
Hochsträß 8
7900 Ulm

James W. Pennebaker
Departement of Psychology
Southern Methodist University
Dallas, TX 75275

Library of Congress Cataloging-in-Publication Data
is available via the Library of Congress Marc Database under the
LC Catalog Card Number 92-074345

Canadian Cataloguing in Publication Data
Main entry under title:
Emotion, inhibition and health
ISBN 0-88937-060-5

2. Repression (Psychology).   2. Inhibition.
3. Psychophysiology.   I. Traue, Harald C., 1950–
II. Pennebaker, James W.

BF175.5.R44E58 1992   152.4   C92-095238-0

Umschlagsgraphik: Bernhard Jäger, geb. 1935, 6000 Frankfurt, Mathildenstraße 1B,
            Ausschnitt aus einer größeren Graphik ohne Titel, 1989.

ISBN 0-88937-060-5
Hogrefe & Huber Publishers, Seattle • Toronto • Göttingen • Bern

ISBN 3-8017-0437-8
Hogrefe • Verlag für Psychologie, Göttingen • Bern • Toronto • Seattle

Set by Wallstein-Verlag GmbH, D-3400 Göttingen.
Printed and bound by Diederische Universitätsdruckerei
W. Fr. Kaestner GmbH & Co. KG, D-3400 Göttingen-Rosdorf.
Printed in Germany on acid-fee paper.

Contents

Contributors

Jens B. Asendorpf	Max Planck Institute for Psychological Research, München, Germany
Ross Buck	University of Connecticut, Storrs, Connecticut, USA
Clayton Culver	New School for Social Research, New York, USA
Wolfgang Fiegenbaum	Christoph-Dornier-Foundation for Clinical Psychology, Marburg, Germany
Irmela Florin	Philipps University, Marburg, Germany
Margit Gramer	University of Graz, Graz, Austria
Jutta Hermanns	Philipps University, Marburg, Germany
Hans Hufnagel	University of Saarland, Saarbrücken, Germany
Helmuth P. Huber	University of Graz, Graz, Austria
Rainer Krause	University of Saarland, Saarbrücken, Germany
Melissa Jenkins	Philipps University, Marburg, Germany
Henri Laborit	Laboratoire D'Eutonologie, Hopital Boucicaut, Paris, France
Carol Z. Malatesta	Long Island University, Brooklyn, USA
Alison Michael	University of Dublin, Dublin, Ireland
James W. Pennebaker	Southern Methodist University, Dallas, USA
Rudolf Schöbinger	Philipps University, Marburg, Germany
Evelyne Steimer-Krause	University of Saarland, Saarbrücken, Germany
Lydia Temoshok	Henry M. Jackson Foundation, Behavioral Medicine HIV Research Program, Rockville, Maryland, USA
Harald C. Traue	University of Ulm, Ulm, Germany
Günter Wagner	University of Saarland, Saarbrücken, Germany
Heike Winter	Philipps University, Marburg, Germany

It is dangerous to supress emotions. People who continuously suppress their feelings will break.

Sinéad O'Connor, 1990

Preface

Within the last decade, a growing number of researchers in psychology and medicine have discovered that issues surrounding emotional expression are directly related to mental and physical health. Beginning in 1988, a group of psychologists interested in emotion, inhibition, and psychosomatics met in Sydney, Australia, as part of an International Congress of Psychology. From this meeting an informal network of researchers was established to share theories and findings related to emotion and health. This book is an outgrowth of that first meeting.

We are not the first to discover that the inhibition of emotions can lead to health and psychological problems. Both William James and Sigmund Freud presaged the problems of emotional expression and inhibition in the 1890s. James (1890), for example, noted that the failure to express powerful emotions "could strike into a pathological path when the normal one is dammed," resulting in illness, vengeful brooding, or listlessness. Freud (e.g., 1917), of course, was more graphic in describing the dangers of repressed emotions. The failure to express anger, for example, could lead to depression, obsessive thoughts, a variety of deviant behaviors, and a plethora of hysterical symptoms.

Whereas most of the scientific community within psychology rejected the psychodynamic processes associated with emotion as originally posited by James and Freud, psychosomatic researchers with medical training began reporting important links between emotional expression and disease starting in the 1930s. Helen Flanders Dunbar (1935) ushered in the psychosomatic viewpoint by describing and cataloging hundreds of case studies that suggested that different psychosomatic diseases were related to specific emotions. Beginning in the 1940s and spanning two decades, Harold G. Wolff and his colleagues (see Wolf & Goodell, 1968) developed an experimental method whereby the evocation of specific emotions in a person produced measurable biological changes. For example, a patient who was induced to talk about hostile experiences in Wolff's laboratory evidenced striking increases in muscle tension in the neck, thereby producing a headache.

In perhaps the most detailed theoretical discussion of emotions and psychosomatic processes, Franz Alexander (1950) forcefully argued that when specific classes of emotions were blocked, patients developed clearly identifiable health problems. Blocked anger and hostility, for example, were thought to be associated with cardiovascular disorders. According to Alexander, the blocking of dependency-relevant emotions, on the other hand, resulted in digestive and other parasympathically-controlled problems. As intuitively appealing as Alexander's framework may be, it has not gained much respect within mainstream psychology and medicine due to its lack of an empirical foundation.

The current volume represents a new approach to the links among emotion, inhibition, and health. The research discussed in this book is based heavily on solid scientific experiments. Because the contributors represent a variety of backgrounds and traditions, there is no attempt at promoting a single theoretical explanation. Rather, concepts from cognitive, social, and clinical psychology are used to explain differing aspects of the emotion-health relationship.

This book is intended for both researchers and clinicians in psychology and medicine. The first half of the book focuses on current theoretical issues related to emotion and health. In drawing on their own and others' research findings, the authors of the various chapters address basic emotion-health problems that have been debated since Freud and James. The second half of the book is devoted to more specific clinical problems. We have attempted to bring together an exciting group of thinkers and clinicians who have studied a diverse group of psychosomatic problems, including cardiovascular and gastrointestinal problems, cancer, pain, and asthma.

In many respects, this book represents the state of the art within the area of inhibition, emotion, and health. The strengths of this research area include diverse methodologies and wide-ranging theoretical foundations. Ironically, these strengths are, in many ways, also the primary weaknesses of this research area. As a group, we have not adopted a single paradigm or theoretical doctrine. Many of our working ideas appear to be inconsistent and not fully developed. For example, the definitions of emotion and inhibition vary from researcher to researcher depending on the empirical methods that have been adopted.

Any new area of research brings with it diversity, occasional controversy, and enthusiasm. We invite the readers to share in the excitement of this developing research endeavor. We also express our thanks to Boris Traue and Alison Michael for proofreading. Last but not least, thanks are due to Dr. Michael Vogtmeier, Susanne Schurr and David Emmans from Hogrefe & Huber Publishers

Harald C. Traue
James W. Pennebaker

References

Alexander, F. (1950). *Psychosomatic medicine*. New York: Norton.

Dunbar, H.F. (1935). *Emotions and bodily changes: A survey of the literature: 1910-1933*. New York: Columbia University Press.

Freud, S. (1917/1966). *Introductory lectures on psychoanalysis*. New York: Norton.

James, W. (1890). *The priciples of psychology* (Vol. 2). New York: Holt.

Wolf, S. & Goodell, B. (1968). *Harold G. Wolff's Stress and Disease*. Springfield, Ill.: Thomas.

PART A: THE THEORETICAL DIMENSION

Inhibition and Arousal

H.C. Traue and J.W. Pennebaker

One goal of research in psychology and psychosomatics is to identify those psychological mechanisms that affect bodily responses ranging from transient autonomic activity to chronic disease. Since the 1950s, impressive evidence has been amassed demonstrating the roles of classical and instrumental conditioning in affecting arousal and health. Even before the behavioral revolution, however, scientists from a variety of perspectives were pointing to more complex psychological states that also contributed to somatic activity. James (1890), Freud (1893), Luria (1932), and many others argued that the psychic states of conflict or inhibition were inherently stressful for the organism.

After almost four decades of cognitive psychology and behaviorism, scientists are now returning to their laboratories to investigate inhibition and arousal from a variety of perspectives. In this chapter, we briefly summarize some of the main themes within psychology that are pointing to the health and psychic risks of inhibition. Interestingly, the research on inhibition and arousal does not stem from any single discipline within psychology. Rather, a pattern of overlapping research questions and findings has emerged within clinical, social, cognitive, personality, and developmental psychology as well as psychoanalysis and psychosomatic medicine. As we discuss below, a solid understanding of emotional and behavioral inhibition promises to uncover many basic issues associated with stress and disease.

Biological Mechanisms of Inhibition

The concept of inhibition has a long tradition in psychology. Originally, the concept referred to the reciprocal suppression of muscular protagonist-antagonist-activity and the inhibition of neighboring cells in sensory physiology. Pavlov (1927) described various mechanisms of inhibition as extinction processes of conditioned reactions. Spence (1936) and Hull (1950) expanded the concept of inhibition as an explanation for the weakening of conditioned reactions. According to Pavlov's model of thought, arousal and inhibition of the central nervous system are fundamental to all behaviors in determining their strength, mobility, and equilibrium.

The strength of the nervous system delimits the individual differences in physiological reactions to an environmental stimulus. Pavlov defined a nervous system as weak if a physiological response is strong, and vice versa. The concept of nervous system strength was redefined by Sales (1971) as "need for stimulation". That is, persons with a strong nervous system need strong stimuli for a certain excitation whereas those with a weak nervous system need only weak stimulation. The need for stimulation (or the strength of the nervous system) was operationalized by Zuckerman et al. (1964) through the *Sensation Seeking Scale*. The authors showed a positive correlation of search for stimulation (high levels on the *Sensation Seeking Scale*) with expressive behavior (measured by the *Affect Expression Rating Scale* and by the *Affective Communication Test*). That is to say, persons with a strong nervous system (according to Pavlov) show little physiological activity and much expressive behavior.

Pavlov's concept of the strength of a nervous system was one basis of the personality dimension extraversion-introversion developed by Eysenck (1957). According to this concept, potentials of excitation are more easily stimulated in introverts than in extraverts. These differences have their physiological basis in the ascending reticular system (ARAS) and are considered innate (Eysenck, 1967).

One of the predictions of the introversion-extraversion construct is that, in the case of equal stimulation, introverts show a higher physiological arousal than do extraverts. Eysenck (1967) demonstrated this by assessment of the electrodermal response to psychological stimulation. On the whole, however, the literature reveals a more heterogenous and contradictory situation. In their specification of conditioning, Eysenck and Levy (1972) presumed that introverts are more easily conditioned when the CS is weak, and when intervals between the CS and the UCS are short and only partially reinforced. Since it is unlikely that during the process of socialization these exact conditions will be prevalent, the originally assumed biological foundation of the concept cannot fully apply (Buck, 1976).

Gray (1972) modified the construct of introversion-extraversion by abandoning the former thesis of a generally better status of conditioning in favor of the better status of conditioning by punishment stimuli for introverts. Gray gave different reasons for the biological basis of introversion-extraversion. By employing barbiturates, he identified the hippocampus and septal regions as the inhibitory system which in introverts is especially activated and strongly reacts to punishment stimuli. The more it is activated, the stronger will behavior be inhibited by punishment and the more introverted the individual will be. Figure 1 depicts the modification of Eysenck's theory by Gray.

The re-formulation of the introversion-extraversion concept led to the development of a three-component nervous system: an unspecific arousal system, a behavioral inhibition system (BIS), and a behavioral activation system (BAS). The behavioral inhibition system (BIS) reacts to unidentified stimuli, to aversive stimuli like pain, and to the absence of expected response contingent reward. The neural-anatomic location of the behavioral inhibition system is the septum-hippocampus-frontal-region (SHF). Pharmocological substances, such as barbiturates, alcohol and tranquilizers have an arousing effect on the SHF-region. A lesion of the SHF-region also has an arousing effect. The basic scheme of the experiments with animals by Gray is the approach-avoidance-conflict. The animals learn a response to become reinforced. Once the response is learned, in addition to the incentive, a punishment is introduced in order to activate the BIS and reduce the learned behavior (passive avoidance). If an anxiety-reducing substance is then given, blocking the BIS, the effect of the punishment stimulus is neutralized.

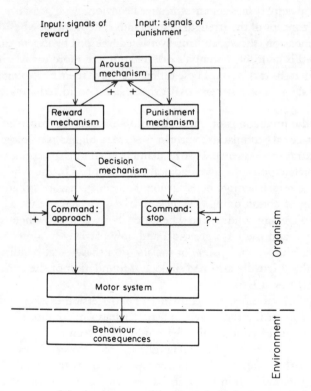

Figure 1: The structure of the development of dysthymic behavior in neurotic introverts and psychopathic behavior in neurotic extraverts, from Gray (1972).

The behavioral activation system (BAS) is activated by reward and punishment. It can be understood as a reward-seeking system, mediating approach, flight, and active avoidance behavior. The BIS and BAS interact with each other in an antagonistic manner. Both have a positive input into the third system of unspecific arousal, anatomically identified with the reticular formation. Gray named only the reticular activation system as arousal system. The unspecific arousal system corresponds with the activation concepts by Lacey (1967) and Routtenberg (1968). The difference, according to Gray, is that the intensity of activation is controlled through the unspecific activation system, once the BAS or BIS is stimulated. Particularly intriguing is the fact that Gray emphasized the fractionating of activation depending on appetitive and aversion stimuli (cf., Duffy, 1957, concerning the reduction of behavior in case of high central activation).

As depicted in Figure 2, the BAS and BIS steer the motoric system with corresponding behavioral consequences. Unfortunately, the system fails to reliably predict the specific behaviors resulting from behavioral activation or behavioral inhibition in humans. Typically, activation in behavior corresponds to an elevated motoric activity. Behavioral inhibition, on the other hand, can be produced by simultaneously elevated activity of protagonist and antagonist muscles, by elevated muscular tension without dynamics, or by relaxation. However, since the BIS reacts to aversive stimuli, a relaxing reaction is not likely, especially since the elevated vegetative and motoric activity in case of anxiety or stress has been proven by experimental studies (Birbaumer, 1977; Traue et al., 1986). It is also known that at least the muscular activity of the forehead is elevated in case of anxiety. Elevated muscular contractions which inhibit behavior as an active process are likely to occur (see also Terrance, 1972).

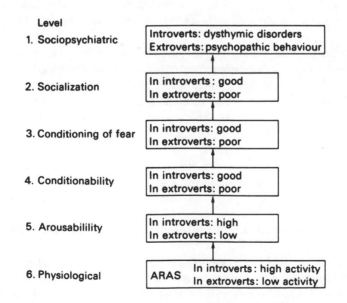

Figure 2: A simplified model of the behavioral inhibition and behavioral activation system (BIS & BAS), adapted from Gray (1975).

Fowles (1980) extended Gray's three components to the area of autonomic and somatic nervous system activity. According to Fowles, cardiovascular activity – such as fluctuations in heart rate (HR) and blood pressure – reflects the action of the behavioral activation system. Ehrlich and Malmo (1967), for example, found significant reductions of HR within a conditioning paradigm as a result of frustration, despite a rise in motoric activity. This suggests that, beyond the cardiosomatic coupling (Obrist, 1976) of motoric system and HR, cardiovascular activity can depend on central activation.

It has been known for some time, for example, that biofeedback is only partially effective in lowering HR (Lang, 1975). It has been observed that the biofeedback signal indicating the success by showing a drop in HR, led to a subsequent rise of HR, while negative feedback, signaling failure, lowered the HR. This correlation between reinforcement and HR was completely independent of motoric activity.

Of particular relevance is the fact that Fowles (1980) linked the behavioral inhibitory system with electrodermal activity (EDA). Indeed, a number of experiments have demonstrated that freezing linked with frightening stimuli is associated with heightened EDA. Similarly, EDA consistently increases when individuals are induced to lie, such as during a guilty knowledge test (Waid & Orne, 1981). Further, when attempting to deceive the experimenter, subjects typically inhibit their eye movement and facial activity (Pennebaker & Chew, 1985). The EDA reacts, however, in response to a large spectrum of stimuli (Edelberg, 1973). Robert (1974) showed that an EDA-reaction follows punishment stimuli and frustrating non-rewards, which nevertheless do not influence HR.

In summary, the literature reviewed by Fowles shows that specific connections between Gray's three arousal systems and psychophysiological reactions of HR and EDA are probable. Conclusions a posteriori of motoric activity due to the differential activation of BIS and BAS may be premature at this time. A reduction of behavioral activity on the level of observable behavior gives no information on the actual motoric activity (Traue, 1989). The stated connections between the arousal systems and physiological activity refer to conditioned reactions and not to responses to stimuli per se. They are thus dependent on conditioning and on socialization processes.

Emotional Expression versus Inhibition and Physiological Activity

A central debate within the emotion literature concerns the degree to which emotional expression is inversely related to physiological activity. Prideaux (1920) noted that "the greater the visible signs of emotion... the less is the response on the galvanometer" (p. 66). In the 1930s, Jones observed the behaviors of children with simultaneous measurement of EDA. He described the inverse relations between expression and EDA-reaction as "internalizer" behavior or "externalizer" behavior. He assumed that expressive behavior is frequently punished during primary socialization, causing emotions to be shifted from overt to covert behavior. In summarizing his work, Jones (1960) reported that "in older children, the increase of inhibition and of apparent emotional control may not imply a diminished emotionality but merely [a] shift from outer to inner patterns of response" (p. 13). Socialization, then, involved the increasing control of expressivity. At the same time, punishment from parents and other socializing agents lead to an increase of physiological and in particular in electrodermal activation. Jones also assumed that constitutional factors might encourage this development.

The relatively undifferentiated emotional dynamics of infancy is extraversive in nature, involving generalized movements and low thresholds for vocal expression in crying. Such overt activities are adaptive only as signals of some difficulty or need, and as demands for succor. In the following years, overt emotional expression tends to bring disapproval and punishment rather than succor. Since the internal awareness of discharge is not disapproved or inhibited, these channels increasingly carry the efferent load of major as well as minor emotional charges. The wider range of emotional patterns which now appears is attributable partly to constitutional factors...and no doubt partly to differences in parental discipline and other social impingements. (Jones, 1950, page 163).

The concept of internalization (or emotional inhibition) and externalization (or emotional expression) has aroused a great deal of interest within the last two decades. Ross Buck and collaborators used pictures to arouse emotional reactions, measuring at the same time EDA and HR. After videotaping the mimic responses of the subjects, raters gave three judgements about mimical and gestical reactions of the subjects. The parameters of expressiveness (communicative accuracy) were: 1. number of pictures which can be identified by the expressive behavior of the subjects; 2. rate of pleasure effect in the response (pleasantness measure); and 3. strength of the response (strength measure).

The experiments using this slide-viewing paradigm showed remarkable sex and individual differences in adults and school children (Buck, 1975, 1977). Expressive behavior in the sense of communication precision correlates with extraversion and self-esteem-rating. The expressive subjects report more personal-emotional aspects (Buck et al., 1972, 1974). Self- and other-ratings of test persons with the *Affect Expression Rating Scale* (AERS) showed that expressiveness correlated with social activity, direct expression of hostility, impulsiveness and friendship. A negative correlation was found in self-ratings with a variety of measures of behavioral inhibition, including shyness, self-ratings of emotional control and inhibition, quiet, reserved, and introversion. Expressive persons were better in taking on a pose of emotional expression (Buck, 1979).

Table 1 reviews the primary findings from Buck's laboratory along with those of other research groups. As can be seen, Buck (e.g., 1977; Buck et al., 1974) and Miller et al. (1975) found negative correlations between pleasantness of expression, number of correct picture identifications and EDA. Lanzetta and Kleck (1970) showed a positive correlation of the EDA with the number of false judgements concerning mimical anticipation to shocks. Some experiments extended the inverse relation between expressiveness and physiological reactivity by including the HR (Buck et al., 1974; Miller, 1974). To complicate matters, Notarius and Levenson (1979) found that generally subjects during stress reacted electrodermally and with an increase of heartbeat rate, independent of whether they were rated as inhibited or expressive. Asendorpf (1981) also failed to verify relations between expressiveness and arousal.

Other studies that are indirectly related to the internalization and externalization dimensions have also found inverse relations between expressiveness and arousal. Learmouth et al. (1959) correlated personality scores resulting from Rorschach responses with changes of skin resistance in 20 subjects. They deduced from their analyses that persons with a personality structure "most consistent with the free expression of feeling" (p. 195), showed less fluctuation in the EDA. Crider and Lunn (1971) found negative relations between lability in the EDA (as a stable individual characteristic) and impulsiveness and extraversion. A secondary analysis found negative relations between the verbal stress report and arousal in persons with high scores on a scale of denial. Waid (1976) investigated the relationship between EDA and socialization processes. The socialization scores of the test persons correlated positively with EDA. Persons who scored as highly socialized persons on the socialization scale by Gough (1960, 1964) and who were exposed to stressful noises and unexpected sounds showed stronger EDA-reactions than subjects with lower scores. Other studies that have examined psychopathy have reported that individuals with low socialization scores (i.e., those individuals defined as sociopathic and openly aggressive) also tend to have low EDA (Lykken, 1957; Waid, 1976).

A newer study by Malatesta et al. (1987) investigated the hypothesis of a differential relation between inhibition of certain emotions and specific symptom patterns. Healthy adults were asked to recall an emotionally moving recent incident (sadness, fear, anger) and report about it. The expressiveness ratings of mimical behavior for the three emotions were coded from the videotaped behavior. These expressiveness ratings were correlated with the scales of a list of physical symptoms. With only one exception, all significant coefficients were negative, indicating that expressiveness was associated with low levels of physical symptoms. In addition, a trend emerged indicating that the total score for arthritis symptoms corresponded with reduced expression of anger. Further, the total score of skin relevant symptoms correlated most with an inhibited expression of sadness. There was no consistent pattern of cardiovascular symptoms, although a negative correlation was found with ratings of general expressiveness. Reduced

Table 1: Experiments using the internalization-externalization dimension

Author	Experimental Procedure	Correlation between expressivness and		
		n	EDA	HR
Lanzetta & Kleck, 1970	30 trials with shock baseline signal, shock/non-shock	12	−.69	—
Buck et al. 1972	25 slides (sexual, scenic, maternal, disgusting, unusual) (10 sec view, 20 sec report)	9 10	−.55 −.91	+.21 -.60
Buck et al. 1974	like Buck et al. 1972	16 16	−.74 −.74	-.27 -.43
Miller, 1974	pharmacological study	8	—	-.71
Miller et al. 1975	(? quoted from Buck, 1979)	10	−.42	-.31
Buck, 1977	16 slides (familiar unfamiliar persons, unusual)	13	−.43	—
Notarius & Levenson, 1979	Unpleasant and stress-ful movie as baseline, expectation of shock	76		

1. Baseline: Expressive Ss higher HR, inhibited Ss higher SCL
2. Inhibited Ss respond with HR increase in stress
3. Expressive and inhibited SS respond with SCL increase in stress

Author	Experimental Procedure	n	EDA	HR
Asendorpf, 1981	Induction of anxiety, happiness, and anger	36	n. s.	

facial expressiveness cannot be equated with low arousal since the subjects reported strong emotions which were caused by the instruction. Beyond the general finding of an inverse relation between expressiveness and physical symptoms, the data favor a symptom-dependent selective inhibition of certain emotions.

Jones (1950) interpreted externalization-internalization in the etiological sense of suppression. Buck (1979), on the contrary, took introversion (similar to Gray, 1972) as a third conditioning variable, sensitizing individuals for socialization conditions. In short, the biological disposition of introversion causes a higher EDA-lability and leads, under certain conditions of socialization, to the inhibition of expressive behavior. This is the so-called Gray-Buck hypothesis, an assumption which Buck explained as follows:

> It is proposed that such systems can account for the data we have considered regarding externalizing-internalizing modes of responses if it is assumed (1) that early in life these are important, stable, individual differences in levels of activity in the excitatory and inhibitory systems; (2) that learning experiences can result in situationally specific changes in these levels of activity; and (3) that activity in the inhibitory system relative to the excitatory system is directly or indirectly associated with increased electrodermal responding and possibly with other kinds of autonomic nervous system arousal (Buck, 1979, p. 159).

Findings in studies of newborns speak for biologically caused individual differences. Field and her co-workers (1982) observed 3-day-old newborns and measured simultaneously their HR. Results showed that expressive infants differ from inexpressive by lower HR activity. More recently, Kagan and his colleagues (1988) selected 54 inhibited and 53 uninhibited 2- and 5-year olds from an original group of 400 children. The inhibited children were defined as timid, quiet, and unlikely to initiate interactions with others. By and large, inhibition among both age groups was stable over a 5-year period. Further, those classified as inhibited exhibited higher resting HRs, cortisol levels, and urinary norepinephrine levels than the non-inhibited children. According to Kagan, these behavioral and physiological effects of inhibition are due, in large part, to genetic factors rather than socialization.

Unfortunately, the precise links between externalizing-internalizing models and those related to behavioral inhibition and activation have not been firmly established. Fowles (1980) showed that EDA and HR covary differentially with the activity of BIS and BAS, while, on the contrary, expressiveness seems to correspond generally to low arousal (EDA and HR). To complicate matters, the inverse relation between expressiveness and arousal is based on interindividual correlations. If, instead of the interindividual correlations, the intraindividual correlations between expressiveness and physiological reactivity are calculated, the direction is reversed. An individual with expressive behavior is physiologically active at the same time. The intraindividual reanalysis of Buck's data

(1979) showed a weak but significant correlation coefficient of r = .15 (p <.01) between EDA and expressiveness. That is, intraindividual relations are completely different from interindividual ones on the situational level. These findings cannot easily be coordinated with Gray's concept of BIS and BAS.

Theoretically, there may be individual differences insofar as some persons have a general imbalance in favor of the BIS or the BAS, which is connected to a general proclivity towards expressiveness. The intraindividual situational variations in EDA may be caused by the unspecific activation components. These are speculations, however. Independent of the connections with Gray's activation system, the empirical evidence for an inverse relationship between expressiveness and arousal in emotion-inducing situations is sufficient to be relevant for an etiological concept of psychophysiological disorders.

Deception, Expression and Physiological Activity

Corresponding to the discrimination between spontaneous (subcortical) and intentional (cortical) expressive behavior, Buck (1984) distinguished between inhibition and deception. Inhibition, in his terms, is based on biological mechanisms. Deception, on the other hand, is based on psychological mechanisms with wide-ranging intentional components. Terrance (1972), who defined inhibition as an active process or "a general process where a given event does not occur due to the action of another event," was closer in his understanding of deceptive behavior than to biological inhibition. Additionally Buck (1984) distinguished between nonemotional deception, stressful deception, and emotional deception. The concept of stressful deception is especially important in this context since it shows that the suppression of expressive behavior is stressful for the organism. The methods of truth recognition by the lie detector depend on this mechanism (DePaulo & Rosenthal, 1979). There are a few often-observed behavioral patterns accompanying deception, such as flickering of eyelids, hesitation before an answer, throat-clearing, and an increase of verbal mistakes. In deception there is also slowness of speech and a reduced rate of speech (Zuckerman et al., 1981).

Waid and Orne (1981, 1982) have used a guilty knowledge test (GKT) to learn the degree to which deception can be reliably identified using various autonomic nervous system channels such as EDA, HR, respiration rate, and blood pressure. Although all autonomic channels are better than chance at detecting deception, EDA is the most stable and robust sign of deceptive behavior. The GKT consists of a series of trials in which test persons tell the truth or lie in random order. There are a number of versions of this test.

With a simple GKT, Pennebaker and Chew (1985) observed 30 subjects during deception. They tried to determine if simultaneous to EDA-reactions there was an inhibition of verbal expression. In addition, the effect of observation was investigated. There were two different observation conditions registered: one with and one without observation. Two important effects emerged. First, subjects who were observed evidenced higher overall EDA levels than subjects not observed. Second, when individuals attempted deception, EDA levels increased at the same time that their eye movements and facial activity decreased.

Unfortunately these studies do not give information on how "freezing" of expressive behavior is accomplished. We only know that a reduction of dynamics occurs, that is, the movement of facial mimicry, since behavior is thus operationalized; it cannot be deduced whether an increase of tension in antagonistic muscles takes place, or just a "holding still" by total relaxation. After consideration of other studies, though, it can be speculated that a muscular relaxation is unlikely, since deception itself is understood as a stressful burden (Buck, 1984; Waid & Orne, 1982).

Expressiveness and Arousal in Infants

Eysenck (1967) interpreted behavioral and response differences in adult introverts and extraverts as partially innate. Introverts possess a lower threshold to activate the ARAS and are therefore more sensitive to socialization influences and conditioning. In other words, their expressive behavior is socialized "away" during their development. According to this interpretation, interindividual differences in infants should occur in physiological responding but not neccessarily in their expressive behavior. Contrary to this (and supporting the Gray-Buck-hypothesis), individual differences in infants can be observed which may be interpreted directly in the sense of the internalization-externalization concept.

In a group of infants with strong HR activation in response to stress Lewis et al. (1978) found low expressive behavior and an inverse relation in infants with strong expressive behavior. In infants from 6 to 24 months of age Hutt and Hutt (1967) found a relation between an orienting reaction and HR variability. Their 22-month old inhibited infants showed higher HR and less HR variability compared to expressive infants.

The questions of spontaneous expressive behavior, the ability for imitating facial expression, the ability for conditioning, and the relation between expressiveness and arousal in 74 new-borns with a normal birth and pregnancy were investigated by Field et al. (1982). The results of the study can be summarized as follows. During the testing of several reflexes and noise reactions, newborn children showed specific expressive behavior (e.g., disgust after soap-taste) far beyond any chance occurrence. Expressiveness showed remarkable individual variations. Infants were able to imitate the expression of sadness, surprise, and pleasure. Raters estimated 76% of the sadness trials to be correct. The precision of expression imitation could be proven by motoric details (lips, mouth, eyes). By means of a global expression-scale infants were classified as expressive and non-expressive. The expressive infants reacted less strongly to stressors (*Brazelton Scale*), showed lower average values of HR, but higher HR variability during sleep. They also reacted more quickly with cries to poking, watched the face of the tester for a longer time during expression imitation, especially in later trials (that is, they were less habituated), and they showed a higher frequency of scanning. Further, their facial expression could be more easily identified. Finally, they imitated the expression behavior more specifically compared to the less expressive group.

The Field data, along with the findings of Kagan et al (1988), point to the heritability of expressive behavior. Further, this same expressiveness appears to have an inverse relation to physiological arousal. As a number of other investigators have found, cardiovascular responsivity to novel stressors is highly stable beginning at a very early age (see Birns et al., 1969). In addition, HR variability is highly correlated at the ages between 6 to 12 and 12 to 24 months (Hutt & Hutt, 1967).

One could assume that the socialization hypothesis would be considerably weakened by these findings. The one area that points to the probable importance of early experience in the development of expressiveness deals with gender differences (Hall, 1979). Among adults, a consistent effect is that females are more emotionally expressive than males, whereas studies of new-born infants find no variations between the sexes. If sex differences are proven not to be innate, socialization processes in the sense of the Gray-Buck-hypothesis will certainly influence the relation between expression and arousal.

The new-born studies are of relevance for theories on stress and illness. Since expressive infants are less irritable and react physiologically weaker to aversive simple stressors, there may be an innate stress resistance. In addition to this factor, there are socialization experiences which enlarge the biological stress resistance, particularly for handling social situations. Through the greater expressiveness of infants, their first few months are characterized by stronger social interaction with their parents. Pre-school-age expressive children are better liked and more popular than their non-expressive comrades (Buck, 1975; Field & Walden, 1982). Expressive children are able to defend their toys against competitors simply by aggressive facial expression (Campos et al., 1975) without the tendency to escalate aggressive acts in case of loss of the toy. On the other hand, children could prevent or conclude aggressive acts by distinctive gestures and signs of submissiveness (Ginsburg et al., 1977). There are many experiments (Bull, 1983) which show that the observations with children are also valid for young adults.

Repression – Sensitization and Physiological Activity

Repression is a psychoanalytic concept describing a mechanism of defense by which inner psychic conflicts are coped with by repressing memories and feelings from consciousness. In his theory of muscular armouring Reich (1973, originally published 1933) saw the somatization of the psychological repression mechanisms. This psychoanalytic concept, in connection with theories of perception (Bruner & Postman, 1947), is the basis of the personality dimension repression-sensitization (Byrne, 1961). Individuals at the poles of this dimension are characterized by rigid defense mechanisms. Repressors block any frightening or stressful information, whereas sensitizers direct their attention towards this information.

Perhaps the largest stumbling block in the study of repression has been in its measurement. By definition, repressed thoughts and feelings are out of the awareness of individuals. Consequently, self-reports of repressed memories or general repression-related personality styles must be inferred rather than directly measured by investigators. Within the personality realm, two measurement strategies have evolved. The first, proposed by Byrne (1961), identified individuals as repressors using the repression-sensitization (RS) scale. On the scale, individuals reported the degree to which they felt a variety of anxiety-related thoughts, moods, and physical symptoms. Repressors, then, reported few symptoms whereas sensitizers reported many. Unfortunately, experiments using the RS scale usually found that sensitizers complained more about health and mood than repressors, with no reliable differences between repressors and sensitizers on measures of objective physical health (e.g. Boucsein & Frye, 1974; Stein, 1971). According to Asendorpf et al. (1983) one of the causes for this failure lies in the high correlation between the RS-scale and measures of anxiety or Negative Affectivity (NA). In other words, the RS-scale "repressor and sensitizer" cannot distinguish between the fearful and the fearless.

The second, and more recent and promising measure of repressive coping style has been proposed by Weinberger and his colleagues (e.g., Weinberger et al., 1979). According to their classification scheme, repressive coping style is two-dimensional and comprised of an anxiety dimension and an inhibition or constraint factor. Anxiety is typically measured using the *Taylor Manifest Anxiety Scale* (MAS) and constraint is tapped using the *Social Desirability Scale* (SDS) developed by Crowne and Marlowe (1960). By using these two dimensions, Weinberger classified individuals into one of four categories:

- repressor (MAS low, SDS high)
- low-level anxious (MAS low, SDS low)
- high-level anxious (MAS high, SDS low)
- defensive-high-level anxious (MAS high, SDS high)

Beginning in 1979, Weinberger, Schwartz, and Davidson compared repressors, low-level-anxious, and high-level anxious. Their male subjects were observed during free associating of sentences with neutral, sexual, and aggressive contents and were measured physiologically with HR, EDA and frontalis EMG. During the experiment, the repressors reacted with significantly higher HR, more spontaneous skin conductance activity, and higher frontalis muscle tensions compared to the low-level anxious subjects. In behavior, the repressive copers showed a prolonged reaction time before answering and more disturbances of speech. Asendorpf (1981) verified these results in a similar study. Instead of EMG of the frontalis muscles, he observed mimicry. Repressors differ from other groups during stress (not during neutral stimuli) by stronger mimicry. This result appears to contradict other studies in which repression and inhibition are connected. Unfortunately, Asendorpf did not take EMG-measurements, thus the relation between mimical activity and muscle tension from this study remains unclear.

Finally, it should be noted that other strategies of measuring repression have also been attempted. For example, Weinstein et al. (1968) found that repressors (as measured by low anxiety reports during a stressful experiment) demonstrated increased arousal during anxiety and stress (as measured by skin conductance and HR). Using a similar measure repression, Parsons et al. (1969) found that in a group discussion repressors showed more skin conductivity reactions than sensitizers compared to the entire group.

Aggression, Inhibition of Aggression, and Blood Pressure

Starting from the frustration-aggression hypothesis of Dollard, Miller and co-workers (1939), the research group under Hokanson at the Florida State University examined the relation between aggression, inhibition of aggression and blood pressure. Hokanson (1961) operationalized the expression of aggression in a series of studies in which subjects believed that they were delivering electric shocks to another individual as part of a learning task. The person they thought would receive the shocks was an experimental confederate who annoyed or insulted the subject prior to the task. In such a setting the amount, time duration, and strength of the shocks correlated consistently (r = .13, .19 and .42) with reductions in systolic blood pressure after the aggressive act. The more aggressive the subjects acted, the more their blood pressure dropped following the aggressive behavior.

A subsequent study (Hokanson & Shelter, 1961) tested changes of blood pressure under "low and high frustration", "low and high status of the frustrator" and "opportunity versus no opportunity for aggressivity" as experimental factors. The researchers found a significant interaction between frustration and the possibility of aggression. That is, if the frustrating person had a low status and the subject was highly frustrated, systolic blood pressure was significantly elevated. If, on the other hand, there was no chance for aggression, blood pressure remained stable.

In a test of the value of actual versus symbolic catharsis, Hokanson and Burgess (1962) investigated the influence of various forms of aggressive expression on blood pressure and HR. Two groups of subjects were exposed to high or low frustration, by criticizing their mental abilities. The highly frustrated were given the chance to release their frustration after the frustrating situation by expressing it towards the frustrator with electric shocks, verbal expression in fantasy (by telling a TAT-story), or not at all. Overall, the possibility for direct verbal or physical anger expression towards the frustrator lowered HR and blood pressure to levels equal to or below baseline. When subjects did not have a chance for anger expression or for only unconscious expression through a TAT-story, HR and blood pressure values remained high.

Finally, Hokanson and his colleagues (1963) investigated the effect of tension reduction through aggressive expression towards the frustrator himself, his assistant (a graduate student), an undergraduate student, or by no chance for aggression. Overall, blood pressure levels were reduced the most when subjects aggressed against the frustrator compared to no chance of aggressive expression. Furthermore, aggression failed to lower blood pressure when the object of retaliation was of lower status. The variations between objects of different status were, however, not significant.

Baker and Schaie (1969) replicated Hokanson's blood pressure findings. Their study confirmed that aggression ought to be shown openly and directly against the aggressor. Interestingly, covert aggression or aggression substitutes through another person instead of the frustrator had no effect. These findings called into question the hypothesis of Dollard et al. (1939) that the occurrence of any act of aggression is assumed to reduce the instigation to aggression. In a direct test of this, Gambaro and Rabin (1969) addressed the issue underlying conceptions of catharsis: Does aggressive expression lower blood pressure if the aggressive act is not directly imposed towards the frustrator, but towards another object? Further, would feelings of guilt following aggression undermine the effect? Indeed, several authors have claimed that guilt inherently inhibits emotional expression (Clark, 1952; Rader, 1957).

In Gambaro and Rabin's study, subjects were randomly assigned to one of four groups: frustration and direct aggression, frustration and aggression against another person, frustration and non-aggression, and non-frustration/ non-aggression. Overall, Hokanson's finding that aggression has to be direct and not displaced was confirmed. In addition, the division of subjects into groups of more and fewer guilt feelings showed that the group with fewer guilt feelings also showed the blood-pressure-lowering effect in the displaced aggression condition.

Alexithymia

Alexithymia is defined as a condition characterized by an individual's inability to feel and show emotions, lacking imagination, and a general inhibition in verbal expression. This constellation of symptoms has variously been labelled alexithymia (Sifneos, 1973), operative thinking or *pensée operatoire* (Marty & De M'Uzan, 1963), and psychosomatic phenomenon. One of the interesting aspects of this disorder is the parallel nature of the assumptions of chronic repression made about psychosomatic patients (Alexander, 1950).

Alexithymia is definitely not a homogenous theoretical concept. Nemiah (1977) already named a number of psychological and neuroanatomical theories. Alexithymia is here referred to in the sense that neuro-anatomic conceptions assume a disturbance in the neuronal connections between cortex and limbic system. There are "...disturbances: (1) in the pathway between the center for psychic elaboration and that for consciousness; (2) in the pathway between the center underlying emotion and that for psychic elaboration, or (3) in the center for psychic elaboration itself" (Nemiah, 1977, p. 203). In reference to McLean (1949) and studies on environmental dependencies (e.g., Borges & Berry, 1976), Nemiah assumed a deficit in communication between limbic system and cortex in psychosomatically disturbed patients. It should be noted critically that Nemiah did not consider his biological deficit model of alexithymia as an hypothesis which needs to be verified, he considered it a loophole, since the classical psychoanalytic models of thought do not suffice for explanation of psychosomatic problems. "It is just here that the structural model comes to rescue, by making possible the translation of intangible, unmeasureable psychoanalytic constructs into the concepts of neurochemical processes taking place in neuronal pathways and centers..." (Nemiah, 1977, p. 205).

Currently, a great deal of controversy surrounds the diagnosis of alexithymia (Ahrens & Deffner, 1984). At present, there are no agreed-upon definitions of the phenomenon. Although promising, the experiments of analysis of verbal materials as a measure or reflection of alexithymia are difficult to evaluate since the various parameters of interview situations are not standardized. Indeed, the verbal structure of psychosomatic patients (e.g., v. Rad et al., 1977) seems to indicate signs of a restricted code.

References

Ahrens, S., & Deffner, G. (1984). Zur Affektverarbeitung bei psychosomatischen Patienten. Teil II. *Zeitschrift für psychosomatische Medizin und Psychoanalyse, 30,* 357-376.

Alexander, F. (1950). *Psychosomatic medicine. Its principles and applications.* New York: Norton.

Asendorpf, J. B. (1981). *Affektive Vigilanz*. PhD thesis at the University of Gießen, Germany.

Asendorpf, J. B., Wallbott, H. G., & Scherer, K. R. (1983). Der verflixte Repressor: Ein empirisch begründeter Vorschlag zu einer zweidimensionalen Operationalisierung von Repression-Sensitization. *Zeitschrift für Differentielle und Diagnostische Psychologie, 4*, 2, 113-128.

Baker, J. W., & Schaie, K. W. (1969). Effects of aggression "alone" or "with another" on physiological und psychological arousal. *Journal of Personality and Social Psychology, 12*, 1, 80-86.

Birbaumer, N. (1977). *Psychophysiologie der Angst*. München: Urban & Schwarzenberg, 2. Auflage.

Birns, B., Barten, S., & Bridges, W. H. (1969). Individual differences in temperamental characteristiscs of infants. *Transactions of the New York Academy of Sciences*.

Birns, B., Barten, S., & Bridges, W.H. (1969). Individual differences in temperamental characteristics of infants. New York: Transactions of the New York Academy of Sciences (cited from Field, 1982).

Borges, S., & Berry, M. (1976). Preferential orientation of the stellate cell dendrites in the visual cortex of the dark-reared rat. *Brain Research 112*, 141-154.

Boucsein, W., & Frye, M. (1974). Physiologische und psychische Wirkungen von Mißerfolgsstreß unter Berücksichtigung des Merkmals Repression-Sensitization. *Zeitschrift für experimentelle und angewandte Psychologie, 21*, 339-366.

Bruner, J. S., & Postman, L. (1947). Tension and tension release as organisation factors in perception. *Journal of Personality, 15*, 300-308.

Buck, R. (1975). Nonverbal communication of affect in children. *Journal of Personality and Social Psychology, 31 (4)*, 644-653.

Buck, R. (1976). *Human motivation and emotion*. New York: J. Wiley & Sons.

Buck, R. (1977). Nonverbal communication of affect in preschool children: Relationships with personality and skin conductance. *Journal of Personality and Social Psychology, 35 (4)*, 225-236.

Buck, R. (1979). Individual differences in nonverbal sending accuracy and electrodermal responding: The externalizing-internalizing dimension. In R. Rosenthal (Ed.), *Skills in nonverbal communication*. Cambridge, MA: Oelgeschlager, Gunn & Hain, Publisher.

Buck, R. (1984). *The communication of emotion*. New York, London: The Guilford Press.

Buck, R., Miller, R. E., & Caul, W. F. (1974). Sex, personality and physiological variables in the communication of emotion via facial expression. *Journal of Personality and Social Psychology, 30*, 587-596.

Buck, R., Savin, V., Miller, R. E., & Caul, W. F. (1972). Nonverbal communication of affect in humans. *Journal of Personality and Social Psychology, 23*, 362-371.

Bull, P. E. (1983). *Body movement and interpersonal communication*. New York: John Wiley & Sons.

Byrne, D. (1961). The repression-sensitization scale. Rationale, reliability and validity. *Journal of Personality, 29*, 334-349.

Campos, J. E, Emde, R., Gaensbauer, F., & Henderson, C. (1975). Cardiac and behavioral interrelationships in the reactions of infants to strangers. *Developmental Psychology, 11*, 589-601.

Clark, R. A. (1952). The projective measurement of experimentally induced levels of sexual motivations. *Journal of Experimental Psychology, 44*, 391-399.

Crider, A., & Lunn, R. (1971). Electrodermal responsibility as a personality dimension. *Journal of Experimental Research in Personality, 5 (2)*, 145-150.

Crowne, D. P., & Marlowe, D. (1960). A new scale of social desirability independent of psychopathology. *Journal of Consulting Psychology, 66*, 547-555.

DePaulo, B. M., & Rosenthal, R. (1979). Telling lies. *Journal of Personality and Social Psychology, 37*, 1713-1722.

Dollard, J., Doob, L., Miller, N. W., Mowrer, O. H., & Sears, R. R. (1939). *Frustration and aggression*. New Haven: Yale University Press.

Duffy, E. (1957). The psychological significance of the concept of "arousal" or "activation". *Psychological Review, 64*, 265-275.

Edelberg, R. (1973). Mechanisms of electrodermal adaptions for locomotion, manipulation or defense. *Progress in Physiological Psychology, 5*, 155-209.

Ehrlich, D. J., & Malmo, R. B. (1967). Electrophysiological concomitants of simple operant conditioning in the rat. *Neuropsychologia, 5*, 219-235.

Eysenck, H. J. (1957). *The dynamics of anxiety and hysteria*. New York: Praeger.

Eysenck, H. J. (1967). *The biological basis of personality*. Springfield, Ill.: Charles C. Thomas.

Eysenck, H. J., & Levy, A. (1972). Conditioning, introversion-extraversion and the strength of nervous system. In V. D. Nebyltsyn and J. A. Gray (Eds.), *Biological bases of individual behavior*. New York: Academic.

Field, T.M. (1982). Individual differnces in the expressivity of neonates and young infants. In: R.W. feldmann (Ed.), Development of nonverbal behavior in children. New York: Springer Verlag.

Field, T. M., & Walden, T. A. (1982). Production and discrimination of facial expressions by preschool children. *Child Development, 53*, 1299-1311.

Field, T. M., Woodson, R., Greenberg, R., & Cohen, D. (1982). Discrimination and imitation of facial expressions in neonates. *Science, 218*, 179-181.

Fowles, D. C. (1980). The three arousal model: Implications of Gray's two factor theory for heart rate, EDA and psychopathy. *Psychophysiology, 17*, 87-104.

Freud, S. (1893). Vortrag über den psychischen Mechanismus hysterischer Phanomene (cited from S. Freud, 1940, *Gesammelte Werke*, London: Imago Publ., pp. 81-98).

Gambaro, A., & Rabin, S. (1969). Diastolic blood pressure response following direct and displaced aggression after anger arousal in high and low guilt subjects. *Journal of Personality and Social Psychology,* 12, 87-94.

Ginsburg, H. J., Pollman, V. A., & Wanson, M. S. (1977). An ethological analyis of nonverbal inhibitors of aggressive behaviors in male elementary school children. *Developmental Psychology,* 13, 417-418.

Gough, H. G. (1960). Theory and measurement of socialisations. *Journal of Consulting Psychology,* 24, 23-30.

Gough, H.G. (1964). Manual for the California Psychological Inventory. Palo Alto, Calif.: Consulting Psychologists Press.

Gray, J. A. (1972). The psychophysiological nature of introversion-extraversion: A modification of Eysenck's theory. In V. D. Nebylitsyn & J. H. Gray (Eds.): *Biological basis of individual behavior.* London: Academic Press.

Gray, J. A. (1975). Elements of a two-process theory of learning. New York: Academic Press.

Gray, J. A. (1979). *Elements of a two-process theory of learning.* London: Academic Press.

Hall, J. A. (1979). Gender, gender roles and non-verbal communication. In R. Rosenthal (Ed.) *Skills in nonverbal communication: Individual differences.* Cambridge, MA: Oelgeschlager, Gunn & Hain.

Hokanson, J. E. (1961). The effects of frustration and anxiety in overt aggression. *Journal of Abnormal and Social Psychology,* 62, 346-251.

Hokanson, J. E., & Burgess, M. (1962). The effects of three types of aggression on vascular processes. *Journal of Abnormal and Social Psychology,* 64, 446-449.

Hokanson, J. E., Burgess, M., & Cohen, M. F. (1963). Effects of displaced aggression on systolic blood pressure. *Journal of Abnormal and Social Psychology,* 67, 214-218.

Hokanson, J. E., & Shelter, S. (1961). The effect of overt aggression on physiological arousal. *Journal of Abnormal and Social Psychology,* 63, 446-448.

Hull, C. L. (1950). Simple qualitative discrimination learning. *Psychological Review,* 57, 303-313.

Hutt, C., & Hutt, S. J. (1967). HR variability: The adaptive consequences of individual differences and state changes. Human behaviors and adaptation. *Human behaviors and adaptation* (cited from Field, 1982).

James, W. (1890). *The principles of psychology (Vol. 1).* New York: Henry Holt.

Jones, H. E. (1950). The study of emotional expression. In M. Reymert (Ed.), *Feelings and emotions.* New York: McGraw-Hill.

Jones, H. E. (1960). The longitudinal method in the study of personality. In I. Iscoe and H. W. Stevenson (Eds.), *Personality development in children.* Chicago: University of Chicago Press.

Kagan, J., Reznick, J.S., & Snidman, N. (1988). Biological bases of childhood shyness. *Science,* 240, 167-171.

Krohne, H. W. (1974). Untersuchungen mit einer deutschen Form der Repressions-Sensitization-Skala. *Zeitschrift für klinische Psychologie,* 3, 238-260.

Lacey, J. I. (1967). Somatic response patterning and stress: Some revisions of activation theory. In M. H. Appley & R. Tramball (Eds.), *Psychological stress: Issues in research*. New York: Appleton-Century Crofts.

Lang, P. J. (1975). Acquisition of heart-rate control: Method, theory and clinical implications. In D. C. Fowles (Ed.), *Clinical applications of psychophysiology*. New York: Columbia University Press.

Lanzetta, J. T., & Kleck, R. E. (1970). Encoding and decoding of nonverbal affect in humans. *Journal of Personality and Social Psychology, 16*, 12-19.

Learmouth, G. J., Acherley, W., & Kaplan, M. (1959). Relationship between palmar skin potential during stress and personality variables. *Psychosomatic Medicine, 21*, 150-157.

Lewis, M., Broods, J., & Haviland, J. (1978). Hearts and faces: A study in the measurement of emotion. In M. Lewis & L. A. Rosenblum (Eds.), *The development of affect*. New York: Plenum Press.

Luria, A.R. (1932). *The nature of human conflicts*. New York: Liveright.

Lykken, D.T. (1957). A study of anxiety in sociopathic personality. *Journal of Abnormal and Social Psychology, 55*, 6-10.

Malatesta, C. Z., Jonas, R., & Izard, C. E. (1987). The relation between low facial expressivity during emotional arousal and somatic symptoms. *British Journal of Medical Psychology, 60*, 169-180.

Marty, P., & de M'Uzan, M. (1963). La "pensée operatoire." *Revue Francais Psychoanalytique, 17*, 345-356.

McLean, P. D. (1949). Psychosomatic disease and the visceral brain. *Psychosomatic Medicine, 1*, 338.

Miller, R. E. (1974). Social and pharmacological influences on nonverbal communication in monkeys and men. In L. Krames, T. Alloway & P. Pliner (Eds.), *Nonverbal communication*. New York: Plenum Press.

Miller, R.E., Gianini, A., & Levine, J. (1975). Nonverbal communication in man with a cooperative conditioning task. Unpublished manuscript, University of Pittsburgh.

Nemiah, J.C. (1977). Alexithymia: Theoretical considerations. *Psychotherapy and Psychosomatics, 28*, 199-206.

Notarius, C. I., & Levenson, R. W. (1979). Expressive tendencies and physiological response to stress. *Journal of Personality and Social Psychology, 37*, 1204-1210.

Obrist, P. A. (1976). The cardiovascular-behavioral interaction: As it appears today. *Psychophysiology, 13*, 95-107.

Parsons, O. A., Fulgenzi, L. B., & Edelberg, R. (1969). Aggressiveness and psychophysiological responsivity in groups of repressors and sensitizers. *Journal of Personality and Social Psychology, 12*, 235-244.

Pavlov, I. P. (1927). *Conditioned reflexes*. London: Oxford University Press.

Pennebaker, J. W., & Chew, C. H. (1985). Deception, EDA and inhibition of behavior. *Journal of Personality and Social Psychology, 49*, 1427-1433.

Porges, S.W., Arnold, W.R., & Forbes, E.J. (1973). Heart rate variability: An index of attentional responsivity in human newborns. *Developmental Psychology, 8*, 85-92,

Prideaux, E. (1920). The psychogalvanic reflex: A review. *Brain, 43*, 50-73.

Rader, G. E. (1957). The prediction of overt aggressive behavior from Rorschach content. *Journal of Projective Techniques, 21*, 294-306.

Reich, W. (1973). *Charakteranalyse.* Frankfurt: Fischer-Taschenbuch-Verlag (Original work published 1933).

Robert, L. (1974). Comparative psychophysiology of the electrodermal and cardiac control system. In P. A. Obrist, A. H. Black, J. Breuer & L. V. DiCara (Eds.), *Cardiovascular psychophysiology – current issues in response mechanisms, biofeedback and methodology.* Chicago: Aldine.

Routtenberg, A. (1968). The two-arousal hypothesis. Reticular formation and limbic system. *Psychological Review, 75*, 51-80.

Sales, S. (1971). Need for stimulation as a factor in social behavior. *Journal of Personality and Social Psychology, 19*, 124-134.

Sifneos, P. E. (1973). The prevalence of alexithymic characteristics in psychosomatic patients. *Psychotherapie and Psychosomatik, 22*, 255-262.

Spence, K. W. (1936). The nature of discrimination learning in animals. *Psychological Review, 43*, 427-449.

Stein, S. H. (1971). Arousal level in repressors and sensitizers as a function of response context. *Journal of Consulting and Clinical Psychology, 36*, 386-394.

Terrance, H. A. (1972). Conditioned inhibition. In R. A. Boakes & M. S. Holliday (Eds.), *Inhibition and learning.* London: Academic Press.

Traue, H. C. (1989). *Gefühlsausdruck, Hemmung und Muskelspannung unter sozialem Streß.* Göttingen: Hogrefe Verlag.

Traue, H. C., Bischoff, C., & Zenz, H. (1986). Sozialer Streß, Muskelspannung und Spannungskopfschmerz. *Zeitschrift für Klinische Psychologie, 15*, 57-70.

v. Rad, M. (1983). *Alexithymie. Empirische Untersuchungen zur Diagnostik und Therapie psychosomatisch Kranker.* Berlin: Springer Verlag.

v. Rad, M., Lalucut, T., & Lolas, F. (1977). Differences of verbal behavior in psychosomatic and psychoneurotic patients. *Psychotherapie and Psychosomatik, 28*, 83-97.

Waid, W. N. (1976). Skin conductance response to both signaled and unsignalled noxious stimulation predicts level of socialization. *Journal of Personality and Social Psychology, 35*, 923- 929.

Waid, W. N., & Orne, M. T. (1981). Cognitive, social and personality processes in the physiological detection of deception. In L. Berkowitz (Ed.), *Advances in Experimental Social Psychology, 14*, 61-106.

Waid, W. N., & Orne, M. T. (1982). Reduced electrodermal response to conflict, failure to inhibit dominant behaviors and deliquent proneness. *Journal of Personality and Social Psychology, 34*, 769-774.

Weinberger, D. A., Schwartz, G. E., & Davidson, R. J. (1979). Low-anxious, high-anxious and repressive coping styles. Psychometric patterns and behavioral and physiological responses to stress. *Journal of Abnormal Psychology, 88,* 369-380.

Weinstein, S., Avervill, J.R., Opton, E.M., & Lazarus, R.S. (1968). Defensive style and discrepancy between self-report and physiological indexes of stress. *Journal of Personality and Social Psychology, 10,* 406-413.

Wolff, H. H. (1977). The contribution of the interview situation to the restriction of fantasy life and emotional experience in psychosomatic patients. *Psychotherapie und Psychosomatik, 28,* 58-67.

Zuckerman, M. Kolin, E. A., Price, L., & Zoob, I. (1964). Development of a sensation seeking scale. *Journal of Consulting Psychololgy, 28,* 477-482.

Zuckerman, M., Larrance, D. T., Spiegel, N. H., & Klorman, R. (1981). Controlling nonverbal displays: facial expressions and tone of voice. *Journal of Experimental Social Psychology, 17,* 506-524.

Emotional Communication, Emotional Competence, and Physical Illness: A Developmental-Interactionist View

ROSS BUCK

The question of the relationship between emotion and physical illness is one of the most important, and at the same time most contentious, issues in the behavioral sciences. In recent years there have been a number of studies suggesting that personality, emotion, and other psychosocial factors may be involved in a wide variety of illnesses, both in the predisposition to those illnesses and in the ability to cope with them once they have occurred. These factors include life changes and other sorts of stress, social support, and personality patterns such as the Type-A pattern associated with heart disease, the Type-C pattern associated with cancer, and the alexithymic personality pattern associated with psychosomatic disorder. Others have disputed these findings, arguing that it is premature to draw definitive conclusions in this area because of extraordinarily difficult problems of measurement, definition, and control (see Angell, 1985).

One of the problems in this area is that the research findings tend to be considered in isolation, without an overall theoretical conceptualization. This chapter will not review these findings in detail, drawing instead upon recent reviews to establish certain basic points (Buck, 1988a; Rodin & Salovey, 1989). Instead, it will present a general theoretical position – developmental interactionist theory – from which, it is argued, these findings can be related to one another in a coherent way. This position will be used to examine the following areas of application: the effects of life stress, the definition and measurement of the phenomenon of alexithymia and social support of illness, the relationship of individual differences and illness.

This chapter will suggest that individual bioregulation involves in part the attainment of *emotional competence*, which is defined as the ability to deal in an appropriate and satisfactory way with one's own feelings and desires. The way to emotional competence is through emotional education, which involves *emotional communication*, which in turn requires a certain level of emotional expressiveness on the part of the individual in question. Emotional communication occurs in the context of personal relationships, and it is argued that the great importance of "social support" in resisting illness is derived from the role of emotional communication in fostering individual emotional competence and bioregulation. This argument implies that the most important individual characteristic from the point of view of successful bioregulation is a moderate level of emotional expressiveness: either too little or too much expressiveness can theoretically contribute to a lack of effective emotional communication and thereby to deficiencies in emotional education, emotional competence, and individual bioregulation.

Developmental-Interactionist Theory

In the contemporary controversy regarding the relationship of cognition and emotion, these terms are rarely defined. I have argued in other contexts that implicitly "cognition" is defined differently by, for example, Zajonc and Lazarus, with Zajonc (1984) regarding cognition as involving relatively complex information processing with a transformation of sensory input, and Lazarus (1984) defining even a "primitive evaluative perception" (p. 124) as cognition. Zajonc's definition of cognition corresponds to "knowledge by description" in epistemological theory, while Lazarus's corresponds to "knowledge by acquaintance" (Buck, 1988a, 1990b).

Emotion as Bodily Information

Developmental interactionist theory defines cognition simply and generally as KNOWLEDGE, and defines emotion as a readout of motivational systems (see Buck, 1985). It does not regard cognition and emotion to be "related" to one another: instead, emotion is seen to be a KIND of cognition, involving particular SOURCES of knowledge. More specifically, biological emotions are seen to often (but not always) involve the possibility of an immediate acquaintance with, or direct knowledge of, certain kinds of internal bodily processes both as subjective experience from within oneself (Emotion III) and as signaled by the displays and expressive behaviors of others (Emotion II).

The Interactionist Component

The interactionist aspect of the theory is analogous in some respects to the traditional Schachter and Singer (1962) view of emotion as involving an interaction between "cognitive" and "physiological" systems. However, the present view recasts the former in terms of general-purpose processing systems (GPPS) and the latter in terms of special-purpose processing systems (SPPS). SPPSs are phylogenetically determined or "built-in," "hard-wired" systems which are structured at the species level over the course of evolution. GPPS are systems that are open to structuring by experience over the course of the development of the organism, or over the course of ontogeny.

SPPSs are not meant to be contrasted in any way with "cognition." Indeed, SPSSs are considered to be *sources* of cognition, or sources of knowledge, of certain sorts. For one, they are sources of structured information about certain bodily processes. SPSSs appear at a variety of levels: indeed reflexes, instincts, drives, primary affects, and effectance motivation are all considered to be SPPSs at different hierarchical levels. Collectively these are termed primary motiva-tional-emotional systems or *primes* (Buck, 1985).

As one proceeds up the hierarchy from reflexes, there is an increasing inter-action between the SPPS in question and GPPSs of association and learning. Thus, reflexes are little influenced by learning; instincts are characterized by highly stereotyped behavior sequences which may require specific sorts of expe-rience for their proper expression; drives are characterized by specific bodily needs and an activation and direction of behavior in directions that tend to facilitate the discovery of circumstances that satisfy those needs, etc. (Buck, 1985). In this way, SPPSs and GPPSs are not considered to be at two ends of a continuum but rather are seen as two types of systems that interact increasingly as one goes up the hierarchy (Buck, 1985, 1988a).

The Developmental Component

This interaction between special-purpose and general-purpose processing sys-tems occurs in a developmental context, hence the term "developmental-inter-actionist." Just as the child must learn about events in the external physical en-vironment, the child must learn about, label, and otherwise come to terms with events within his or her own body (accessible via the Emotion III process) and events within the bodies of others (accessible via the pickup of the expressive, Emotion II displays of the other). This is the process of EMOTIONAL EDU-CATION (Buck, 1983, 1988a).

Emotional Education

Emotional education is defined as the process of learning *about* bodily informa-tion, including information deriving from "drives" (hunger, sex) as well as "af-fects" (the primary affects of happiness, sadness, fear, anger, etc.; the effectance affects of curiosity, cognitive dissonance, understanding, etc; and the social af-fects of pride, shame, guilt, envy, pity, etc.; see Buck, 1985, 1988a). As noted, this information is available via the subjective experience (Emotion III readout) of one's own feelings and desires, as well as the pickup of the spontaneous dis-plays (Emotion II readout) of the feelings and desires of others.

According to Gibsonian theory, events in the external environment consti-tute affordances: they can be "picked up" directly because they afford actions of an important sort and are therefore dealt with by perceptual systems that have evolved as phylogenetic adaptations. Developmental-interactionist theory sug-gests that the notion of affordances can be generalized as *social affordances*: dis-plays that are "picked up" directly because they afford interpersonal actions of an important sort (Buck, 1988b). More speculatively but equally importantly, the theory argues that the Emotion III readout – the subjective experience of feelings and desires – involves the perception of an "internal ecology" of structured information that can be usefully regarded as AFFECTIVE AFFORDANCES.

It might be objected that, in the original Gibsonian conception, the pickup of affordances is regarded as VERIDICAL, while there seems to be much more doubt about the veridicality of the pickup of social and affective affordances. This objection, however, may confuse sensitivity and accessibility with veridicality. Very sensitive perceptual systems have evolved – for good reason – to deal with, say, events in the general visual environment (for human beings and other primates) compared to events in the social and bodily environments. This being so, it is easier to make discriminations and descriptions of the visual world, and, together with the fact that the visual world is accessible to all human beings, this makes it much easier to reach consensus about the nature of such events. Social and affective affordances are more comparable in sensitivity to, for example, taste and smell, whereas in human beings discrimination is much more difficult in comparison with vision.

The affordances associated with taste and smell are similar perhaps to social affordances for human beings, in that there is not much of a "common vocabulary" to describe such events, but such a vocabulary CAN be learned. The perfumer or wine taster learns a special vocabulary of smells or tastes, together with an "education of attention" that allows finer discriminations to be made. Similarly, a vocabulary of expressive behavior can be learned – FACS, MAX, dance notation systems, etc., are examples of such vocabularies – and an individual can learn to note the expressive behaviors of others and to make finer discriminations. However, all of these are different from affective affordances on the matter of accessibility.

Accessibility. Emotional education differs from education in the usual sense because information specifying bodily events is not objectively accessible in the same way as is information specifying events perceived in the external environment. It is accessible only to the responder: only the responder KNOWS (by acquaintance) his or her feelings and desires: hunger, warmth-cold, sexual arousal, happiness, sadness, anger, etc. It is an important tenet of developmental-interactionist theory that such information consists of VERIDICAL affective affordances, although they may be sensed only dimly. It is also a tenet of the theory that this information is ALWAYS ACCESSIBLE to the individual, even though it is normally attended to when it is at relatively high levels. Just as we ignore the feel of comfortable shoes, we ignore our feelings and desires when they are relatively weak and unchanging. However, these feelings and desires – of a certain level of warmth or chill, of hunger or satiety, of sexual arousal, of happiness, of anger – are ALWAYS ACCESSIBLE when our attention is drawn to them, just as is the feel of comfortable shoes. The reader can easily test this proposition to her or his satisfaction by taking a moment to examine these feelings and desires within her/himself.

If it is acknowledged that subjective experience – the Emotion III readout – is accessible to self more than other (even leaving the question of veridicality aside), the question remains how the child learns ABOUT warmth and cold, sexual desire, happiness, and anger: to label them, understand them, and know what they are and what to do when they occur. The child has direct access to the feelings and desires (Emotion III), but the socialization agent has access only to the child's EXPRESSION (Emotion II) of those feelings and desires. The child, I suggest, has less access to his/her own Emotion II expression than does the socialization agent, a proposition illustrated and supported by the well-known attribution experiment of Storms (1973).

The child does, however, have access to the expressive behavior of the other, and it is through exposure to such social affordances that the essentials of emotional education occur. The other responds to the expressive behavior of the child in such a way that the emotional experience of the child is (or is not) clarified in a socially appropriate manner. For example, if the child screams and throws things, and the socialization agent typically labels the reaction with the English word "angry," the child will learn to associate that particular pattern of subjective experience with the label "anger," and also hopefully learn what the culture expects him/her to do when such feelings occur. The socialization agent's response is analogous in many respects to biofeedback, and I have termed this sort of feedback learning SOCIAL BIOFEEDBACK (Buck, 1988a). The other major way by which the child learns about feelings and desires is, of course, by imitation and modeling, and this, I think, is one of the motivating factors behind the choice and use of mass communication media (Buck, 1988c).

Emotional Communication

Emotional education, whether it proceeds via social biofeedback or via imitation and modeling, depends upon emotional COMMUNICATION, and more specifically upon spontaneous emotional communication (Buck, 1988d). Communication is seen as occurring in two simultaneous streams. The symbolic stream is communication in the conventional sense: it is learned and culturally patterned, used intentionally, composed of symbols, and propositional. Spontaneous communication, in contrast, is biologically based in both its sending and receiving aspects, is nonvoluntary, composed of signs rather than symbols, and it is nonpropositional. Spontaneous communication involves the communication of motivational and emotional states (desires and feelings) via phylogenetically structured displays and expressive movements: it is, in essence, a conversation between limbic systems in which both sending and (given attention) receiving occur automatically.

Spontaneous communication is based upon SPSSs, while symbolic communication is based upon GPSSs. The two are NOT usefully considered to be at opposite ends of a continuum: rather they are two qualitatively different sorts of systems that interact. Their interaction can best be conceptualized as in Figure 1. Spontaneous communication is present in all communication situations, while symbolic communication may be entirely absent or may be much more impor- tant in the overall communication process than is spontaneous communication.

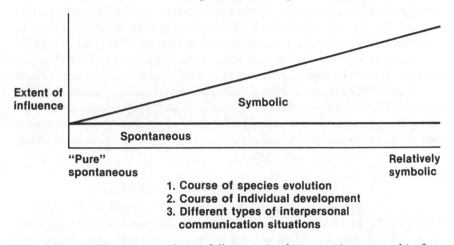

The ordinate of Figure 1 can be usefully conceived as a continuum, and in fact this helps to illustrate the relationship not only between spontaneous and sym- bolic communication, but the more general relationship between SPSSs and GPPSs. It can represent different sorts of communication situations, from unbridled passion on the left to a dry lecture on the right; it can represent the development of the individual, with the newborn infant on the left and the adult on the right; or it can represent the phylogenetic scale with simple crea- tures (ants, bees) on the left and human beings on the right. In each case, the example on the left represents a situation dominated by SPSSs that are biologi- cally structured and unlearned, while on the right these systems are still present, but dominated by the functioning of GPPSs, including in human beings lan- guage.

Emotional Competence

In emotional education, the individual learns to label and understand his or her own feelings and desires. In effect, the individual learns via GPPSs ABOUT the Emotion III information that is known directly via SPSSs. However, unlike other learning where the phenomenon in question is accessible to all, emotional education concerns a phenomenon that is known directly only by the subject. This makes it possible to learn "incorrect" lessons concerning Emotion III in- formation, where the criterion of correctness involves the natural functioning of the emotional system in question.

For example, if the socialization agent responds to screaming and throwing things by labeling it as "anger," the child will gain a "correct" label for the subjectively experienced Emotion III state (which presumably involves neurochemical activity in the region of the amygdalae). However, it is conceivable that if the socialization agent consistently responds to such behavior by saying "You're a bad girl" and acting accordingly with punishment and hostility, a very different sort of lesson would be learned, one which might encourage the individual to regard such Emotion III information with shame, guilt, fear, and/or anxiety. The extent to which emotional education results in a correct and useful understanding of one's feelings and desires, as defined by the ability to express such states openly and appropriately in a variety of social contexts, is EMOTIONAL COMPETENCE. Emotional competence is to bodily information what competence in general is to information in the external physical environment, what and social competence is to information in the social environment (Buck, 1991).

Emotional Competence and Bioregulation

Emotional competence implies that the individual knows how to respond when feelings and desires occur: that he or she understands what these mean in his/her socio-cultural context and how to express them appropriately and effectively. If this is not the case, it is probable that the third type of emotional response – Emotion I, or the autonomic/endocrine/immune system response – may be activated, with possibly negative consequences for health.

Developmental-interactionist theory recognizes three sorts of emotional response: Emotion I (physiological responses associated with bodily adaptation, including the "fight or flight" response), Emotion II (spontaneous expressive displays), and Emotion III (subjective experience). The theory predicts dynamic relationships between these responses based in part upon their accessibility during the social learning process. Specifically, Emotion II and III responses are, as we have seen, differentially accessible to the self and the socialization agent. Emotion I responses – autonomic, endocrine, and immune system responses – are unique in that they are relatively inaccessible. Socialization agents cannot punish the child for having such responses because neither they nor the child are normally aware of their existence.

I suggest that it is for this reason that physiological and overt responses are often negatively correlated in between-subject analyses (Buck, 1979, 1980; Buck, Miller, & Caul, 1974; Buck, Savin, Miller, & Caul, 1972). When overt behavior of any sort is punished and thereby inhibited or suppressed, it is likely both that such punishment will in itself cause conditioned emotional responses in similar situations in the future, and that emotional competence will be compromised in that the individual will not in the future know how to effectively handle the feelings and desires involved. The result would be a kind of helplessness. Such inhibition may, of course, be based upon temperament in interaction with social learning (Buck, 1979, 1984, 1988a).

In sum, I am proposing that a lack (or surfeit) of emotional expressiveness will hinder emotional communication, emotional education, and consequent emotional competence, resulting in failure of bioregulation of various sorts. This has implications for the bioregulatory functions of personal relationships. Assuming that a lack of emotional competence is indeed related (indirectly) to heightened Emotion I responses, and that emotional competence varies with different personal relationships, it follows that the activation of Emotion I responses will be affected by the nature of the personal relationship that is salient at the moment. This in turn may help to explain the strong relationships between social support and resistance to illness, which shall be considered below.

Personal Relationships and Emotional Competence

The child learns to deal with his or her feelings and desires in interaction with other persons – parents, teachers, peers, siblings – and emotional education is affected by the qualities of the particular relationships that he or she establishes. Moreover, as each relationship becomes deeper or more intimate, it is increasingly characterized by shared expectations that can become RULES specific to that relationship. This phenomenon is well established in the literature on personal relationships (Duck et al., 1984). This has important implications for emotional education and competence, for it suggests that the "rules" one learns about emotion may differ with different interaction partners. Thus, one may be more emotionally expressive and competent with some persons than others (see Buck, 1989a).

The notion that emotional expression and communication is specific to particular personal and social relationships has important implications as far as the observation and measurement of expressive behavior is concerned. First, it implies that those close to a person may often have a distorted view of that person's actual level of expressiveness because their observation of expressive behavior is affected by relation-specific rules. Thus, those close to a person may not always be the best judges of that person's actual feelings unless they know the person very well, in a variety of social contexts. The same point applies to persons with a formal relationship, as in doctor-patient or student-teacher relationships. Here, the expressive behavior is influenced by general expectations about what is role-appropriate.

A second implication of this notion is that expressive behavior would be expected to be influenced in relationship-specific ways whenever a given personal or social relationship is salient, so that observations of expressive behavior may be less generally valid when the person is with a significant other than when he or she is alone or in a situation where social expectations are minimized. Both of these considerations are important when considering the measurement of emotional expression and its relationship with health/disease, as we shall see.

The Implications of Inhibition

Rules about emotional expression, such as Ekman and Friesen's (1975) "facial management techniques" and "display rules", produce learned patterns of non-verbal expression which are symbolic rather than spontaneous: a nonverbal version of Goffman's "presentation of self". We learn to CONTROL our expressive behavior, allowing us to present ourselves nonverbally in socially appropriate ways in a variety of settings. I suggest that such control is not harmful or stressful in any medical sense, particularly if one has close friends or family with whom one can "let one's hair down" and express one's true feelings. The control of nonverbal behavior thus produces symbolic behaviors, although these may be virtually identical to spontaneous behaviors. We have evolved to be highly effective liars, for good reason (see Buck, 1984). Emotional expression can be controlled in a variety of ways: an existing motivational/emotional state can be modulated (increased or decreased), a nonexisting state can be simulated, or an existing state can be falsified by masking it with the expression of a nonexisting state (Ekman & Friesen, 1975).

There is another sort of acquired influence on the display that may, however, be stressful and medically problematic. This is INHIBITION as opposed to control (Buck, 1984). Inhibition is the conditioned SUPPRESSION of the spontaneous display. Display rules do not affect the spontaneous display: such behavior is symbolic by definition (see Buck, 1984). The spontaneous display can however be inhibited, as when expression leads to general social disapproval and punishment – "Big boys don't cry;" "Young ladies don't hit." The effects of such inhibition are, unlike the effects of the display rules, unidirectional. The display is in all cases lessened – suppressed. There is a great deal of speculation, backed up by considerable data, that such suppression may be associated with psychophysiological responses that are stressful to the body. The notion that the inhibition of spontaneous emotional expression is stressful is the SUPPRESSION HYPOTHESIS (see Buck, 1984).

This, then, is a summary of those principles of developmental-interactionist theory that are relevant to issues of emotional expression and health. What follows is a summary of some of the major findings in the literature on emotional expression and health which may be addressed by these principles.

The Stress-Illness Relationship

The relationship between stress and bodily symptoms has long been recognized. The Greek physician Galen estimated that 60% of his patients had symptoms of emotional rather than physical origin, which is close to the current estimate of 60-80%. However, psychological factors in disease have been minimized in the recent growth of scientific medicine. Miller (1983) pointed out that for many centuries the available drugs were either worthless or harmful, and that "the continued prestige of physicians rested on purely psychological factors such as the placebo effect and the remarkable capacity of the body to heal itself" (p. 3). The discovery of effective anesthetics, vaccines, antibiotics, and other drugs tended to emphasize the physical and technological side of illness and treatment. Ironically, it also tended to downgrade the emotional factors in illness, and the personal side of medical treatment, and Miller argued that many of the important psychosocial functions of the physician therefore came to be neglected. The study of emotional factors in illness can be organized into at least three major areas: the study of life change and illness, the relationship of social support to illness, and the role of individual differences in illness.

Life Events and Illness

One of the first suggestions that various illnesses are related to stress was the discovery of illness clusters: within a few years an individual may experience a wide range of illnesses of various causes involving a variety of bodily systems (Hinkle & Wolff, 1958; Rahe, 1990). These illness clusters seem to be related to the individual's adaptation to his current life situation. One of the most common events calling for adaptation by the individual is a change in one's life. Such changes may be seen by the individual as positive (a raise, marriage, an outstanding personal achievement, etc.) or negative (the death of a friend or family member, divorce or separation, being fired, etc.). Studies have related such life changes to the occurrence of a wide variety of illnesses (see Buck, 1988a).

The studies of life change and illness have been critically examined in recent years, and this has helped to clarify the issues involved. Many of the criticisms have centered on the methodological problems involved in the measurement of life change (see Creed, 1985). These criticisms are more methodological than substantive, in that none seriously questions the existence of a basic relationship between life change and illness. The volume of evidence makes it clear that the assessment of life change "will lead to a more complete understanding of how psychosocial factors interact with bodily functioning" (Creed, 1985, p. 113).

One kind of study of life change that avoids the problems of measuring events focuses upon the health effects of a single, definable event, such as the 1979 nuclear accident at Three Mile Island (TMI) in Pennsylvania. Most such studies find significant health effects, and they support the general notion that it makes sense to regard such effects as involving stress-induced immunosuppression (see Baum, Gatchel & Schaeffer, 1983; Fisher, 1985). However, there are large individual differences in that some people appear to cope successfully with the event while others do not.

These conclusions are bolstered by prospective studies which follow a number of subjects for a period of time and relate changes in health to life changes occurring within that time. For example, Totman, Kiff, Reed, and

Craig (1980) found the occurrence of common colds to be related to life stress in the previous 6 months, and Meyer and Hoggarty (1962) found that strepto-coccal infections were related to periods of family tension as reported indepen-dently by parents. A number of prospective studies have been conducted on the effects of life events on the outcomes of pregnancy. Most have found that preg-nancy complications (premature delivery, low birthweight infants, etc.) are asso-ciated with a relatively high incidence of life stress. However, it is noteworthy that Omer, Friedlander, Palti and Shekel (1986) found a *decrease* in premature deliveries in four Israeli hospitals during and after the 1973 Yom Kippur War. A similar finding was noted in Finland during World War II: the incidence of low birthweight deliveries decreased (Corsa, Pugh, Ingalls, & Gordon, 1952). Omer et al. suggested that this may be due to an increase in social support during war-time. Indeed, there is evidence that changes involving relationships with other people can have particularly dramatic health effects.

Social Factors and Illness

Findings from both animal and human studies suggest that the supportive pre-sence of others can have a beneficial effect upon the physiological response to stress and increase resistance to illness (see Bovard, 1959; Cobb, 1976). Con-versely, a loss of a significant personal relationship – as in bereavement – can have disruptive effects upon the body (Hofer, 1984). The influence of such so-cial factors depends both upon the nature of the relationship with the other and the nature of the stressful circumstance (Buck & Parke, 1972).

Kiecolt-Glaser et al. (1984a, b) have investigated the combined effects of stress, social support, and life change on immune system functioning. They found that an important measure of immune system functioning – natural killer (NK) cell activity – was significantly related to both life change and reported loneliness, as well as the stress of an examination. Also, Kiecolt-Glaser et al. (1987) found relationships between marital quality, marital disruption, and im-mune system functioning in married and divorced women. Sarason and his colleagues have also emphasized the importance of social support in the suscep-tibility to illness (Sarason, Sarason, Potter, & Antoni, 1985). Other studies gen-erally confirm the importance of social support in the management of stress (Buck 1988a).

This importance of social relationships in the link between stress and illness highlights the fact that adaptation is not a process that occurs wholly within the individual. Developmental-interactionist theory views expression and commu-nication to be a fundamental feature of motivation and emotion, and this view implies that other organisms participate directly in the adaptation of the indi-vidual: that personal relationships have BIOREGULATORY functions (see Blanck, Buck, & Rosenthal, 1986). I suggest that this is related to the increase in emotional competence afforded by the relationship (Buck, 1989a).

Individual Differences and Illness

Although there is evidence that both life events and social support contribute to the individual's tendency to become ill, it is clear that there are individual differences in such susceptibility. For example, there is evidence that people who are socially skilled develop stronger and more effective social support networks (Sarason, et al., 1985). Also, the degree of *control* that an individual has (or thinks he or she has) is an important determinant of the effects of stress (see Stewart et al., 1986).

There may also be individual differences in resistance or susceptibility to specific illnesses. In particular, there is evidence that two of the most serious and widespread illnesses – cardiovascular disease and cancer – are at least sometimes associated with particular personality patterns.

The Type-A personality and cardiovascular disease

The description of the Type-A behavior pattern (TABP) is based upon the "expressive style" of the individual: such an individual walks briskly; has a tense, teeth-clenching, jaw-grinding facial set; has "hostile" eyes that look unflinchingly at others; has loud, terse, explosive, and accelerating speech with few mid-sentence pauses (Hall, Friedman, & Harris, 1986). A study comparing the facial expressions of Type-A and non-Type-A (Type-B) individuals concluded that the TABP is associated with facial expressions of glare and disgust (Chesney, Ekman, Friesen, Black, & Hecker, 1990). Chesney et al. suggested that these expressions reflect the increased hostility of Type-A individuals.

The research on the TABP includes that of the Western Collaborative Study Group, a prospective study which first assessed Type-A tendencies on 3,000 individuals and then followed them for 8 1/2 years. The competitive and hard-driving Type-A individuals were found to be twice as likely as others to have heart attacks, even when risk factors such as obesity, smoking, and hypertension were statistically controlled (Rosenman, Brand, Scholtz, & Friedman, 1976). Such results led a National Heart, Lung, and Blood Institute review panel to conclude that the TABP is significantly associated with an increased risk of heart disease (Cooper, Detrie, & Weiss, 1981).

With the question of the importance of the TABP as a risk factor apparently resolved, there was increased interest among researchers in theoretical and measurement issues. The preferred measure of the TABP is the structured interview (SI), which involves a provocative and challenging confrontation between the subject and a specially trained interviewer. The SI has been described as "behavioral assessment in the rough" (Chesney, Eagleston & Rosenman, 1980). Particular emphasis is placed on the speech mannerisms of the subject, including the loudness, explosivity, rapidity, and quickness of response (Hall et al., 1986). However, the relationship between the operationally defined measure (involving speech style) and the conceptual definition of the TABP is by no means clear (see Dembroski et al., 1985; Scherwitz, Berton & Leventhal, 1977; Schucker & Jacobs, 1977).

Because the SI is complex and expensive, there have been at least 10 attempts to measure the TABP by self-report questionnaires (Rodin & Salovey, 1989). However, these scales have not been as successful as the SI in predicting coronary disease.

A recent large-scale prospective study, the Multiple Risk Factor Intervention Trial (MRFIT: "Mister Fit") involving over 12,500 high risk men, failed to find a relationship between the TABP and heart disease. In 3,100 of these subjects the TABP was measured by the SI; in the remainder, it was measured by questionnaire. Some have used this failure to question the validity of the TABP and its relationship with heart disease, while others have argued that some of the SI interviews in the MRFIT study were flawed (see Fischman, 1987). Specifically, it has been suggested that some of the MRFIT interviewers asked questions too quickly and interrupted the subject. This may have turned off the relatively suspicious and hostile Type A's so that they hid their hostile feelings and appeared to be the more placid Type B's. Conversely, the more socially sensitive Type B's may have played along by responding more quickly and automatically, and thus appeared to be Type A's (Scherwitz, reported in Fischman, 1987). Whatever the case, this controversy is interesting because it both emphasizes the *interactive* nature of the SI and suggests that the TABP may be affected by the presently existing interpersonal environment. This in turn suggests a need to relate the TABP to the real-life behavior of the subject in the home and workplace in the context of the *actual personal relationships* of the subject with other people.

A variable possibly related to the TABP concept but not formally assessed in the SI has also successfully predicted coronary disease. This is the "Anger-In" dimension, described as a tendency to withhold the expression of anger even when such expression is appropriate. For example Dembroski et al. (1985) studied patients in the standard SI, but used a component scoring system which included ratings of Anger-In and also Potential for Hostility, which was defined as a disposition to experience anger, irritation, and/or annoyance to such frustrating events as being caught behind a slow-moving car. Of the measures taken in the SI only Anger-In and Potential for Hostility were significantly related to coronary disease. Also, their effects were interactive, in that Potential for Hostility was associated with disease only among patients high on the Anger-In dimension. Dembroski et al. concluded that hostility and anger suppression may be the most important elements in the TABP, and that the other attributes of the TABP may be "relatively benign" (1985, p. 231).

McClelland (1982) noted similarities between the TABP and his notion of a *need for power*, which involves the need to exert control. McClelland suggested that men high in the need for power may often be in a state of chronic sympathetic nervous system arousal. Such people have shown increased epinephrine levels in the urine, particularly if they report distress over their inability to exert control, which McClelland termed *power stress*. McClelland suggested that a high need for power in and of itself is not necessarily unhealthy, but if the expression of power is frustrated or blocked, either by internal inhibition or external power stress, it will be associated with chronic sympathetic activation, disruption of the immune system, and disease. He reported that subjects with a high need for power but low power stress were found to be healthy compared to those with high power stress, who were lower on measures of immune system functioning. High vs. low power stress was not associated with immune system functioning in subjects with low need for power.

Interestingly, the relationships between the need for power and illness occur only if the individual involved has a relatively low need for affiliation. McClelland (1982) hypothesized that the need for affiliation may lead to the formation of personal relationships that ameliorate the potentially disruptive effects of the need for power; and that caring for others in effect counteracts the harmful effects of the need for power.

A recent study seems to support the notion that the effects of the TABP may be related to social support. Orth-Gomer and Unden (1990) reported in a 10-year follow-up of a study of 150 middle-aged men that the mortality rate for men showing Type-A and Type-B behavior was similar (24% and 22% respectively). However, a lack of social support was found to be an independent predictor of mortality in Type-A men, but not Type-B men. The authors use this finding to suggest a possible explanation for the inconsistencies between intervention studies of the TABP – which generally show positive outcomes when Type-A behavior is reduced – and follow-up investigations like the MRFIT study which often have been unable to demonstrate negative effects of the TABP. Specifically, they suggest that Type-A modification programs may work by increasing the availability of social support, and that this may be "the mechanism through which Type-A modification exerts its main effects on cardiovascular health" (p. 59).

This interpretation of the effects of the TABP in terms of social support is consistent with the findings of strong relationships between social support and health, and in particular with McClelland's findings, and they are also consistent with the emphasis of developmental-interactionist theory on the importance of emotional communication for emotional self-regulation. Thus, the TABP, which has been conceptualized as an INDIVIDUAL "personality" characteristic, may actually have its effects through SOCIAL forces that operate via emotional communication. There is certainly no attempt here to discount the importance of individual characteristics, but rather to point out that the effects of such characteristics often operate via their impact upon social relationships (Buck, 1990c). There is evidence that other individual differences related to health outcomes can be explained in a similar manner.

The Type-C personality and cancer

Psychological and social factors have been implicated in both the predisposition to cancer and the ability to cope with the disease. Depression, helplessness, anxiety, and grief have been cited as frequent precursors of cancer, and there have been reports that feelings of hopelessness, and the loss of a significant personal and dependent relationship often occur near the time of the clinical onset of cancer. Prospective studies have suggested that a limited ability to express depression, anger, and anxiety may be associated with a predisposition to cancer, and one prospective study found a strong relationship between "rationality vs. antiemotionality" measured in 1965-1966 and cancer mortality occurring years later (Grossarth-Maticek et al., 1985). Rationality vs. antiemotionality was measured by a self-report scale indicating whether the person showed emotional spontaneity or "cognitive censoring", with items asking whether the person tries to operate according to reason and logic, even when to do so is contrary to his or her feelings. Cancer incidence was 40 times higher among those high in reason and logic as opposed to spontaneity.

Psychological and social factors are also important in the process of coping with cancer, and may play a significant role in its clinical course. Weisman and Worden (1976) found that the specific diagnosis or prognosis was less important than psychosocial distress in predicting the patient's ability to cope with cancer. Also, several studies have suggested that a certain "coping style" involving the denial of illness and a resolution to fight the disease (fighting spirit) may be associated with decreased morbidity and mortality of cancer (Pettingale, 1984). The personality pattern most closely associated with cancer is like that associated with cardiovascular disease in that both involve the expression of emotion, and particularly, anger. However, in contrast to the impatient "pent-up" aggressiveness of the TABP, the personality pattern associated with cancer has been termed "pathological niceness" (Renneker, 1981). This has been termed the cancer-prone personality or the "Type-C behavior pattern" (Greer & Watson, 1985).

The Type-C pattern involves the suppression of emotional responses, particularly when angry, combined with conformity, compliance, unassertiveness, and patience. Such people appear to be aware of negative emotions, but suppress them behind a facade of pleasantness and calmness, and appear as compliant, submissive, selfless, passive, and anxious to please.

It should be emphasized that the "Type-C" personality pattern, assuming it exists, is not *responsible* for cancer. Cancer is after all a disorder that occurs at the level of single cells which causes them to grow out of control. Few would argue that the Type-C personality initiates this process, or that it is necessary or sufficient to promote it. The suggestion is rather that for *some* cancers, in *some* situations personality factors can influence the cancer process in interaction with biological mechanisms.

Studies of the biological mechanisms that may mediate this influence have emphasized the immune system (see Bammer & Newberry, 1982). Animal research has shown that stress which impairs immune system functioning can lead to the development and rapid spread of experimentally induced cancer, and depression in humans has been associated with increased cortisol levels and depressed function of T cells. In a review of this literature, Peterson, Popkin, and Hall (1981) suggested that "immunosuppression associated with depression may be a mediating factor in cancer" (p. 779).

Pettingale (1985) has noted many possible mechanisms in addition to immune system mechanisms by which psychological processes may affect cancer. Such mechanisms may vary for different kinds of cancer and different stages of tumor development. For example, emotional suppression may be associated with increased autonomic and hormonal responding which may exacerbate the effects of stress. Grossarth-Matticek and his colleagues (1985) have also suggested that the blocked expression of needs and feelings plays a central role in the effects of stress upon cancer. They also argued that psychosocial risk factors in cancer have been "grossly underestimated" (p. 175).

We have seen a common link in the psychological factors associated with cardiovascular disease and cancer: they both involve difficulties in the expression of emotion. Such difficulties are also implicated in the classic psychosomatic disorders.

Alexithymia and psychosomatic illness

The "classic" psychosomatic illnesses are those in which psychological factors have been implicated as major factors in the etiology of the disorder. These include certain forms of ulcer, colitis, asthma, and headache. Although there is no clear evidence that these are closely associated with particular conflicts, there is evidence that they may be associated with a general lack of emotional expression. Marty and de M'Uzan (1963) called attention to the preoccupation of psychosomatic patients with minute details, which they termed operational thinking ("la pensée operatoire"). Sifneos (1967, 1973) noted that such patients have a remarkable inability to describe their own feelings in words. He coined the term *alexithymia* (literally "no words for mood") to describe this inability to express verbally one's feelings.

A number of studies have found alexithymic characteristics in patients with psychosomatic illnesses. Anderson (1981) suggested in a review of this literature that "impairment in the expression of affect is a necessary but not sufficient factor in the development of psychosomatic disease" (p. 149). Lesser (1981) pointed out in another review that, although alexithymia is a relatively new term, the concept is firmly grounded in psychoanalytic theory and a large body of consistent clinical observations. He also suggested that alexithymia should be more precisely defined, and that methods of measurement should be developed and validated (see Paulson, 1985).

Alexithymia may be related to deficits in the spontaneous expression and communication of emotion (Buck, 1979, 1988a). First, there is the evidence already noted that spontaneously expressive persons tend to have smaller skin conductance and heart rate responses in between-subjects analyses than do non-expressive persons (Buck, 1984). Similarly, subjects high in alexithymia were found in one study to have relatively high levels of sympathetic nervous system responding and a dissociation between subjective and physiological stress responses (Martin & Pihl, 1986), and in another study to have higher levels of electrodermal arousal and slower recovery times in novel situations compared with low alexithymic persons (Rabavilas, 1987). Second, a recent study has shown that alexithymia (measured psychometrically) is related to deficits in the spontaneous expression of negative affects, but not to symbolic (i.e., posed) expression (McDonald & Prkachin, 1990). Third, both alexithymia and a lack of spontaneous expressiveness have been associated with deficits in right hemisphere processing (Buck, 1990a; Buck & Duffy, 1980; Shalev et al., 1988; TenHouten et al., 1985, 1987, 1988). These findings have important implications for the understanding of both the neurological basis and the wide-ranging effects of emotional expression and suppression (Buck, 1984, 1988a).

Conclusions

Any attempt to understand the relationship between stress and disease must take into account the nature of the events being experienced in the life of the individual, the nature of the social support network available to the individual, and the personal qualities of the individual. There is a significant thread running through the discussion of the latter involving the extent to which feelings are "held in" or expressed openly: in cardiovascular disease, cancer, and psychosomatic illness a lack of spontaneous emotional expression appears to exacerbate the stress-disease link.

Developmental-interactionist theory offers a theoretical orientation within which these phenomena may be viewed systematically. First, the emphasis upon emotional communication in the attainment of emotional competence is compatible with the evidence that illnesses of various sorts are linked with problems in emotional expression. Second, the findings regarding the importance of personal relationships are consistent with the notion that emotional expression and communication are specific to such relationships. This fact may also explain some problems in replicating research in this area: the failure to consistently measure emotional expression may be caused by differences in the interpersonal situations in which expressiveness is assessed. Finally, the notion of emotional competence can be used to conceptualize situations in which a lack of ability to respond overtly to one's own feelings and desires might result in the activation of physiological response systems normally associated with adaptation – the fight or flight response – involving the autonomic, endocrine, and immune systems. These "Emotion I" responses can reasonably be predicted when the organism is in a situation in which an overt response is, for one reason or another, not available (Buck, 1989b, 1985, 1988a).

Thus, if it is difficult to express and communicate a given motivational/emotional state, as when expression is actively inhibited or, more passively, when few cultural models are provided showing how to deal with certain feelings or the language is so constructed that a given sort of expression is difficult, the state does not "go away". Developmental-interactionist theory suggests that the inability effectively to deal with one's feelings and desires can be sufficient to arouse autonomic and other physiological responses (i.e., the fight-or-flight response) simply because a lack of competence (i.e., helplessness) is an aversive state. Also, if the social inhibition has been active (as in the intimidating "Big boys don't cry," or "Young ladies don't hit"), it is likely that the situation in which inhibition occurs is in itself aversive and apt to create conditioned emotional responses (CERs) which have an autonomic component.

In addition, a lack of competence, or active inhibition, in a given area of emotional expression will disrupt emotional communication and consequent social support in that area. Indeed, it may create a vicious circle in which a lack of expressiveness makes it difficult to form openly expressive personal relationships. It is possible in fact that much of the stress and increased susceptibility to physical illness associated with a lack of expression is due to the consequent lack of authentic spontaneous emotional communication with others and the bioregulation that such communication engenders.

This leaves us with a question whose answer is at present unresolved. To what extent are the harmful effects of emotional inhibition due to "intraorganismic" causes – the inappropriate activation of Emotion I responses – as opposed to social causes – a lack of authentic spontaneous communication with others and subsequent individual disregulation? These two explanations are not, of course, mutually exclusive, but it does appear that social and intraorganismic factors may play different roles in different disorders. Thus, if our analysis of the TABP is correct, it suggests that "suppressed" hostility is in fact expressed in ways – negative facial expressions and tones of voice – that tend to turn others away. If others are NOT turned away, the negative effects of the TABP seem not to occur. With the Type-C pattern, in contrast, social competence seems to be quite adequate and the individual is perceived by others as very pleasant and accommodating. The problems here seem at first glance to be intraorganismic, with the lack of expression of negative emotion in some way causing inappropriate Emotion I responding. However, it is conceivable that it is the lack of COMMUNICATION of the negative affect that is the real culprit. The same issue arises with respect to alexithymia: the overall inhibition of expression probably leads to both direct intraorganismic effects on Emotion I responses, and to deficits in emotional communication.

In the end, it seems likely that emotional inhibition negatively impacts disease through both intraorganismic and social processes, that the effects of these processes are interactive, and that both sorts of processes must be considered in designing plans for amelioration and treatment.

A Note on Measurement

Measurement issues are of fundamental importance in the study of the relationship between emotional expression and illness. There is no simple, replicable, externally valid, generally accepted procedure for measuring any of the styles of emotional expression that we have considered. The measurement of the TABP by the SI is fundamentally a measurement of an expressive style, and it is perhaps the best developed of any of the measurement procedures in this area. However, we saw that the exact way that the SI is conducted may have a major impact upon the results, and there seems to be no fully satisfactory self-report scale available. There is no generally recommended procedure for measuring the Type-C personality. Alexithymia is measured in the BIQ interview situation, but this is not as well documented or described as is the SI, and the available self-report scales do not correlate well with it. The self-report scales of alexithymia have had psychometric problems, some of which may be corrected by the Taylor, Ryan and Bagby (1986) *Toronto Alexithymia Scale* (TAS: Bagby, Taylor & Parker, 1988; Morrison & Pihl, 1989). Nevertheless, there are difficulties in using a relatively transparent self-report scale such as this to measure emotional expression, since at least some inexpressive people may not admit, indeed may not even realize, their own lack of expression.

One of the factors that must be taken into account in the measurement of emotional expressiveness is that the social situation should be expected to markedly alter the individual's pattern of expressiveness. An individual who is normally unexpressive may be very expressive in the presence of a significant other, and on the other hand a normally expressive person may "clam up" in the presence of a certain person. In general, any measure of expressiveness that is made in the presence of another person is both a measure of individual expressiveness and a measure of the nature of the personal relationship involved. An effective measure of emotional expressiveness must either minimize social cues, standardize the nature of the social situation, or provide an independent means for assessing the nature of the personal relationship.

Another factor that should be taken into account is the nature of the emotional stimulus which is causing the expression in question. There is little standardization in the field in this regard.

Both of these factors are addressed in the slide-viewing technique, in which a person views a series of slides, and describes his/her emotional response, while being filmed by a hidden camera (Buck, 1989, 1984). The resulting expressions can be analyzed by objective communication scores, the stream of expression can be segmented to reveal points of significant expression, and the resulting points of expression analyzed by a notation system such as FACS, MAX, or dance notation systems (see Buck, 1990a). The study by McDonald and Prkachin (1990), showing that alexithymia (measured by the TAS) was negatively correlated with spontaneous expression (measured via the slide-viewing technique) but not symbolic expression, is consistent with this suggestion. Potentially, styles of expression corresponding to the Type A, Type C, and alexithymic patterns as well as "healthy" patterns of expressiveness may be objectively defined via the slide-viewing technique.

References

Anderson, C.D. (1981). Expression of effect and physiological response in psychosomatic patients. *Journal of Psychosomatic Research, 25,* 143-149.

Angell, M. (1985). Disease as a reflection of the psyche. *New England Journal of Medicine, 321,* 1570-1572.

Bagby, R.M., Taylor, G.J., & Parker, J.D.A. (1988). Construct validity of the Toronto Alexithymia Scale. *Psychotherapy and Psychosomatics, 50,* 29-34.

Bammer, K., & Newberry, B.H. (1982). *Stress and cancer.* Toronto: Hogrefe.

Baum, A., Gatchel, R.J., & Schaeffer, M.A., (1983). Emotional behavior and physiological effects of chronic stress at Three Mile Island. *Journal of Consulting and Clinical Psychology, 51,* 565-572.

Blanck, P.D., Buck, R.W., & Rosenthal, R. (Eds.). (1986). *Nonverbal communication in the clinical context.* University Park: Pennsylvania State University Press.

Bovard, E. (1959). The effects of social stimuli on the response to stress, *Psychological Review, 66,* 267-277.

Buck, R., (1979). Individual differences in nonverbal sending accuracy and electrodermal responding: The externalizing-internalizing dimension. In R. Rosenthal (Ed.), *Skill in nonverbal communication: Individual differences.* Cambridge, MA: Oelgeschlager, Gunn, and Hain.

Buck, R. (1980). Nonverbal behavior and the theory of emotion: The facial feedback hypothesis. *Journal of Personality and Social Psychology, 38,* 811-824.

Buck, R. (1983). Emotional development and emotional education. In R. Plutchik & H. Kellerman (Eds.), *Emotions in early development.* New York: Academic Press.

Buck, R. (1984). *The communication of emotion.* New York: Guilford Press.

Buck, R. (1985). Prime theory: An integrated view of motivation and emotion. *Psychological Review, 92,* 389-413.

Buck, R. (1988a). *Human motivation and emotion.* 2nd Edition. New York: John Wiley & Sons.

Buck, R. (1988b). The perception of facial expression: Individual regulation and social coordination. In T.R. Alley and L.S. Mark (Eds.), *Social and applied aspects of perceiving faces*. Hillsdale, NJ: Lawrence Erlbaum Associates.

Buck, R. (1988c). Emotional education and mass media: A new view of the global village. In R. Hawkins, J. Weimann, & S. Pingree (Eds.). *Advancing communication science: Merging mass and interpersonal processes*. Vol. 16, Sage Annual Reviews of Communication Research. Beverly Hills, CA: Sage Publications.

Buck, R. (1988d). Nonverbal communication: Spontaneous and symbolic aspects. *American Behavioral Scientist, 31*, 341-354.

Buck, R. (1989a). Subjective, expressive, and peripheral bodily components of emotion. In H.L. Wagner and A. Manstead (Eds.), *Handbook of psychophysiology: Emotion and social behavior*. Chichester, Sussex, UK: John Wiley and Sons, Inc.

Buck, R. (1989b). Emotional communication in personal relationships: A developmental-interactionist view. In C.D. Hendricks (Ed.), *Close relationships. Review of personality and social psychology*, Vol. 10. Newbury Park, CA: Sage Publications.

Buck, R. (1991). Temperament, social skills, and the communication of emotion: A developmental-interactionist perspective. In D. Gilbert and J.J. Conley (Eds.), *Personality, social skills, and psychopathology: An individual differences approach*. New York: Plenum.

Buck, R. (1990a). Using FACS vs. communication scores to measure spontaneous facial expression of emotion in brain-damaged patients: A reply to Mammucari et al. (1988). *Cortex, 26,*. 275-280.

Buck, R. (1990b). William James, the nature of knowledge, and current issues in emotion, cognition, and communication. *Personality and Social Psychology Bulletin.*

Buck, R. (1990c). Emotional education and the persistence of dysfunctional personal relationships. Paper presented at the International Conference on Personal Relationships, St. Catherine's College, Oxford University, England.

Buck, R., & Duffy, R. (1980). Nonverbal communication of affect in brain-damaged patients. *Cortex, 16*, pp. 351-362.

Buck, R.W., Miller, R.E., & Caul, W.F. (1974). Sex, personality and physiological variables in the communication of emotion via facial expression. *Journal of Personality and Social Psychology, 30*, 587-596.

Buck, R., & Parke, R. (1972). The behavioral and physiological response to the presence of a friendly or neutral person in two stressful situations. *Journal of Personality and Social Psychology, 24*, 143-153.

Buck, R., Savin, V.J., Miller, R.E., & Caul, W.F. (1972). Nonverbal communication of affect in humans. *Journal of Personality and Social Psychology, 23*, 362-371.

Chesney, M.A., Eagleston, J.R., & Rosenman, R.H. (1980). The Type A structured interview: Behavioral assessment in the rough. *Journal of Behavioral Medicine, 2,* 255-272.

Chesney, M.A., Ekman, P., Friesen, W.V., Black, G.W., & Hecker, M.H.L. (1990). Type-A behavior pattern: Facial behavior and speech components. *Psychosomatic Medicine, 53,* 307-319.

Cobb, S. (1976). Social support as a moderator of life stress. *Psychosomatic Medicine, 38,* 300-314.

Cooper, T., Detrie, T., & Weiss, S.M. (1981). Coronary prone behavior and coronary heart disease: A critical review. *Circulation, 63,* 1199-1215.

Corsa, L., Pugh, T.F., Ingalls, T.H. & Gordon, J.F., (1952). Premature birth as a problem in human populations. *American Journal of Medical Science, 242,* 343-360.

Creed, F. (1985). Invited review: Life events and physical illness. *Journal of Psychosomatic Research, 29,* 113-123.

Dembrowski, T.M., MacDougall, J.M., Williams, R.B., Haney, T.L., & Blumenthal, J.A. (1985). Components of Type A, hostility, and anger in relationships to angiographic findings. *Psychosomatic Medicine, 47,* 219-233.

Duck, S., Lock, A., McCall, G., Fitzpatrick, M, & Coyne, J.C. (1984). Social and personal relationships: A joint editorial. *Journal of Social and Personal Relationships, 1,* 1-10.

Ekman, P., & Friesen, W.V. (1975). *Unmasking the face.* Englewood, Cliffs, NJ: Hall.

Fischman, J. (1987). Type-A on trial. *Psychology Today, 21,* 42-50.

Fisher, K. (1985). Psychoneuroimmunology. *APA Monitor, 16,* 8-56.

Greer, S., & Watson, M. (1985). Towards a psychobiological model of cancer: Psychological considerations. *Social Science Medicine,* 20 (8), 773-777.

Grossarth-Maticek, R., Bastiaans, J., & Kanazin, D.T. (1985). Psychosocial factors as strong predictors of mortality from cancer, ischaemic heart disease and stroke: The Yugoslav prospective study. *Journal of Psychosomatic Research, 29,* 167-176.

Hall, J.A., Friedman, H.S., & Harris, M.J. (1986). Nonverbal cues, the Type A behavior pattern, and coronary heart disease. In P.D. Blanck, R.W. Buck, & R. Rosenthal (Eds.), *Nonverbal communication in the clinical context* (Chap. 6). University Park: Pennsylvania State University Press.

Hofer, M.A. (1984). Relationships and regulators: A psychobiologic perspective on bereavement. *Psychosomatic Medicine, 46,* 183-198.

Hinkle, L.E., & Wolff, H.G. (1958). Ecological investigations of the relationship between illness, life experiences and the social environment. *Annals of Internal Medicine, 49,* 1373.

Kiecolt-Glaser, J.K., Fisher, L.D., Ogrocki, P., Stout, J.C., Speicher, C.E., & Glaser, R. (1987). Marital quality, marital disruption, and immune function. *Psychsomatic Medicine, 49,* 13-14.

Kiecolt-Glaser, J.K., Garner, W., Speicher, C., Penn, G., Holliday, J., & Glaser, R. (1984a). Psychosocial modifiers of immunocompetence in medical students. *Psychosomatic Medicine, 46,* 7-13.

Kiecolt-Glaser, J.K., Ricker, D., George, J., Messick, G., Speicher, C.E., Garner, W., & Glaser, R. (1984b). Urinary cortisol levels, cellular immunocompetency and loneliness in psychiatric inpatients. *Psychosomatic Medicine, 46,* 15-16.

Lazarus, R.S. (1984). On the primacy of cognition. *American Psychologist, 39,* 124-129.

Lesser, I.A. (1981). A review of the alexithymia concept. *Psychosomatic Medicine,* 531-543.

Martin, J.B., & Pihl, R.O. (1986). Influence of alexithymic characteristics on physiological and subjective stress responses in normal individuals. *Psychotherapy and Psychosomatics, 45,* 66-77.

Marty, P., & de M'Uzan, M. (1963). La pensée operatoire. *Revue francaise Psychoanal., Suppl.,* 27.

McClelland, D. C. (1982). The need for power, sympathetic activation and illness. *Motivation and Emotion, 6,* 31-41.

McDonald, P.W., & Prkachin, K.M. (1990). The expression and perception of emotion in alexithymia: A pilot study. *Psychosomatic Medicine, 52,* 199-210.

Meyer, D.J., & Hoggarty, R.J. (1962). Streptococcal infection in families: Factors altering individual susceptibility. *Pediatrics, 29,* 539-549.

Miller, N.E. (1983). Behavioral medicine: Symbiosis between laboratory and clinic. *Annual Review of Psychology, 34,* 1-31.

Morrison, S.L., & Pihl, R.O. (1989). Psychometrics of the Schalling-Sifneos and Toronto Alexithymia Scales. *Psychotherapy and Psychosomatics, 51,* 83-90.

Omer, H.O., Friedlander, D., Palti, Z., & Shekel, I. (1986). Life stress and premature labor: Real connection or artifactual findings? *Psychosomatic Medicine, 48 (5),* 362-369.

Orth-Gomer, K., & Unden, A-L. (1990). Type-A behavior, social support, and coronary risk: Interaction and significance for mortality in cardiac patients. *Psychosomatic Medicine, 52,* 59-72.

Paulson, J.E. (1985). State of the art of alexithymia measurement. *Psychotherapy and Psychosomatics, 44,* 57-64.

Peterson, L.G., Popkin, M.L., & Hall, R.C.W. (1981). Psychiatric aspects of cancer. *Psychsomatics, 22,* 778-793.

Pettingale, K.W. (1984). Coping and cancer prognosis. *Journal of Psychosomatic Research, 28 (8),* 363-364.

Pettingale, K.W. (1985). Towards a psychobiological model of cancer: Biological considerations. *Social Science and Medicine, 20 (8),* 779-787.

Rabavilas, A.D. (1987). Electrodermal activity in low and high alexithymia neurotic patients. *Psychotherapy and Psychosomatics, 47,* 101-104.

Rahe, R.H. (1990). Life change, stress responsivity, and captivity research. *Psy-*

chosomatic Medicine, 52, 373-396.

Renneker, R. (1981). Cancer and psychotherapy. In J.G. Goldberg (Ed.), *Psychotherapeutic treatment of cancer patients.* New York: Free Press.

Rodin, J., & Salovey, P. (1989). Health psychology. *Annual Review of Psychology, 40*, 533-579.

Rosenman, R. H., Brand, R. J., Scholtz, R. I., & Friedman, M. (1976). Multivariate prediction of coronary heart disease during 8.5 year follow-up in the Western Collaborative Group Study. *American Journal of Cardiology, 37*, 903-910.

Sarason, I.G., Sarason, B.R., Potter, E.H., & Antoni, M.H. (1985). Life events, social support and illness. *Psychosomatic Medicine, 47*, 156-163.

Schachter, S., & Singer, J. (1962). Cognitive, social and physiological determinants of emotional state. *Psychological Review, 69*, 379-399.

Scherwitz, L., Berton, K., & Leventhal, H. (1977). Type A assessment and interaction in the behavior pattern interview. *Psychosomatic Medicine, 39*, 229-240.

Schucker, G., & Jacobs, D.R. (1977). Assessment of behavioral risk for coronary disease by voice characteristics. *Psychosomatic Medicine, 39*, 219-228.

Shalev, A., Attias, J., Bleich, A., & Shulman, H., et al. (1988). Audiological evaluation of nonalcoholic, drug-free posttraumatic stress disorder patients. *Biological Psychiatry, 24(5)*, 522-530.

Sifneos, P.E. (1967). Clinical observations on some patients suffering from a variety of psychosomatic diseases. *Acta Medicine Psychosomatic, 1*, 1-10.

Sifneos, P.E. (1973). The prevalence of "alexithymic" characteristics in psychosomatic patients. *Psychosotherapy and Psychosomatics, 22*, 255-262.

Stewart, A.J., Sokol, M., Healy, J.M. Jr., & Chester, N.L. (1986). Longitudinal studies of psychological consequences of life changes in children and adults. *Journal of Personality and Social Psychology, 50(1)*, 143-151.

Storms, M. D. (1973). Videotape and the attribution process: Reversing actors' and observers' points of view. *Journal of Personality and Social Psychology, 27*, 165-175.

Taylor, G.J., Ryan, D., & Bagby, R. (1986). Toward the development of a new self-report alexithymia scale. *Psychotherapy and Psychosomatics, 44*, 191-199.

TenHouten, W.D., Hoppe, K.D., Bogen, J.E., & Walter, D.O., (1985). Alexithymia and the Split brain: I. Lexical-Level Content Analysis *Psychotherapy and Psychosomatics. 43*, 202-208.

TenHouten, W.D., Walter, D.O., Hoppe, K.D., & Bogen, J.E. (1987). Alexithymia and the split brain: V. EEG alpha-band interhemispheric coherence analysis. *Psychotherapy and Psychosomatics, 47*, 1-10.

TenHouten, W.D., Walter, D.O., Hoppe, K.D., & Bogen, J.E. (1988). Alexithymia and the split brain: VI. Electroencepalographic correlates of alexithymia. *Psychiatric Clinics of North America, 11(3)*, 317-329.

Totman, R., Kiff, J., Reed, S.E., & Craig, W. (1980). Predicting experimental colds in volunteers from different measures of recent life stress. *Journal of Psychosomatic Research, 24,* 155-163.

Weisman, A.D., & Worden, J.W. (1976). The existential plight in cancer: Significance of the first 100 days. *International Journal of Psychiatry in Medicine, 7,* 1-15.

Zajonc, R.B. (1984). On the primacy of affect. *American Psychologist, 39,* 10-103.

Acknowledgements: Preparation of this paper was supported by NIMH grant MH-40753 and by the University of Connecticut Research Foundation.

Inhibition of Action:
Interdisciplinary Approach to its Mechanism and Physiopathology

HENRI LABORIT

Between 1949 and 1951, the experimental and clinical study of hemorrhagic and traumatic shock syndroms led us to the following opinion: What was previously called our "means of defense" merely facilitated motor activity of the organism in its environment (Laborit, 1952, 1954). As Cannon (1932) already conceived, they facilitated flight or fight via a vasomotor activity depending primarily on circulating catecholamines (CA). These mediators cause a shift in the blood mass from cutaneous and splanchnic organs towards those necessary for motor activity (muscles, heart, lungs, brain). This reaction could insure survival only if the flight or fight was rapidly effective by removing the organism from the environmental aggression. If ineffective, however, the persistence of the reaction would lead to anoxia of the splanchnic organs, and, via vasomotor and metabolic mechanisms extensively studied, to acidosis and death. If we admit this hypothesis, we are no longer led to consider shock syndroms as an "exhaustion" of the means of defense, but rather the result of their mobilization and the persistence of their action when fight or flight is ineffective. A therapeutic consequence implied that rather than attempting to compensate inadequacies of the defense mechanisms, particularly the adrenosympathetic reaction, it could be useful to control them. This is what has been done by using molecules which inhibit the activities of the autonomic nervous system, combined in what we have called lytic cocktails, leading to "neuroplegia". Among these pharmacological means, the value of certain phenothiazine derivatives (phenergan, diparcol) was the basis of our introduction of chlopromazine, another pheothiazine derivative, in the therapeutic armamentarium in 1952. We called the decreased metabolic requirements of tissues caused by cold after blockade of the body temperature control mechanism by lytic cocktails "artificial hibernation".

Furthermore, these neuroendocrine reactions to various agressions had many points in common with those resulting from psychosocial aggression. This led us to propose the use of these molecules, especially chlorpromazine, in clinical psychiatry (Laborit, Huguenard & Allaume, 1952). At that time, however, our understanding of the neuropsychological and biochemical relations between physical and psychosocial aggression was not sufficient.

I will not describe the course of our research since that time, or how the vast body of research collectively known as the "Neurosciences" contributed worldwide to this progress. I will only schematically describe the main steps. Our complete work and our concepts in this field have been dealt with in the volume entitled *L'inhibition d'action* (Inhibiton of action) (Laborit, 1st edition 1979, 2nd edition 1986).

Shock Versus Stress

A large number of recent publications have dealt with "stress" rather than "shock". The experimental methods used to provoke stress never cause a state of shock. Regardless of whether it be inescapable footshocks, variable duration restraint, forced swimming, isolation, fighting, etc., experiments are always performed on a conscious animal and not one under general anesthesia. These experiments always involve the hypothalamo-pituitary-adrenal axis (HPA) and the adrenergic sympathetic system, in those involving shock. On the other hand, disturbances in the homeostatic equilibrium, the acid base and electrolyte balance, metabolic disturbances, vasomotor and arterio-capillary phenomena, for example, are rarely considered. Shock was primarily concerned with these phenomena, whereas in the case of stress, there are only few studies on biochemical and central neurophysiological activities. It is probable that our increased knowledge of brain biochemistry during the past several decades has enabled us to realize that this is the essential factor in the variations of our behavior. We thus sought to use experimental tests involving an "active" or a "passive" behavior against the aggressive agent, a behavior which no longer occurs in states of shock, even if there was originally a fight or flight attempt.

The brain will thus make possible certain responses to the stressing agent. It will first attempt to control or neutralize it, either by flight (active avoidance) or fight (struggle, defensive aggressiveness). It will record the result of the experience: the success or failure of this control. This learning process will have important consequences for its subsequent behavior, which will thus depend on a *memory* process.

We were able to show that if control is effective, there are but few biological or physiological disturbances, central or peripheral, or else they are very temporary. It is only when the motor action of environmental control becomes impossible that stable physiopathological disturbances appear (Laborit, Kunz, & Valette, 1974a).

In summary, between shock and stress, we go from a syndrome where the *lesion* is primary and triggers a nonspecific *reaction* which favors fight or flight, to a syndrome where the lesion is secondary to a reaction caused by the learning of the *ineffectiveness of the action.*

In the case of *shock,* the syndrome progresses rapidly with no prior learning and the nervous response is limited above all to the hypothalamus and the brain stem. In *stress,* memory has a predominant role and the limbic system and associative cortex are required for establishing physiological and biological disturbances.

Action Inhitory System (AIS)

The work described above was carried out in the 1950s. For several years afterward, we held the opinion that the pathology could result from the mobilization of a so-called defense system which protects our lives only by permitting motor autonomy. We considered that this system becomes ineffective in technologically developed urban societies where the individual can neither flee from nor fight against his socio-cultural environment. While remaining functional, it is responsible for reactions which become purposeless and whose persistence could be deleterious.

More recently, we have revised this opinion and noted experimentally that it is not this reaction which commands fight or flight and then becomes purposeless that is the origin of chronic physiopathological disorders, but rather another reaction commanding *inhibition of action,* when the action is judged impossible or ineffective. This reaction may still be considered as " adaptive", since it may obviate the destruction of the aggressed by the aggressor. It enables the aggressed to make himself forgotten, to avoid confrontation. Its danger arises from its duration if the environmental conditions are prolonged.

(A) Self Stimulation Experiments: Reward and Reinforcement

Electrical stimulation of the lateral hypothalamus and certain structures related to it such as the basal ganglia, paleocortex and tegmentum, causes a positive reinforcement of learning (Fig. 1). Physiological stimulation of the median forebrain bundle (MFB) in the normal state arises from the coincidence between the intent and the result of the action. The intent arises from the synthesis of the endogenous need and the entire prior experience of the subject. We may consider that the MFB is activated by the reestablishment of the homeostatic equilibrium, or by its maintenance. This biological equilibrium is accompanied by a sensation of pleasure.

We should remember that the chemical mediation that controls the MFB is primarily catecholaminergic (dopaminergic and noradrenergic). The control catecholaminergic system inhibits the hypophyseo-pituitary-adrenal alarm reaction and norepinephrine release from peripheral sympathetic nerve fibers. But it also activates locomotor activity and thus faciliates action when its result is favorable for maintaining the structure of the organism.Thus, when the active response of an animal leads to stimulation, it is regarded as significant if the stimulation results in survival. If not, it leads to habituation. In the first case, the animal is rewarded for its action and it learns that this action is a rewarding one.

A large body of work, starting with that of Olds and Milner (1954), showed the role of the MFB and of catecholamines, dopamine and norepinephrine (NE), in both motor activity and in the reinforcement of a gratifying action. Nevertheless, the first can be dissociated from the second. Franklin (1978) stat-

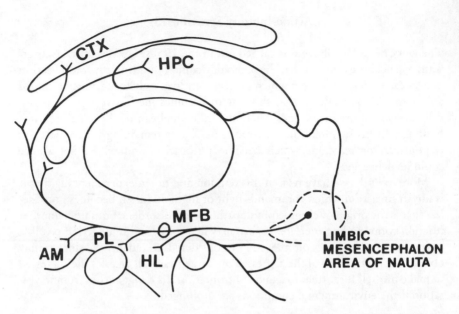

Figure 1:   Ascending adrenergic pathway of the reward mechanism. MFB: median forbrain
             bundle. HL: lateral hypothalamus. PL: preoptic region. AM: amygdala. HPC:
             hippocampus. CTX: neocortex. (From Stein, 1967).

ed that self-stimulation and reward behavior depend on dopaminergic mediation, wheras locomotor activity depends on NE. Inversely, Mason and Fibiger
(1979) observed that 6-hydroxydopamine (6-OHDA) injected into the dorsal
noradrenergic bundle decreases the NE concentration in the MFB and delays
the extinction of a passive avoidance behavior. Heffner and Seiden (1980), on
the other hand, showed that operant behavior performances are associated with
an increased rate of CA synthesis in these selective regions on the central nervous system. Bracs, Jackson, and Gregory (1982) showed that alpha-methyl-p-
tyrosine depresses the conditioned avoidance response (CAR) that is restored
when DA is applied directly on the nucleus accumbens.

(B) Punishment

Some authors tend to oppose the reward systems to a *punishment system.* The
anticipation of or search for reward, resulting from a stimulus previously shown
to be gratifying, causes the facilitation of the previously rewarded behavior. This
is a learning process. Inversely, the anticipation of fear of punishment, already
experienced to be such, leads to the suppression of the previously punished behavior: this is also a learning process (Stein, 1968). These authors tend to render
two functionally antagonistic formations responsible for the action or inhibiti-

on behaviors: the MFB which we discussed above, and the periventricular systems (PVS), described by Molina and Hunsperger (1962).

(C) Behavioral Inhibition

We have nonetheless considered that this was an incomplete description and interpretation. Punishment can in fact trigger either flight/fight (defensive aggressiveness) or inhibition. The system described by Molina and Hunsperger (1962), however, commands a flight or fight reaction following aversive stimulation and involves the central gray matter; it is a cholinergic system with an unconditioned response of the final common pathway. In other terms, this system is an *activator of action*. Inhibition of action, on the other hand, occurs when the punishment cannot be avoided by flight or fight. In order to determine that this avoidance is impossible, we showed that learning is necessary: *learning the ineffectiveness of the action*. This was demonstrated (Laborit, Kunz, & Valette, 1974) by the following experiment. In a previous study (Kunz, Valette, & Laborit, 1974), we showed that stable high blood pressure could develop in rats subjected to aversive stimuli (footshocks) at the rate of 10 cycles of 21 seconds per day for 7 consecutive days when the animal could not flee the punishment (active avoidance) or fight (combat with another animal of the same species). It was thus seen that the action inhibitory system had to be responsible for this stable cardiovascular disturbance. However, this system does not seem to be immediately mobilized by the animal subjected to an aversive stimulus, which first responds by flight or defensive aggressiveness. It seems that the animals first have to memorize the ineffectiveness of flight or fight by learning to be inhibited. In this case, it can be supposed that stable traces of long term memory are established. We thus sought to determine if electroconvulsive shocks, followed by shortlasting coma, applied immediately after each experimental session, could prevent the occurrence of the chronic hypertension. It is known that this type of shock prevents the passage from short to long term memory (Dawson & McGaugh, 1969). This technique has the advantage of not superimposing a pharmacological process on mechanisms concerning inhibition of memorization phenomena which are still insufficiently defined. In addition, it has the advantage of utilizing a traumatic means capable of triggering what is called a "defense reaction". The results obtained are shown in Table 1. It is evident that if we prevent shock after each session of aversive stimuli without the possiblity of fight or flight, the stable hypertension normally arising in animals that cannot flee or fight does not develop.

These facts suggest that inhibition phenomena result from a learning process and that the limbic areas are required for its occurrence. Devenport, Devenport, and Holloway (1981) believed that the hippocampus opposes the effects of reward by opposing the catecholaminergic mechanism. Animals with hippocampal lesions or those receiving amphetamines present an extinction delay, an improved active avoidance, and a suppressed passive avoidance. Black, Sand-quist, West, Wamsley, and Williams (1979) showed that cholinergic agonists in-crease the concentration of cGMP in the hippocampus, an increase which is prevented by atropine.

Table 1: Variations in blood pressure in rats caused by inescapable footshocks or flight in 7 consecutive daily series of 10 stimulations, in the presence or absence of an electroconvulsive shock at the end of each sequence (P with Student's test).

	Blood Pressure					
	Initial	After 2 stimula-tions	After 4 stimula-tions	After 7 stimula-tions	After a one week rest	On day 30
Controls	13.25 ± 0.12	14.40 ± 0.39	14.40 ± 0.26	14.40 ± 0.39	16.43 ± 0.26	16.00 ± 0.27
electric	13.06	13.03	*13.53	*13.96	**14.43	*13.70
Shock	± 0.12	± 0.20	± 0.15	± 0.13	± 0.12	± 0.20

Results compared with Student's t test:
*P <0.10; **P <0.01

10 animals per group

Action Inhibitory System and Acetycholine

A large body of now old studies led to the suspicion that the cholinergic system plays a role in this inhibition. We will mention here only the most recent find-ings. Anisman, Remington, and Sklar (1979) showed that treatment with a catecholaminergic stimulant, L-dopa, or a cholinergic blocker, scopolamine, antagonizes the escape deficit (inhibition) caused by the prior learning of in-escapable footshock.

Russel and Macri (1979) showed the intimate relation between the levels of cerebral ACh and motor activity. 3'-hemicholinium intracerebroventricularly (icv) reduces the ACh concentration and causes hyperactivity. If an initial hy-peractivity is noted after the septal lesions which reduce ACh levels, it disappears with time, suggesting the progressive reestablishment of a balance between neuromediators.

Mason and Fibiger (1979) noted that anticholinergic drugs (scopolamine, atropine) cause motor stimulation in rats. Stephens and Herberg (1979) reported that scopolamine and benyatropine (ip) increase self stimulation. Scopolamine does not inhibit the uptake of dopamine (DA) by synapses, as does benyatropine. The stimulating action of these drugs can thus be attributed only to the inhibition of a reward by a cholinergic inhibitory system.

Schmidt, Cooper, and Barrett (1980) reported the interesting finding that strain F-344 rats are highly capable of actively avoiding a footshock, while those of strain Z-M become inhibited and reduce their motor activity. Cholinergic activity increases in the dorsal hippocampus of Z-M and not in F-344 after footshocks. The authors concluded that a cholinergic mechanism controlled the behavioral stress-suppressing response. Zolman, Mattingly, and Sahley (1978) also observed in chicks that scopolamine increases motor activity and the resistance to extinction of an active conditioning to obtain food. Similarly in this case, the animals have difficulty in learning a passive avoidance, thus demonstrating the similarity of (a) the results obtained in rats and of (b) the role of a cholinergic system in inhibition.

Action Inhibitiory System and Serotonin

Using rats trained to stop nociceptive stimulation caused by electrodes implanted in the mesencephalic gray matter Schenberg and Graeff (1978) reported that two 5-HT antagonists (methysergide and cyproheptadine) faciliate the response and decrease latency. Tachiki, Tateishi, Nishiwaki, Nakamura, Nagayama, and Takahashi (1978) showed that small doses of the serotonin precursor 5-HTP decrease motor activity and that inactive doses of tetrabenazine combined with inactive doses of 5-HT decreased motor activity. pCPA opposes sedation due to tetrabenazine, which is thus due to an excess of functional 5-HT. Graeff and Silveira-Filho (1978) showed that stimulation of the seronotinergic raphe nucleus inhibited the behavior of rats trained to press a lever to obtain water.

pCPA inhibits 5-HT synthesis and restores this behavior. 5-HTP + benerazide antagonize the action of pCPA. Thus, the mesencephalic serotoninergic pathway which originates in the median raphe nucleus and which projects onto the septal region and the hippocampus seems to be involved in behavior inhibition. Similarly, Redgrave (1978), after creating a self stimulation behavior by lever pressing and implanting an electrode in the MFB and ventral mesencephalic tegmentum (VMT), observed that 5-HT reduces the number of pressings and increases their duration, while DA causes the opposite, as does norepinephrine (NE). The reward system thus seems to be stimulated by catecholamines

(CA) and inhibited by a serotoninergic system. Plaznik, Kostowski, Bidzinski, & Hauptmann (1980) created lesions in the dorsal and medium raphe nuclei and noted that active avoidance and overall activity of the animals are faciliated with a massive decrease of 5-HT level. Inversely, Thornton and Goudie (1978) used pCPA and lesions in the median raphe nucleus to prevent acquisition of a passive avoidance response. Yamamoto and Ueki (1978) also observed motor hyperactivity in animals with lesions of the median raphe. Since it is suppressed by alpa-methyltyrosine (α-MT) which blocks CA synthesis, they believed that this hyperactivity results from the activation of a catecholaminergic system secondary to the inhibition of sertoninergic activity. Lesions of the raphe, on the other hand, seemed to be responsible for muricidal behavior. An identical opinion was formulated by Waldbillig (1979). The inhibitory serotoninergic system arising in the dorsal raphe has projections onto the amygdala, whose lesions thus cause muricidal behavior.

Montanero (1979) reported that the antiamnesic effects of antiserotoninergic drugs towards passive avoidance are related to an anti-punishment effect caused by an antiserotoninergic treatment.

Giambalvo and Snodgrasse (1978), however, formulated the opinion that serotoninergic pathways emanating from raphe nuclei exert a tonic inhibition on the nigrostriatal pathway at the level of the substantia nigra by directly forming a synapse with DA neurons, while their neostriated endings have an indirect effect on the DA neuron endings, perhaps via an interaction with cholinergic or GABA-ergic neurons. If DA is involved in locomotor activity and reward behavior, then serotonin would inhibit these behaviors (Tayler, 1976; Warbritten, Steward, & Baldessarini, 1978).

Thus, after considering the role of the AIS in physiopathology, some of our work has led us to invoke the participation of the cholinergic and serotoninergic systems in the mechanism of motor inhibition.

Brain Areas Involved in Inhibition of Action Behavior

Without going into the details of the physiological experimentation, we would like to mention the following areas at least briefly which have been implicated in inhibition behavior, as shown in Figure 2.

(I) An area in which a final common pathway arises towards the motor neurons, the ventromedian hypothalamus (VHM), has been clearly implicated in inhibition.

(II) Likewise, bundles converging towards this area and arising from the caudate nucleus, from the dorsal septal region, from the dorsal hippocampus (Laborit, Baron, & Laurent, 1977) and from the lateral amygdala have also been associated with inhibition. The latter two areas appear to play an important role. Gray (1972) noted the correlation between an inhibition behavior and the

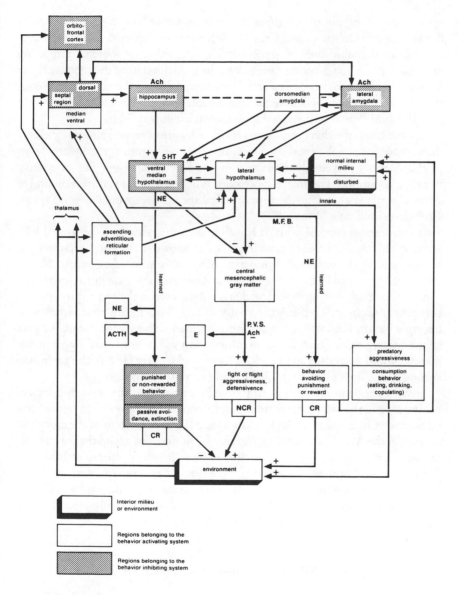

Figure 2: General scheme of the neurophysiology of behavior.
MFB: median forebrain bundle.
E: epinephrine.
NE: norepinephrine.
ACh: acetylcholine.
CR: conditioned response.
NCR: nonconditioned response

appearance of hippocampal theta waves of intermediate frequency, 7.5 to 8.5 Hz. Graeff, Quintero, and Gray (1980), however, reported that these waves depend on the activation of a mesolimbic serotoninergic system, projecting onto the septum and hippocampus. The effect of stimulating the median raphe nuclei (MR) and the neocortical activity is comparable to the action of a conditioned stimulus (CS), signalling an unavoidable shock. They cause a freezing, a behavioral inhibition and a slow hippocampal rhythm at 7 Hz.

In both cases, the theta response is blocked by atropine and altered by chlordiazepoxide or amobarbital. A serotononergic antagonist, methysergide or pCPA, does not prevent the theta response to MR stimulation. They are sensitive to scopolamine. The freezing behavior is believed to act via the mesolimbic serotoninergic system, but the hippocambal theta waves would depend on an ascending cholinergic system.

(III) In certain cortical areas, it is well known that area 4 of the frontal lobe activates striated and smooth muscles. It is also known that motor responses can be provoked by the electrical stimulation of visual or somesthesic areas. Nevertheless, the increased latency of response shows that in this case much longer circuits are involved. Arising in sensorial areas of the cortex, they pass through subcortical connections, reaching the motor cortex. This means that rather than having a "control center" commanding movements, the motor cortex is above all the last step from which sensorial information will be converted into a motor manifestation. According to Pycock, Kerwin, and Conter (1980), the prefrontal cortical DA system plays an inhibitory role in motor behavior.

Serotoninergic projections from the raphe nuclei onto the septo-hippocampal system and the prefrontal cortex, and the cholinergic projections to the frontal neocortex from the reticular formation and the basal nucleus of the amygdala are part of the AIS. The ascending cholinergic projections excite the frontal cortex and stimulate ACTH and cortisol release. Inversely, fronto-striatal projections decrease exploratory activity by inhibiting dopaminergic neurons in the caudate nucleus. Furthermore, ascending projections from the raphe nuclei inhibit dopaminergic nigrostriatal neurons. Figure 2 schematically represents the main relations among the cerebral regions leading to a behavior.

Role of AIS in the Involvement of the HPA Axis

It is not within the scope of the present work to review the experimental data demonstrating the involvement of the VMH in the mobilization of the hypothalamo-pituitary-adrenal cortex axis. The same is true for the glucocorticoids (Gcs) which stimulate certain regions in the SIA, leading to a positive retroreaction which would appear to be shown by the dexamethasone escape test in a number of cases. Nor will we develop the experimental reasons for suggesting that the stimulation of the adrenal medulla and the peripheral sympathetic ner-

vous system depends on a nicotinic cholinergic stimulation of the hypothalamus.

It is sufficient to mention that all data lead us to believe that the involvement
of the AIS in environmental situations preventing gratifying action or passive
avoidance of punishment is the intermediate between behavior and chronic
neuroendocrine disturbances (Figure 3).

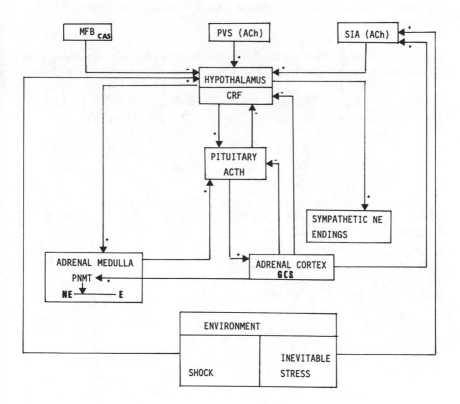

Figure 3:   Negative feedback reactions in the hypothalamo-pituitary-adrenal system (con-
            trolled system) and its control by the nervous behavioral system in response to
            the environment (self mechanism).

Central Biochemical Implications of the Inhibition of Action

We have considered that the ratio between DOPAC/HVA, two main metabolites of intraneuronal degradation, is useful, since the DOPAC level expresses its
intraneuronal degradation and that of HVA mainly its extraneuronal degradation after synaptic release. Using HPLC, we measured the levels of these meta-

bolites in whole brains and in more precisely defined brain areas of rats subjected to inhibition of action in the form of inescapable footshocks 13 minutes
per day for 16 consecutive days.

Under these conditions (see Table 2), there is an increase of DA, a significant
decrease of HVA and no change in DOPAC. Hermann, Guillonneau, Dantzer,
Seatton, Semerdjian-Rouquier, and Le Moal (1982) found an increase in DO-
PAC in several brain areas after a single session of inescapable footshocks.

Table 2: Brain biogenic amines and metabolites. The results are expressed as nmoles/g tissue.
The test animals were subjected to inescapable footschocks for 13 min/day during 16 days.

	NE	DOPA-MINE	DOPAC	HVA	SERO-TONIN	5-HIAA
Controls (n = 8)	1.09± 0.02	3.18± 0.05	0.28± 0.01	0.16± 0.006	1.26± 0.07	0.58± 0.07
Inescapable footschocks (n = 10)	1.09± 0.04	3.58± ** 0.12	0.27± 0.01	0.13± *** 0.006	1.27± 0.08	0.47± * 0.01

The results were compared with Student's t test:
P<0.10; * P<0.01; * * *p <0.001.

These results suggest an increase in the intrasynaptosomal amino oxidation of
DA. In addition, Stolk, Robert, Levine, and Barchas (1974) studied NE metabolism and CA synthesis in rats subjected to inescapable footshocks in the presence or absence of another rat. The paired animals engaged in fighting, while
the single rats were in a state of inhibition. Among the latter, the turnover of
(^{3}H)NE in the spinal bulbar pons showed that the levels of normetanephrine
decreases significantly, also suggesting that metabolism is primarily intraneuronal and deaminating via monoamine oxidase (MAO). In the fighting animals
on the other hand, it was noted that there is a trend towards the formation of
normetanephrine, thus towards synpatic O-methylation of NE by COMT. It
thus appears that in the case of inhibition of action, less is released at synapses
where COMT is responsible for their degradation and is preferentially amino
oxidated by intramitochondrial MAO. In the latter case, amino oxidation will
produce hydrogen peroxide (H_2O_2) and amonia (NH_3), while in a situation of
behavioral activity, COMT is activated and the CA undergoes degradation by

methylation. In the first case, Maker, Weiss, Silider, and Cohen (1981) showed the oxidation of GSH in brain homogenates incubated with DA or 5-HT. The process is blocked by pargyline (a MAO inhibitor) or by catalase which traps hydrogen peroxide. Similarly, Sinet, Heikkila, and Cohen (1980) confirmed the production of H_2O_2 by brain mitochondria in vivo with 5-HT and DA as substrates.

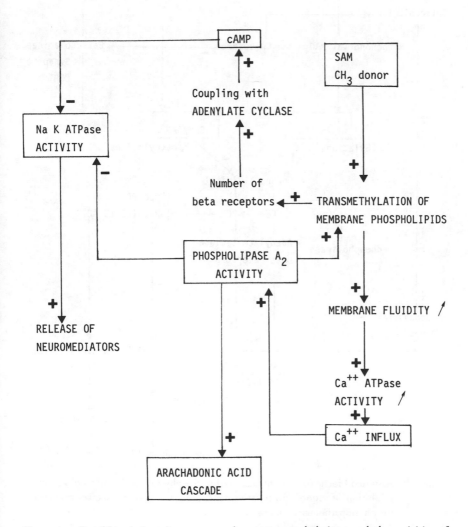

Figure 4: Possible relations between membrane transmethylations and the activities of Na K ATPase, adenylate cyclase and phospholipase A_2.

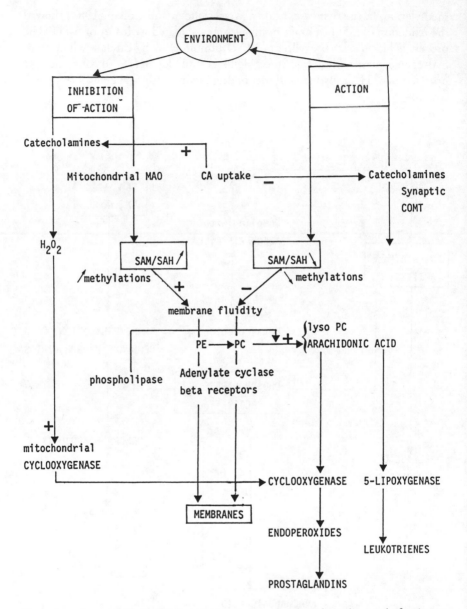

Figure 5: Assumed biochemical events involved in the physiological control of action vs. inhibition of action with putative development of toxic substances responsible for physiopathological states.

Seregi, Serfozo, and Mergl (1983) showed the existence of a mitochondrial cyclooxygenase in rat brains. It is sensitive to H_2O_2 which activates it, and yields endoperoxides and prostaglandins from endogenous arachidonic acid (AA). The authors admitted the interdependence between MAO that produces H_2O_2 and the cyclooxygenase that the latter activates. Moreover, phospholiphase A_2 (PLA_2) which releases AA is, similar to the two enzymes above, primarily mitochondrial. Its activity is Ca^{2+} dependent. Calcium ions that penetrate neurons with depolarization stimulate PLA_2 activity which starting from phosphatidylcholine is the origin of the AA cascade (Fig. 5).

The administration of exogenous L-dopa thus leads to its methylation by COMT, which increases the membrane concentration of S-adenosylhomocysteine (SAH) at the expense of S-adenosylmethionine (SAM), a methyl group donor (Baldessarini, 1975). SAH in turn inhibits membrane methylations and decreases membrane fluidity and permeability, limiting the uptake of neuromediators (Samet & Rutledge, 1984). In a situation of inhibition of action (inescapable footshocks), we have observed the reverse process, i.e. an increase in the SAM/SAH ratio (unpublished data). Membrane methylations are facilitated, with resulting metabolic consequences (Hirata & Axelrod, 1980). These methylations control calcium penetration and thus the activation of PLA_2 and the AA cascade. These processes are schematically represented in Figures 4 and 5.

Table 3: Changes in blood pressure (in mm Hg) in rats subjected to electric footshocks after an audible alarm with no possibility of active avoidance, and subjected or not to a prior injection (24 h) of nialamide (10 mg/kg subcutaneous). Controls received 0.5 ml/kg of isotonic saline in the same conditions and via the same route. Blood pressure was measured in the tail 24 hours after the test, i.e. immediately before the next. One group of 7 animals sacrificed on the last day of the experiment (for assay) and having lived in the laboratory in the same conditions had a mean blood pressure of 136± 2.1.

	D0	D1	D2	D3	D4	D5	D6	D7
Nialamide 10 mg-Kg s.c.	137 ±2.1	132 ±2.1	136 ±2	127 ±1.7	128 ±2.2	128 ±1.5	128 ±2.3	128 ±1.9
Isotonic saline	136 ±2.1	145 ±2.5	155 ±2.7	167 ±2.0	160 ±3	160 ±3.6	158 ±2.4	161 ±4.1

A complex physiological control sets in, in which the synaptic utilization of CAs leads to their methylation by COMPT, to a decrease in SAM, and a corresponding increase in SAH. The decrease in the uptake of CAs caused by the latter will increase their synaptic efficiency. Inversely, amino oxidation by MAO in a situation of inhibition of action will favor membrane methylation and the release of mediators which will then be taken up more easily by the deaminated substances. If the inhibition of action persists, it all happens as if the increase in membrane methylations, due to the increase in the SAM concentration, commanded all the processes controlling the AA cascade. This leads to the formation of endoperoxides, prostaglandins and leukotrienes, whose free radical and prooxidizing properties are increasingly considered as being the origin of a number of physiopathological conditions. We thus observed (Laborit, Valette, & Laurent, 1975) that rats in inhibition of action caused by inescapable footshocks no longer exhibited chronic hypertension if they received a MAO inhibitor (nialamide) (Table 3).

Hypotheses on the Mechanism of Intrasynaptosomal Retention of CA in Inhibition of Action

Since inhibition of action is not primary, but rather secondary to a learning of the ineffectiveness of action, the CAs released first in the synaptic slit cannot command an efficient behavior, and this causes secondary inhibition. It may be supposed that the conflict between the action activator system and the AIS is the basis of anxiety, i.e. the expectancy under tension of the moment when action will become possible. The hypothesis may be proposed that, if this moment occurs with a delay, the CAs released could act on their autoreceptors in the pathways that contain them (mesolimbic and nigrostriatal for DA) and that, in this case, their autooxidation will result from the secondary inhibition of their release and this is what would take place in depression. The DA mesocortex system apparently does not have autoreceptors and so the activity of certain cortical areas will remain high.

It may also be admitted (Laduron, 1985) that the increased activity of the cholinergic system in inhibition of action could involve *presynaptic heteroreceptors*, which would block the synaptic release of CA. The same is true for the serotoninergic system starting at the raphe nuclei which is a known inhibitor of the dopaminergic nigrostriatal neuron.

Phosphoinositide Cycle, Neuromediators and Inhibition of Action

For the past several years, another aspect of membrane phospholipid metabolism has raised considerable interest outside the scope of this discussion. Under the action of phospholipase C, membrane phosphoinositides furnish inositol triphosphate (IP_3) and diacylglycerol (DG). It has been shown that IP_3 mobilizes intracellular Ca^{2+} from the endoplasmic reticulum and that free Ca^{2+} combines its action with that of DG to stimulate protein kinase C (PKC). This enzyme participates indirectly in cell metabolism and the activity of certain nuclear genes by phosphorylating certain enzymes.

The activity of the phospoinositide cycle, which involves the formation of cGMP, generally antagonizes the cAMP formation cycle by adenylate cyclase which is stimulated by beta receptor agonists. This cycle also activates a protein kinase, but in this case cAMP dependent, which phosphorylates certain enzymes.

The phosphoinositide cycle is activated by M_1 acetylcholine and a_1 norepinephrine receptors in particular. Recently, we have shown that direct stimulation of PKC by phorbolesters antagonizes the amnesia of an inhibition behavior caused by scopolamine (Laborit & Zerbib, 1987). The memory of the ineffectiveness of action would thus be dependent on the stimulation of the phosphoinositides cycle by M_1 acetylcholine (ACh) receptors. This stimulation could be the mediator of the presynaptic inhibitory action of the cholinergic system on DA release. We have seen that intrasynaptosome retention of DA could cause an increase in membrane methylations and of the AA cascades from phosphatidylcholine. Now, it has been shown that depressive states are generally accompanied by an accumulation of cAMP. Antidepressants generally decrease the number of beta receptors and the formation of cAMP.

It is still too soon to define the correlations among the nervous pathways involved in the inhibition of action, the neuromediators involved, the membrane receptors stimulate and the resulting metabolic responses that are at the origin of a particular behavior. The general ideas we have schematically presented are only the first step in the understanding of these correlations.

Inhibition of Action, Neuroimmunomodulation and Somatic Physiopathology

The volume *Inhibition of Action* (Laborit, 1986) contains the physiological applications of the preceding experimental observations. We will limit ourselves here to mentioning that the AIS leads to the release of Gcs and peripheral NE. This will have primarily two types of consequences:

(1) Gcs lead to a blockage of the immune system. It can be deduced that if microbial infection or abnormal cells appear, which normally would be controlled by immune defenses, then an infectious or neoplastic episode may develop unhindered. This explains the relation between infections and neoplasms in behavioral situations where gratifying action is inhibited. It also shows that the infectious agent or cancer-causing factor are not the only ones involved.

(2) The peripheral release of NE at sympathetic system terminals will cause a generalized vasoconstriction, thus a decrease in the vascular container. Also, Gcs lead to a retention of salts and water and so there is an increase in the vascular contents. The combination of these two factors leads to hypertension. This could be shown by placing the animal in a situation of inefficiency of action (Laborit, Kunz, & Valette, 1974a). Experimental observations also suggest that numerous somatic disturbances are generated by the same process: atherosclerosis, gastric ulcers, renal lesions, etc.

(3) Concerning mental pathology, it is not in the scope of the present work to develop the consequences of inhibition of action. They may be summarized by saying that, in our opinion, anxiety and its neurotic consequences result from the conflict between the impulse to act and the inhibition of action, in this case from learning that punishment will follow the satisfaction of the impulse. Psychosis could be a flight into the imaginary when the inhibition is too painful to bear.

(4) It is also interesting to note that in the scheme we have outlined, free radicals (H_2O_2, leukotrienes, endoperoxides) are capable of destroying cellular membranes, those of lysosomes in particular, which may cause neuronal death. This could be a primary and fundamental step in progression towards the chronic state of certain diseases (Parkinson, Alzheimer), just as in acute lesions caused by cerebal anoxia.

From a Therapeutic Standpoint

Depressions constitute one of the clinical forms of inhibition. They are generally treated by facilitating the activity of inhibitors, or else tricyclic antidepressants are used. The latter, among other effects, decrease the neuronal concentration of cAMP and inhibit synaptosomal reuptake of the CA released at the synapse. This therapy is the logical consequence of the hypocatecholaminergic theory of depression. However, we can equally well envision a hypercholinergic theory for depressive states, states aggravated by cholinomimetic and anticholinesterase drugs. In this case, inhibitors of ACH release must be used. We have attempted this with minaprine (Cantor) (Laborit & Bonifacj, 1984; Laborit, Brunaud, Savy, Baron, Vallèe, Lamotte, Thuret, Muyard, & Cavino, 1972). As mentioned above, it is also possible that cholinergic hyperactivity is partly responsible for the presynaptic inhibition of the catecholaminergic pathways. An inhibitor of inhibition thus becomes an indirect antidepressant. Similarly, the mechanism of action of anti-anxiety drugs such as the benzodiazepines, whose receptors form a complex with those of GABA, may be interpreted in the framework of the hypothesis previously proposed for a conflict between activating and inhibiting pathways in action. It is known that GABA inhibits the serotoninergic neurons of the raphe, themselves inhibitors of the dopaminergic negrostriatal neurons.

Conclusions

In this general review, we have summarized only the main points of the interdisciplinary consequences of the concept of inhibition of action. This concept must be based on consistent experimental findings on the metabolic, membrane, neurophysiological, neuroendocrine and general biological levels of behavior. The results obtained at these different levels of organization should also be capable of shedding new light on clinical data concerning individuals whose pathology expresses only their difficulties in living in a particular sociocultural framework. These subjects are inserted in this framework with their memory, their learning experiences transformed into automatic motor, conceptual and language actions which have become unconscious. This is undoubtedly responsible for the difficulty, the empiricism and the nonuniform results of therapies seeking the source of disease in a factor of linear and simplistic causality, since we cannot so simply erase the entire prior experience of those who come for relief from a present illness.

Summary

The author reviews the work of his group during the past 3 decades and relates how studies of shock led him to distinguish between shock and stress on both the physiological and biological levels. Stress according to the author involves a memory process, i.e. learning the ineffectiveness of the action to modify the characteristics of the environment. This learning process involves brain territories and nervous pathways whose behavioral result is inhibition of action. On the neurophysiological level, he stresses the importance of the cortex, the dorsal hippocampus, the lateral amygdala and the ventromedian nucleus of the hypothalamus in these mechanisms. He shows why it seems evident that the mediators of the action inhibitory system (AIS) are acetylcholine and serotonin. He also reviews the numerous experimental findings enabling the AIS to be incriminated in the triggering of the hypothalamo-pituitary-adrenal cortex reaction and the peripheral sympathetic adrenergic reaction to aggression. Finally, he shows the role of these two systems in the origin of major pathological processes. He also mentions the discovery and therapeutic introduction of an original molecule, minaprine, which he considers as an inhibitor of AIS and thus as an indirect antidepressant. So-called psychosomatic disturbances thus become a pathological manifestation of inhibition of action, where the unconscious memory of prohibition and prior failures links the subject and his present reaction to the environment to his entire psychosocial past.

References

Anisman, H., Remington, G., & Sklar, L. (1979). Effect of inescapable shock on subsequent escape performance: catecholaminergic and cholinergic mediation of response initiation and maintenance. *Psychopharmacology, 61,* 107-124.

Baldessarini, R.J. (1975). Biological transmethylations involving S-adenosyl-methionie; Development of assay methods and implications for neuropsychiatry. *International Review of Neurology, 18*, 41-47.

Black, A.C., Jr., Sandquist, D., West, J.R., Wamsley, J.L., & Williams, T.S. (1979). Muscarinic cholinergic stimulation increases cyclic GMP in rat hippocampus. *Journal of Neurochemistry, 33*, 1165-1168.

Bracs, P.U., Jackson, D.M., & Gregory, P. (1982). Methyl-p-tyrosine inhibition of a conditioned avoidance response reversal by dopamine applied to the nucleus accumbens. *Psychopharmalogy, 77*, 159-163.

Cannon, W.B. (1932). *La sagesse du corps (Vol, I).* New York: W.W. Morton & Co.

Dawson, R.G., & Mc Gaugh, J.L. (1969). Electroconvulsive shock effects on a reactivated memory trace: further examination. *Science, 166*, 525-527.

Devenport, L.D., Devenport, J.A., & Holloway, F.A. (1981). Reward-induced stereotyp: modulation by the hippocampus. *Science, 4500*, 1288-1289.

Franklin, B.J. (1978). Catecholamines and self stimulation: reward and performance effects dissociated. *Pharmacology, Biochemistry and Behavior, 9*, 813-820

Giambalvo, C.T., & Snodgrasse, S.R. (1978). Biochemical and behavioral effects of serotonin neurotoxins on the negrostriatal dopamine system: comparison of injection sites. *Brain Research 152*, 555-566.

Graeff, F.G., Quintero, S., & Gray, J.A. (1980). Median raphe stimulation, hippocampal theta rhythm and threat-induced behavioral inhibition. *Physiology and Behavior, 25*, 235-262.

Graeff, E.G., & Silveira-Filho, N.G. (1978). Behavioral inhibition induced by electrical stimulation of the median raphe nucleus of the rat. *Physiology and Behavior, 21*, 477-484.

Gray, J.A. (1972). The psychophysiological nature of introversion-extraversion: A modification of Eysenck's theory. In: V.D. Nebylitsyn & J.A. Gray (Eds.), *Biological bases of individual behavior.* New York: Academic Press.

Heffner, T.G., & Seiden, L.S. (1980). Synthesis of catecholamines from tritium-labeled tyrosine in brain during performance of operant behavior. *Brain Research*, 403-420.

Hermann, J.P., Guillonneau, D., Dantzer, R., Seatton, B., Semerdjian-Rouquier, L. & Le Moal, M. (1982). Differential effects of inescapable footshocks and of stimuli previously paired with inescapable footshocks on dopamine turnover in cortical and limbic areas of the rat. *Life Sciences, 30*, 2207-2214.

Hirata, F., & Axelrod, J. (1980). Phospolipid methylation and biological signal transmission. *Science, 209*, 1082-1090.

Kunz, E., Valette, N., & Laborit, H. (1974). Rôle antagoniste de l'activité motrice d'évitement ou de lutta à l'égard de l'hypertension arterielle chronique provoquée chez le rat par l'application journalière d'un choc électrique plantaire. *Agressologie, 15*, 333-339.

Laborit, H. (1952). *Réaction organique à l'aggression et choc (Vol. 1)*. Paris: Masson.

Laborit, H. (1954). *Résistance et soumission en physiobiologie. "L'hibernation artificielle" (Vol. 1)*. Paris: Masson.

Laborit, H. (1974). Proposition d'un modéle intégrè des comportements normaux et anormaux à partir de donées biochimiques, neurophysiologiques, éthologiques, cliniques et sociologiques. *Annals of Medical Psychology, 1*, 47-60.

Laborit, H. (1979, 1986). L'inhibition d'action (1st ed. 1979, 2nd ed. 1986).

Laborit, H., Baron, C., & Laurent, J. (1977). Faits expérimentaux neurophysiologiques et biologiques montraut l'existence d'activités fonctionnelles sèparées pour l'hippocampe dorsal et ventral. *Agressologie, 18*, 11-15.

Laborit, H., & Bonifacj, J.F. (1984). Effect of 3-(-2-Morpholinoethylaminol)4-methyl-6-phenyl-pyridazine (minaprine) on plasm corticosterone levels of physostigmine treated rats. *Research Communications on Chemical and Pathological Pharmacology, 44*, 63-67.

Laborit, H., Brunaud, M., Savy, J.M., Baron, C., Vallée, E., Lamotte, C., Thuret, F., Muyard, J.P., & Cavino, B. (1972). Etude biochimique et pharmacologique du 3-(2-morpholinoethylamino)4-méthyl-6-phényl-pyridazine, dichlorhydrate (Agr 1240). *Agressologie, 13*, 291-318.

Laborit, H., Huguenard, P., & Alluaume, R. (1952). Un nouveau stabilisateur végétatif (le 4560 RP). *Presse Médicale 60*, 206-208.

Laborit, H., Kunz, E., & Valette, N. (1974 a). Róle antagoniste de l'activité motrice d'évitement ou de lutta à l'egard de l'hypertension arterielle chronique provoquée chez le rat par l'application journalière d'un choc électrique plantaire. *Agressologie, 15*, 333-339.

Laborit, H., Kunz, E., & Valette, N. (1974 b). Róle de l'apprentissage dans le mécanisme d'inhibition comportemental et de l'hypertension artérielle consécutives à l'application de stimulus aversifs sans possibilité de fuite ou de lutte. *Agressologie, 15*, 381-385.

Laborit, H., Valette, N., & Laurent, J. (1975). Action d'un inhibiteur de la monoamine oxydase (nialamide) sur l'hypertension artérielle consécutive a l'application de stimulus aversifs et sur l'activité de la ß-glycuronidase cérébrale. *Agressologie, 16*, 355-359.

Laborit, H., & Zerbib, R. (1987). Phobol esters antagonize scopolamine-induced amnesis of a passive avoidance. *Research Communications on Psychology, Psychiatry and Behavior, 12*, 105-117.

Laduron, P.M. (1984). Lack of direct evidence for adrenergic and dopaminergic autoreceptors. *Trends in Pharmacological Science* 459-461.

Maker, H.S., Weiss, C., Silider, D.J., & Cohen, G. (1891). Coupling of dopamine oxidation (monoamide oxidase EC 1.4.3.4.) activity to gluthathione oxidation via the generation of hydrogen peroxide in rat brain homogenates. *Journal of Neurochemistry, 36*, 589-593.

Mason, S.T., & Fibiger, H.C. (1979). Interaction between noradrenergic and cholinergic systems in the rat brain: behavioral function in locomotor activity. *Neuroscience, 4,* 517-526.

Molina, De A.F., & Hunsperger, R.W. (1962). Organisation of subcortical system governing defence and flight reaction in the cat. *Journal of Physiology 160,* 200-213.

Montanero, N., Dall'Olio, R., & Gandolfi, O. (1979). Bromolysergide and methysergide protection against ECS-induced retrograde amnesia. *Neuropsychobiology, 5,* 174-180

Olds, J., & Milner, P. (1954). Positive reinforcement produced by electrical stimulation of septal areas and other regions of rat brain. *Journal of Comparative Physiological Psychology, 47,* 419-427.

Plaznik, A., Kostowski, W., Bidzinski, A., & Hauptmann, M. (1980). Effects of lesions of the mid brain raphe nuclei on avoidance learning in rats. *Physiology and Behavior, 24,* 257-262.

Pycock, C.J., Kerwin, R.W., & Conter, C.J. (1980). Effect of lesion of cortical dopamine terminal on subcortical dopamine receptors in rats. *Nature, 286,* 74-76.

Redgrave, P. (1978). Modulation of intracranial self-stimulation behavior by local perfusions of dopamine, noradrenaline and serotonin within the caudate nucleus and nucleus accumbens. *Brain Research, 155,* 277-296.

Russel, R.W., & Macri, J. (1979). Central cholinergic involvement in behavioral hyperactivity. *Pharmacology, Biochemistry and Behavior, 10,* 43-48.

Samet, M.R., & Rutledge, C.D. (1984). Correlation between phospholipid methylation and neuronal catecholamine transport. *Biochemistry and Pharmacology, 33,* 3547-3551.

Schenberg, L.C., & Graeff, F.G. (1978). Role of the periaqueductal gray substances in the anti-anxiety action of benzodiazepines. *Pharmacology, Biochemistry and Behavior, 9,* 287-296.

Schmidt, D.E., Cooper, D.O., & Barrett, R.J. (1980). Strain specific alteration in hippocampal cholinergic function following acute footshock. *Pharmacology, Biochemistry and Behavior, 12,* 277-280.

Seregi, A., Serfozo, P. & Mergl, Z. (1983). Evidence for the localization of hydrogen peroxide stimulated cyclooxygenase activity in rat brain mitochondria: a possible coupling with monoamine oxidase. *Journal of Neurochemistry, 40,* 407-413.

Sinet, P.M., Heikkila, R.E., & Cohen, G. (1980). Hydrogen peroxide production by rat brain in vivo. *Journal of Neurochemistry, 34,* 1421-1428.

Stein, L. (1968). Chemistry of reward and punishment. In: D.H. Efron (Ed.), Psychopharmacology: A review of progress (1957-1967) (Vol. 1) (pp. 105-123). Washington, D.C.: U.S. Government Printing Office.

Stephens, D.N., & Herberg, L.J. (1979). Dopamine actylcholine "balance" in nucleus and corpus striatum and its effects on hypothalamic self-stimulation.

European Journal of Phamacology, 54, 331-344.

Stolk, J.M., Robert, R.L., Levine, S., & Barchas, J.D. (1974). Brain Norepine-phrine metabolism and shock induced fighting behavior in rats: differential effects of shock and fighting on the neurochemical response to a common footshock stimulus. *Journal of Pharmacology and Experimental Therapy, 190,* 193-209.

Tachiki, K.H., Tateishi, T.T., Nishiwaki, K., Nakamura, E., Nagayama, H., & Takahashi, R. (1978). Animal model of depression: III Mechanism of action of tetrabenazine. *Biological Psychiatry, 13,* 429-444.

Tayler, M. (1976). Effect of L-tryptophan and L-methionine on activity of the rat. *British Journal of Pharmacology, 15,* 449-455.

Thornton, E.W., & Goudie, H.K. (1978). Evidence for the role of serotonin in the inhibition of spectic motor responses. *Psychopharmacology, 60,* 73-80.

Waldbillig, J.R. (1979). The role of the dorsal and median raphe in the inhibi-tion of muricide. *Brain Research, 160,* 341-346.

Warbritten, J.D., Steward, R.M. & Baldessarini, R.J. (1978). Decreased loco-motor activity and attenuation of amphetamine hyperactivity with intraven-tricular infusion of serotonin in the rat. *Brain Research, 143,* 373-382.

Yamamoto, T., & Ueki, S. (1978). Effects of drugs on hyperactivity and aggres-sion induced by raphe lesions in rats. *Pharmacology, Biochemistry and Beha-vior, 9,* 821-826.

Zolman, J.F., Mattingly, B.A., & Sahley, C.L. (1978). Cholinergic involvement in inhibitory behavior of the young domestic chick. *Behavioral Biology, 23,* 415-432.

Social Inhibition: A General-Developmental Perspective

JENS B. ASENDORPF

Inhibition of social behavior is discussed from a general-developmental perspective with a particular focus on the author's recent studies on social inhibition among children and young adults. In a conceptual section, inhibition is distinguished from unsociability and from active avoidance. Drawing on Gray's concept of a behavioral inhibition system, literature is reviewed on developmental changes in the response to three different classes of inhibiting situations: unfamiliar persons, cues for punishment, and cues for frustrative nonreward. This developmental perspective reveals important developmental changes in the nature of inhibition. Based on recent empirical evidence, it is assumed that early acquired as well as later acquired inhibitory processes can simultaneously affect social behavior; social inhibition is conceptualized as a final common pathway to different kinds of inhibitory processes.

Becoming inhibited, or shy, in social-interactional situations is a ubiquitous experience. Zimbardo, Pilkonis, and Norwood (1974) asked approximately 800 18-21-year-old U.S. citizens whether they had been shy in some social situation; 99% remembered such a situation. A similarly high rate was found in various other cultures as well (cf. Zimbardo, 1977). In this chapter I review the existing literature on this ubiquitous experience from a general-developmental perspective: When does social inhibition occur for the first time during infancy, and how does the nature of the eliciting situations, of the response, and of the inhibitory processes mediating this response change between infancy and adulthood?

Thus, in this chapter I take an intraindividual perspective on inhibition. Inhibition is conceived of as a situation-bound, transient emotional state (with the short-term process characteristics typical for emotional states). In this chapter I do not discuss interindividual differences in inhibition and their development (inhibition as a trait).

A Behavioral Systems View of Social Motivation

Lay-psychological terms such as shy, coy, and inhibited refer to a rather fuzzy concept of nonengagement in social interaction. It is necessary therefore to begin with a psychological conceptualization of social motivation that allows for defining social inhibition more clearly and that enables us to distinguish social inhibition from similar concepts such as unsociability and social avoidance.

Referring to general systems theory (Miller, 1978) and its application to development in general (Sameroff, 1983; Thelen, 1989) and social-emotional development in particular (Sroufe, 1979), I assume that human emotional behavior is the resultant of the activation of various behavioral systems, that is, domain-specific, informationally encapsulated, inferential information-processing subsystems of the nervous system ("modules"; Fodor, 1985). These modules have evolved during the evolution of the human species and serve fundamental functions for survival. In this chapter, four such behavioral systems are relevant: those serving attachment, affiliation, sexuality, and inhibition. These systems are activated by specific extra- as well as intraorganismic cues and, if activated, give rise to a specific response tendency. Overt behavior is the final common pathway of these response tendencies (as well as volitional tendencies); thus, emotional social behavior is a joint function of different behavioral systems. If their response tendencies are contradictory, motivational conflicts have to be resolved.

The first three systems (attachment, affiliation, and sexuality) may be called behavioral activation systems (cf. Gray, 1982a, for a similar concept) because their activation evokes a tendency to approach certain conspecifics. On the basis of many conditioning and pharmacological studies, Gray (1982a,b) put forward the hypothesis that another system, the behavioral inhibition system, serves to inhibit the activation of *all* behavioral activation systems; in particular, the same inhibition system inhibits attachment, affiliation, and sexual motivation. This premise also underlies the following discussion of social inhibition.

Social Inhibition, Unsociability, and Social Avoidance

Building upon this behavioral systems perspective, social inhibition is conceived here as the inhibition of social "approach-motivation". Thus, social inhibition requires some social approach motivation in the first place. This requirement distinguishes social inhibition from the simple absence of social approach motivation (*unsociability*; cf. Asendorpf, 1990a, for a more detailed discussion). For example, people may be unsociable because they are tired or at this moment prefer nonsocial activities.

Sometimes it is difficult for observers to decide whether another person is inhibited or merely unsociable if only subtle cues are available indicating that the person may be approach-motivated but at the same time inhibited. And sometimes people label others "shy" or "inhibited" not because they note some clues for inhibition in their behavior but simply because they *expect* these people to be more sociable than they are; within the terminology proposed here, this would be an instance of mislabeling.

Another conceptual problem arises if inhibition is equated with active avoidance. From a functional perspective it is rather obvious that these are different behavioral phenomena. In animal conditioning research and human psycho-pharmacology, some authors proposed a distinction between active and passive avoidance that can be applied directly to active social avoidance versus inhibition (Fowles, 1987; Gray, 1982a; Mackintosh, 1974). According to this view, in active avoidance situations, safety cues (conditioned stimuli for nonpunishment) activate an escape response so that the organism can avoid punishment. Thus, active avoidance is functionally equivalent to approach-motivated behavior: An alternative is approached. For example, a child moves close to mother when a stranger appears in the room.

In passive avoidance situations, inhibitory cues inhibit approach behavior so that the organism can avoid the potential dangers involved in the situation. For example, a child stops playing when a stranger enters the room, and looks at the stranger from a distance for a long time without moving. This type of behavior involves both an approach and a passive avoidance component. Gray (1982a) has convincingly suggested that active and passive avoidance involve different psychophysiological systems and are differentially influenced by drugs such as the minor tranquilizers or alcohol. I also conceive social inhibition to be a form of passive avoidance, not of active avoidance (cf. also Asendorpf, 1989a,b).

Situational Antecedents of Inhibition

Gray (1982a,b) assumed that inhibition is aroused by three different classes of inhibitory cues: novelty, conditioned cues for punishment, and conditioned cues for frustrative nonreward. He based this assumption on the results of many studies conducted predominantly with animals within a conditioning paradigm. If his model of inhibition is applied to human behavior, the conditioning paradigm must be transcended by including more complex situational evaluations such as checking one's coping potential or comparing one's behavior with social norms or self-presentational goals (cf. Scherer, 1984, for a model of emotional behavior that takes such evaluations into account).

Despite this expansion of the mediating processes between situation and response, the tripartite classification of inhibition-relevant situations proposed by Gray (1982a) can be maintained: Social inhibition is triggered by (a) the unfamiliarity of interaction partners (*inhibition toward strangers*), (b) the anticipation of negative evaluation, or (c) the anticipation of insufficiently positive evaluation; the latter two forms of inhibition refer to "punishment" and "frustrative nonreward" and might be both called *social-evaluative inhibition*. Thus, children may become inhibited if they meet strangers or anticipate being rejected or ignored by peers if they try to play with them.

In all three types of inhibiting situations, potential social interaction partners are evaluated for self-relevant characteristics: Is this person familiar to me, and how will this person react to me? Both kinds of evaluation involve memory, but the "novelty check" is much easier to perform than the "social-evaluation check". Only in the most primitive form of this social-evaluation check might particular persons become conditioned cues for punishment or frustrative non-reward. Older children and adults are capable of more complex and more deliberate forms of evaluating another's evaluation.

The self-presentation approach to social anxiety of Schlenker and Leary (1982) is concerned with these higher-order evaluative processes. According to this view, social anxiety arises when people are motivated to make a particular impression on others but doubt that they will do so, because they expect unsatisfactory impression-relevant reactions from others. Such unsatisfactory reactions might be called punishment or frustrative nonreward, but the process by which people form and enact expectations about the impressions of others cannot be accounted for by a conditioning paradigm. Forming expectations about the impressions of others requires cognitive capacities for reflecting upon one's own behavior as well as upon the impressions that others might form about this behavior. In particular, it requires us to take the perspective of others, and to judge one's own behavior from this perspective. As we will see later in this chapter, this requirement has interesting implications for the development of inhibition.

To summarize the conceptual framework achieved so far, social inhibition refers to an emotional state that is characterized by an inhibited approach motivation. The approach component distinguishes social inhibition from unsociability. The avoidance component of inhibition can be further specified as passive avoidance; this specification distinguishes social inhibition from active social avoidance. The tripartite classification of inhibiting situations that was proposed by Gray (1982a) within a conditioning framework can be extended to encompass more complex evaluations of social situations such as self-presentational concerns according to Schlenker and Leary (1982). Social inhibition, then, is conceived of as an emotional reaction to three classes of social situations: being confronted with strangers; and anticipating a negative or an insufficiently positive evaluation from others that is highly valued.

Within this conceptual framework, we will now ask how inhibition develops from infancy through adulthood. This task is facilitated if we first discuss inhibition toward strangers and social-evaluative inhibition separately, and only later ask how unfamiliarity and social evaluation might interact in arousing inhibition.

The Development of Inhibition Toward Strangers

Many studies have consistently demonstrated that around the age of 8 months, infants begin to display "wary" reactions toward adult strangers (see Horner, 1983, and Sroufe, 1977, for reviews). Although considerable individual differences exist in the beginning, duration, and intensity of this reaction, it seems almost universal among infants of all cultures. Most of these studies used the following observational procedure: An adult stranger approaches mother and infant rather quickly and finally takes up the baby. The infant's reaction to the approaching stranger can be classified on a continuum of wariness from a slightly negative reaction ("wary brow") via avoidance movements of eyes, head, and body to intense crying. Typically, a baby's behavior shifts along this continuum from low wariness to some point of maximum wariness that can be taken as a measure of the intensity of the whole process of responding (cf. Waters, Matas, & Sroufe, 1975, for a detailed description). This process often corresponds to the process of the stranger approach; the nearer the stranger comes and the faster the approach is, the more likely is the infant to react with intense wariness.

Infant wariness to strangers is not a simple reflex-like reaction; its intensity depends on various contextual cues such as whether a parent is present or not, how unfamiliar the observation room is, and whether the stranger is male or female (cf. Sroufe, 1977). In an intriguing study, Brooks and Lewis (1976) found that infants reacted with most wariness to adult strangers, with medium wariness to an adult midget, and rarely with wariness to an unfamiliar child. This finding rejects the interpretation of Spitz (1965) that infant wariness depends upon the discrepancy between acquired schemata for known versus unknown persons (a midget is most discrepant from any acquired person schema but arouses only medium wariness). Instead, the wariness reaction appears to depend on a complex evaluation of the whole situation in terms of cues signalling danger (nearness and body size of the stranger, fastness of the approach) as well as safety (nearness of the parent, familiarity of the room).

Infant wariness toward strangers is the first instance of social inhibition during ontogenesis because often (though not always) infants initially smile when the stranger appears at the door and only subsequently react wary, or react for short periods of time with ambivalent behaviors that contain both approach and passive avoidance components. In fact, Bretherton and Ainsworth (1974) found that 85% of 106 12-month-olds reacted to an approaching stranger with some behavioral signs of an approach-avoidance conflict.

Greenberg and Marvin (1982) showed that with increasing age, children's response to an approaching adult stranger becomes particularly ambivalent because older children show not only fleeting expressions of ambivalence but often long-lasting ones such as lengthy coy expressions of smiling accompanied by gaze aversion. Thus, preschool children become able to remain in a state of simultaneous approach and passive avoidance motivation for longer periods.

This kind of social inhibition is preserved through adulthood. Kaltenbach, Weinraub, and Fullard (1980) made the puzzling observation that the mothers who accompanied their babies also displayed an initial wariness toward the approaching stranger as coded by the same procedure that was applied to their infants. On average, they even reacted somewhat more strongly than their babies.

Unfortunately, the authors did not code ambivalent responses of the mothers directly; but the reported frequencies of behaviors (e.g., 54% smiles and 83% wary averted gaze) suggest that the mothers did indeed react with overt ambivalence to the stranger.

These studies of inhibition toward an approaching stranger suggest a continuity of the reaction between infancy and adulthood. But they leave two unresolved issues for further investigation. First, they focus on a very specific type of stranger confrontation that evokes a very specific inhibitory reaction. They do not provide a picture of the wide variety of reactions that can occur when people are confronted with strangers in different contexts. Second, they do not answer the question why infants respond to children with little wariness, and how inhibition toward unfamiliar peers develops. Studies that have been directly concerned with inhibition toward unfamiliar peers suggest that this form of inhibition develops later than wariness toward strangers. However, this conclusion is presently based on only a few, methodologically quite heterogeneous, and largely unpublished studies. Amsterdam and Greenberg (1977) did not observe aversive responses to a videofilm of peers at the age of 10 months, but at the age of 15 and 20 months. Kagan, Kearsley, and Zelazo (1978) found that over 80% of a sample of 1-2-year-olds reacted to the entrance of an unfamiliar peer with inhibited play and vocalization and more proximity to their mother; inhibition was strongest at 20 months of age. Zaslow (1977, cited in Kagan et al., 1978) reported the same result for Israeli children. Jacobson (1977; cited in Kagan et al., 1978) compared the behavior of young children between familiar and unfamiliar peers and already found more inhibition and proximity to mother at 10-15 months of age, in the presence of an unfamiliar peer.

Thus, it seems that inhibition toward unfamiliar peers develops later than inhibition toward adults, reaching a peak around 20 months of age. At this age, a major shift in children's cognitive ability takes place: Children can recognize themselves in a mirror (Amsterdam, 1972; Lewis & Brooks-Gunn, 1979), and they become able to *spontaneously* take the perspective of others as evidenced in an increasing rate of empathic responding to the distress of others (Bischof-Köhler, 1988). Gallup and Suarez (1986) and, in a more sophisticated way, Bischof-Köhler (1989) put forward the hypothesis that the onset of self-recognition and the onset of spontaneous perspective taking might be due to the same fundamental shift in cognitive ability: Children become able to coordinate two different synchronous points of view (self and mirror image; one's own perspective and others' perspective). In particular, Bischof-Köhler (1989) emphasized that this form of perspective taking can be differentiated both from earlier emotional contagion and from later voluntary perspective taking as investigated in the classic studies of Flavell, Botkin, Fry, Wright, and Jarvis (1968).

Asendorpf (1989b) has proposed the hypothesis that the emergence of the ability to spontaneously take the perspective of another person might be responsible for the peak of inhibition toward unfamiliar peers around 20 months of age because it induces an uncertainty about the intentions of the partner. We are presently testing this hypothesis empirically. If it is confirmed, this would suggest that around the age of 20 months a new form of inhibition toward strangers develops that applies to both peer and adult strangers, and that might be quite different from infant wariness because it involves higher-order cognitive processes. Whereas infants' wariness toward adult strangers appears to be triggered by certain cues signalling physical danger (fast approach, body size), later-developing inhibition toward unfamiliar persons might be a response to a cognitive uncertainty about the stranger's intentions.

For older children beyond the second year, strong inhibiting effects of peer unfamiliarity have been more clearly established. Schwarz (1972) found that 4-year-olds expressed less positive affect toward an unfamiliar peer as compared to a familiar peer, moved less through space, and talked less with the partner. Doyle, Conelly, and Rivest (1980) showed that kindergartners looked more at unfamiliar peers from a distance than at familiar peers, and played more solitarily and less interactively; their cognitive play behavior was not affected except for a lower rate of pretense play (role play) with the unfamiliar peer.

Table 1: Effects of Peer Unfamiliarity on Social Participation and Cognitive Play in Dyadic Free Play Sessions

| | Means in session | | | | Unfamiliarity effect | |
| | Unfamiliar | | Familiar | | | |
Variable	1	2	1	2	$F(1,64)$	p
Social participation						
– unoccupied	.03	.02	.02	.01	4.51	.04
– solitary play	.40	.38	.20	.20	36.42	.0001
– looking at partner	.13	.05	.05	.03	21.72	.0001
– parallel play	.20.	24	.31	.31	17.72	.0001
– conversation	.16	.24	.27	.34	19.74	.0001
– interactive play	.02	.05	.13	.09	43.14	.0001
Cognitive play quality						
– rough-and-tumble	.01	.05	.00	.01		ns
– functional	.14	.16	.15	.12		ns
– exploratory	.23	.26	.20	.18	7.90	.01
– constructive	.54	.55	.53	.61		ns
– dramatic	.09	.02	.12	.07	8.69	.005

Note. N=65. Reported are data for two play sessions with unfamiliar peers and two sessions with familiar peers (mean age for both types of session 6.5 years). The unfamiliarity effect was tested within a multivariate analysis of variance treating play sessions as repeated measurements.

In a longitudinal study with 65 children, Asendorpf (1989b) replicated the findings of Doyle et al. (1980) and extended them by a process analysis of children's behavior. Children played at age 5 with an unfamiliar peer, 6 months and 18 months later with a familiar peer, and again 6 months later with an unfamiliar peer (a longitudinal ABBA-design). Assuming linear age-related changes in children's behavior, this design allows an analysis of the effect of unfamiliarity because children had the same mean age when they played with unfamiliar versus familiar peers (cf. Table 1).

As compared to a familiar partner, in the presence of an unfamiliar peer, children were more unoccupied, played more alone, looked more to the partner from a distance, and were less engaged in parallel play, conversations, and particularly less engaged in interactive play. In the presence of an unfamiliar peer, the cognitive quality of their play was not affected except for a somewhat higher rate of exploratory activity and less pretense play.

These overall effects were complemented by analyses of behavior change during the play sessions. Figure 1 illustrates these analyses by depicting the changes in the percent of different behaviors for the first play session.

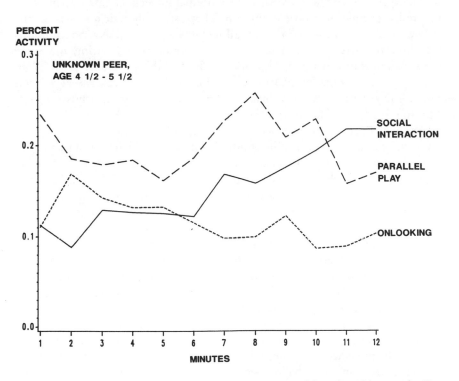

Figure 1:   Changes in social behavior during 12 minutes of free play with an unfamiliar peer (adapted from Asendorpf, 1989b, Fig. 10; Copyright by Springer-Verlag).

Looking at the partner from a distance peaked in the second minute and then decreased steadily; parallel play peaked in the eighth minute and then decreased, and social interaction increased steadily until it surpassed parallel play at the end of the session. These changes apparently reflect the solution of an approach-avoidance conflict evoked by the peer stranger. Inhibition initially led to pro-longed looking to the peer from a distance. Later, the conflict was partially resolved in terms of parallel play as a compromise between approach and avoid-ance (in parallel play, children play with similar toys in close proximity, are vi-sually oriented about each other's activity, but do not interact; cf. Parten, 1932). Finally, inhibition ceased and gave way to social interaction. It should be noted that this interpretation rests upon data sampled at the aggregate level (group means) and hence reflects only average tendencies of behavior; individual chil-dren might deviate strongly from this overall picture.

For adults, an unstructured social setting that is comparable to some extent with the free play sessions of children is a casual conversation between two part-ners. Many studies have used a "waiting-room paradigm" for studying individu-al differences in inhibition. The subject meets another subject or a confederate of the experimenter who pretends to be a normal subject. The two partners are unfamiliar in order to arouse inhibition. They ostensibly wait together for the "real experiment" but in fact they are filmed by a hidden camera. Social norms urge both partners to have some casual conversation in this setting; otherwise the situation is unstructured. The rationale behind this procedure is similar to the one underlying the free play procedure for children: Because the situation is not strongly structured, individual differences become particularly strong (cf. Monson, Hesley, & Chernick, 1982, for empirical evidence).

Although dozens of these experiments are reported in the literature, only very few have systematically varied the familiarity of the two partners. One is the stu-dy of Asendorpf (1989a). In a between-group design, student dyads ostensibly waited together for the "real study"; partner familiarity was systematically varied by pairing strangers, good friends, and strangers who were made familiar with each other. Self-ratings, partner-ratings and observer-ratings of inhibition con-firmed the hypothesis that strangers were most inhibited, recent acquaintances less so, and good friends least of all. In addition to these rating measures, an objective coding of closed body posture showed the same effect. The less fami-liar the partner was, the more closed was the arm position of the students during the conversation. Because body position is a much less reactive measure than ratings, this result strongly confirmed the validity of the results.

After the situation, subjects were debriefed and individually watched the videorecording of the situation. They were asked to remember as accurately as possible the thoughts and feelings they had had during the situations shown on the video screen and to verbalize them continuously. This instruction was aimed at maximizing the information from the subjects as well as somewhat undermi-ning their self-presentation or defense strategies. The audiotaped spontaneous

reports of the subjects were coded for various categories, including any referen-
ces to the partner's unfamiliarity, and any reports of fear of the partner's unfamiliarity. For obvious reasons, good friends did not mention the partner's unfamiliarity. Of the remaining subjects, those recently acquainted with the partner
mentioned the partner's unfamiliarity *more* than complete strangers did, and
none of the 48 subjects in the stranger and acquaintance groups explicitly reported fear of strangers. This is a surprisingly low rate because these subjects spontaneously reported 0.7 instances of fear on average.

These data suggest that subjects felt uneasy in the presence of strangers but
they *did not experience this uneasiness as fear*. They mentioned the unfamiliarity
of their partner more often if it was made salient to them by the acquaintance
procedure, than if it was less obtrusively introduced (but in fact more strongly
so) in the stranger condition, but they never referred to it as fear. Asendorpf
(1989a) interpreted this finding as suggesting that adults' inhibition toward
strangers is due to the *same* inhibitory processes that give rise to stranger wariness among infants.

This might be an overly bold hypothesis because, as we have seen above,
around the age of 20 months a more cognitively mature form of inhibition toward strangers might develop that could also influence adults' reactions toward
strangers. Whichever form of inhibition shows continuity from childhood to
adulthood, the inhibitory processes might operate below awareness if the evaluation of the stranger is done as automatically as in infancy or if it is characterized
by the *spontaneous* perspective taking of two-year-olds (cf. also the work of
Zajonc and associates on subliminal effects of familiarity on pattern recognition; Zajonc, 1980).

If this hypothesis is correct, it is not surprising anymore that subjects had dif-
fuse feelings of uneasiness in the presence of strangers but did not verbalize
them as fear and did not attribute them to objects in their environment. It
might be that inhibition toward strangers sneaks into adult social interaction
beneath the level of awareness because it is based on cognitive evaluations that
develop early in life and that might not reach the level of awareness even in
adults. This interpretation will receive more credibility below when the findings
for inhibition toward strangers are complemented by the quite different results
for social-evaluative inhibition.

The Development of Social-Evaluative Inhibition

Social-evaluative inhibition refers to inhibition triggered by the anticipation of a
negative or an unsufficiently positive evaluation by others. In its most primitive
form, this anticipation is implemented by conditioning: Particular persons become conditioned cues for punishment or frustrative nonreward according to
Gray (1982a). Thus, a chronic alcoholic who frequently beats his infant might

become a conditioned cue for punishment. In a series of studies with adults, Öhman and associates showed that angry faces are very powerful stimuli for the classical conditioning of fear responses, and that the conditioned response is evoked by the physiognomy of the angry person, not by the angry expression itself (Öhman, 1986; Öhman & Dimberg, 1984). Adults appear to be biologically prepared to acquire fear responses to angry conspecifics, and it is very likely that this is true for infants as well.

A later developing form of social-evaluative inhibition requires taking the perspective of others, realizing that they have certain behavioral standards, and evaluating one's own behavior according to these standards. As outlined in the preceding section, spontaneous perspective taking emerges around the age of 20 months. Thus, social-evaluative inhibition should begin at this age or later.

Kagan (1981) provided ample empirical evidence, based on short-term longitudinal studies during the second year of life, that indeed toward the end of the second year children begin (a) to adapt behavioral standards from adults, (b) to show proudness or shame after having solved tasks successfully or unsuccessfully, and (c) to verbally comment on their own behavior. Thus, children of this age begin to understand what another person feels, wishes, and wants, and particularly what she feels *about them* and what he wants *from them*.

A specific relation between the cognitive shift around 20 months and social evaluation was established by Lewis, Sullivan, Stanger, and Weiss (1989). They showed that mirror self-recognition was strongly related to the occurrence of embarrassed reactions among 20-month-olds when these children were overpraised or asked to dance in the presence of their mother and an experimenter: Nonrecognizers rarely reacted embarrassed whereas recognizers did so much more frequently.

Embarrassment is a social-evaluative emotion similar to social-evaluative inhibition and requires the same cognitive capacities. Schlenker and Leary (1982) and Asendorpf (1990c) have suggested that the major difference between embarrassment and inhibition is that embarrassment is a *reactive* emotion whereas inhibition is an *anticipatory* emotion. Embarrassment is aroused by a perceived discrepancy between one's behavior and social norms or individual self-presentational goals (cf. Edelmann, 1987); it is a reaction to self-presentational problems. Social-evaluative inhibition, on the other hand, is evoked by the anticipation of self-presentational problems.

Although this distinction appears to fit the lay psychological usage of the terms "embarrassment" and "inhibition" and also makes sense from a theoretical perspective, embarrassment and social-evaluative inhibition may often be highly correlated empirically because embarrassment makes further social-evaluative inhibition more likely and vice versa. In any case, the finding of Lewis et al. (1989) suggests the hypothesis that social-evaluative inhibition also starts around the age of 20 months when children become cognitively able to spontaneously take the perspective of others and to evaluate their own behavior from the other's perspective. This hypothesis awaits further empirical confirmation, though.

We know little about the later development of social-evaluative inhibition from preschool age until late childhood as well. So far, perhaps the best empirical evidence that the anticipation of being rejected or ignored by peers arouses inhibition was provided by Asendorpf (1990b). In a longitudinal study, 99 children were observed during free play in their preschool/kindergarten class during a three-year-period (as usual in Germany, most children stayed in the same class with the same teacher for 3 years). Detailed codings of children's behavior while trying to initiate contact with others revealed that the observed rate of being rejected or ignored by the partners during these contact initiation attempts was related to the rate of "wait-and-hover" in contact initiations in the same year as well as in following years, but not in preceding years. According to Gottman (1977) who first introduced this code, "wait-and-hover" was coded whenever a child approached others, but then stopped and looked toward them for at least 3 seconds without speaking. This is a clear instance of inhibition.

Thus, experiences of being ignored or rejected by others in class led to increased inhibition later on. Because these results are based on correlational analyses, they await confirmation by studies that systematically vary social evaluation (e.g., intervention studies that try to decrease the incidence of rejection and neglect in peer groups).

During middle and late childhood, the nature of social-evaluative inhibition changes because the reflection about others' impressions reaches the level of *self-awareness*: children become aware that they reflect about another's evaluation of their own actions, and they begin to reflect about their *public self*, that is, how they appear to others.

Buss (1980) as well as Carver and Scheier (1981) assumed that self-related attention can be either primarily directed toward one's own person and behavior ("state of private self-awareness"), or primarily to one's public self ("state of public self-awareness"). Buss (1980) noted that public self-awareness requires the ability to take the perspective of others and hence assumed that public self-awareness and social-evaluative anxiety emerge around the age of 4 years when children become able to (deliberately) take the perspective of others (cf. Flavell et al., 1968). As empirical evidence, Buss (1980, 1986) cited Buss, Iscoe, and Buss (1979) who found that, according to parental reports, children begin to react embarrassed (as judged by behaviors such as blushing or embarrassed smiles) around the age of 4-5 years.

As Lewis et al. (1989) have shown, however, embarrassed reactions can be observed much earlier in situations that arouse embarrassment in adults (e.g., being asked to dance). Furthermore, Darwin (1872) in his classic study on the expression of emotions did the first systematic study on blushing and found that blushing was reported already at age 2.5 years. Buss et al. (1979) relied upon parental reports of questionable validity, and therefore they overestimated the onset of embarrassment. More importantly, Buss (1980) as well as Carver and Scheier (1981) did not distinguish between spontaneous perspective taking and conscious perspective taking, particularly volitional perspective taking.

In line with the view of Bischof-Köhler (1989) I assume that Buss (1980) and Carver and Scheier (1981) are correct as far as *social-evaluative anxiety* is concerned: a conscious experience of fear related to the evaluation of others which is accompanied by public self-awareness. Social-evaluative anxiety indeed requires the ability to consciously reflect about the impressions of others, and this ability may emerge around the age of 4 years. But this form of social-evaluative inhibition must be distinguished from the earlier form that is based on spontaneous perspective-taking.

Social-evaluative anxiety becomes particularly strong during adolescence. Many studies have found a peak of social-evaluative concerns around the age of 13 years, that is, shortly after the average onset of sexual maturity. For example, Simmons, Rosenberg, and Rosenberg (1973) developed a "Self-Consciousness Scale" containing items such as "If you were to wear the wrong kind of clothes to a party, would that bother you?" or "When I'm with people I get nervous because I worry how much they like me". Twelve-to-fourteen-year-olds had higher scores in this scale than both 8-11- and above-15-year-olds. Elkind and Bowen (1979) assessed 4th, 6th, 8th, and 12th graders with a modified version of this scale and found that both boys and girls had highest scores in grade 8. These self-report data suggest a similar peak of inhibited social behavior around the age of 13 years, although as far as I know no study has tested this hypothesis empirically.

The close temporal relationship between the peak of social concerns (and probably of social-evaluative inhibition) and sexual maturity suggests the hypothesis that the self-perceived biological changes during adolescence stimulate thoughts about one's sexual attractiveness; because of the lack of experience with the new role of a woman or a man, many adolescents will doubt that they are attractive and that they are able to handle this new role adequately; and this, in turn, might arouse social-evaluative inhibition.

Although this is a very plausible hypothesis, many developmental psychologists concerned with adolescence have warned against too quickly explaining psychological change during this age period only by sexual maturity. In Western societies, other role ambiguities are closely tied to sexual maturity, such as taking the role of an adult as far as non-sexual aspects are concerned (e.g., economy, responsibility for one's actions, detachment from one's family, or expectations of having to enter the job market). All these role ambiguities may contribute to the peak of social-evaluative inhibition in adolescence.

Although the frequency and intensity of social-evaluative inhibition appears to decrease between adolescence and early adulthood, there is ample evidence that social-evaluative inhibition remains a major – if not the most important – form of inhibition throughout adulthood. Many studies have designed social-evaluative situations in the laboratory in order to study individual differences in inhibition. Most of these studies lack a control situation, though, that allows studying general psychological effects of social evaluation.

One of the few exceptions is the study of Asendorpf (1989a) already mentioned in the preceding section. In addition to the variation of the unfamiliarity of the partner, social evaluation was varied between groups as follows. In the control condition, subjects just waited for the "real experiment" to come. In the evaluation condition, the experimenter instructed nonfriends to get to know each other, and friends to again make up their minds about the friend's personality, in order to evaluate the partner's personality in a questionnaire later on. As Figure 2 indicates, this instruction induced an inhibiting effect of nearly the same size as the variation of familiarity.

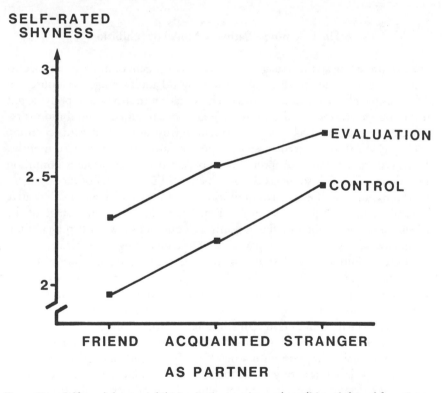

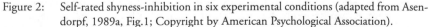

Figure 2:   Self-rated shyness-inhibition in six experimental conditions (adapted from Asendorpf, 1989a, Fig.1; Copyright by American Psychological Association).

Partner- and observer-ratings of inhibition confirmed this effect. Furthermore, the 70 subjects in the evaluation condition spontaneously reported during the video-reconstruction session 0.41 instances of social-evaluative fear; in the control condition this rate was significantly lower. On the other hand, only 2 of the 48 nonfriends in this condition reported fear of strangers. This discrepancy between a rather high rate of (spontaneously!) recalled evaluative fear and a near-to-zero rate of recalled fear of strangers indicates that many subjects were aware of social-evaluative fear whereas nearly none of the subjects in the unfamiliarity conditions was aware of fear of strangers. This discrepancy further supports the interpretation of the familiarity effect that was already put forward in the preceding section: Adults are susceptible to inhibition toward strangers but they do not experience this inhibition as fear.

A Final Common Pathway Model of Inhibition

The two preceding sections suggest that the development of inhibition proceeds in three stages. In the first stage, inhibition toward adult strangers is aroused by rather simple physical characteristics of the situation (nearness and body height of the stranger, fastness of the approach), and social-evaluative inhibition is restricted to conditioned cues for punishment or frustrative nonreward according to Gray (1982a). In the second stage, beginning around the age of 20 months, the emerging new ability of spontaneous perspective taking arouses inhibition toward peer and adult strangers due to a perceived uncertainty of the strangers' intentions, and social-evaluative inhibition due to the anticipation of negative or insufficiently positive social evaluation. Later on, in the third stage of the development of inhibition, the reflection about one's own self-presentation reaches awareness and becomes particularly intense during adolescence.

Thus, inhibition toward strangers and social-evaluative inhibition are assumed to proceed from cognitively rather simple forms in infancy to cognitively more complex forms later on. Furthermore, it is hypothesized that in the third stage of development, a discrepancy arises between inhibition toward strangers and social-evaluative inhibition. Only if potential social interaction partners are perceived as likely sources of non-positive social evaluation, does reflection about their possible impressions of oneself reach awareness and give rise to positive feedback loops resulting in acute public self-awareness and, if negative evaluations are anticipated, in the experience of fear of social evaluation.

The interaction between these different forms of inhibitory processes is, according to my present view, characterized by a clear continuity of early acquired forms of inhibition well into later life. Thus, infant-like inhibition toward approaching adult strangers can be observed also among adults (cf. the study of Kaltenbach et al., 1980, cited above), and adults' reactions to nonevaluative strangers are based on the same inhibitory processes that characterize 20-

months-olds' responses to strangers (cf. the study of Asendorpf, 1989a). I presently assume that the interaction between the various forms of inhibitory processes among adults has the most simple form: Early acquired and late acquired forms of inhibition exert an additive influence on adults' behavior (cf. Figure 2 for empirical evidence). Future empirical studies on the interaction of the various inhibitory processes might modify this suspiciously simple picture.

In analogy to the concept of a final common pathway in physiology, I have suggested regarding inhibited behavior among adults as the final common pathway of different kinds of inhibitory processes (Asendorpf, 1989a). Despite their distinctness in terms of developmental (and, ultimately, evolutionary) history, in terms of the underlying cognitive processes, and in terms of their availability to awareness and verbal self-report, these different forms of inhibitory processes might lead to some similarities in felt uneasiness and inhibited behavior; lay psychological terms such as "shy", "coy", or "inhibited" refer to these similarities. However, this chapter has shown that the psychological analysis extends well beyond these similarities.

Conclusions

The developmental view of inhibition urges us to transcend both the "cognitivistic" self-presentational approach to social inhibition of Schlenker and Leary (1982) that ignores early developing forms of inhibition, and the "biologistic" conditioning model of inhibition proposed by Gray (1982a) that ignores the higher-level cognitive processes involved in the self-presentation of older children and adults, and to reconcile both the "cognitivistic" and the "biologistic" approaches in a psychobiological model of social inhibition that accounts for the full complexity of adult human social interaction and its development.

At a more general level, this chapter may have demonstrated that a developmental perspective is quite useful for understanding social behavior even if one is only interested in adults. In my view, many present social-psychological approaches miss major aspects of human social interaction. They were taylored to describe and to explain adult social interaction in a parsimonious way. Given a very unparsimonious state of affairs due to the fact that nature has evolved but has not been designed, they are in fact too parsimonious. Higher-order living systems such as we are have a long and rather erratic evolutionary history which is recapitulated to some extent in the long and not always straightforward process of individual development. Ignoring this double history makes research easier but in the long run less effective.

The developmental perspective helps us to recognize the complexity of human social behavior as well as to disentangle some of this complexity by applying either a bottom-up or a top-down procedure. We can begin with "simple" functions that characterize infancy, and then proceed to higher-order functions, being guided by developmental principles such as searching for continuities, for the differentiation, and for the integration of early acquired functions. Or we can start with adult behavior, analyze its components, and ask when and how these components may have developed.

In any case, age serves as a guideline for decomposing the complexity of adult behavior into more simple units as they emerge during ontogeny. Furthermore, because the developmental perspective urges us to confront a particular psychological function at different age levels, and not only in its most developed form in adulthood, we are less likely to miss major aspects of this function. Hopefully, this chapter has provided readers with some of the flavor of this developmental perspective on human social behavior.

References

Amsterdam, B.K. (1972). Mirror self-image reactions before age two. *Developmental Psychobiology, 5*, 297-305.

Amsterdam, B., & Greenberg, L.M. (1977). Self-conscious behavior of infants: A videotape study. *Developmental Psychobiology, 10*, 1-6.

Asendorpf, J.B. (1989a). Shyness as a final common pathway for two different kinds of inhibition. *Journal of Personality and Social Psychology, 57*, 481-492.

Asendorpf, J. (1989b). *Soziale Gehemmtheit und ihre Entwicklung [Social inhibition and its development]*. Berlin: Springer-Verlag.

Asendorpf, J.B. (1990a). Beyond social withdrawal: Shyness, unsociability, and peer avoidance. *Human Development, 33*, 250-259.

Asendorpf, J.B. (1990b). Development of inhibition during childhood: Evidence for situational specificity and a two-factor model. *Developmental Psychology, 26*, 721-730.

Asendorpf, J.B. (1990c). The expression of shyness and embarrassment. In R. Crozier (Ed.), *Shyness and embarrassment: Perspectives from social psychology* (pp. 87-118). Cambridge: Cambridge University Press.

Bischof-Köhler, D. (1988). Über den Zusammenhang von Empathie und der Fähigkeit, sich im Spiegel zu erkennen [On the relationship between empathy and mirror self-recognition]. *Schweizerische Zeitschrift für Psychologie, 47*, 147-159.

Bischof-Köhler, D. (1989). *Spiegelbild und Empathie [Mirror image and empathy]*. Bern, Switzerland: Huber.

Bretherton, I., & Ainsworth, M.D.S. (1974). Responses of one-year-olds to a stranger in a strange situation. In M. Lewis & L.A. Rosenblum (Eds.), *The origin of fear* (pp. 131-164). New York: Wiley.

Brooks, J., & Lewis, M. (1976). Infants' responses to strangers: Midget, adult, and child. *Child Development, 47*, 323-332.

Buss, A.H. (1980). *Self-consciousness and social anxiety.* San Francisco: Freeman.

Buss, A.H. (1986). A theory of shyness. In W.H. Jones, J.M. Cheek, & S.R. Briggs (Eds.), *Shyness: Perspectives on research and treatment* (pp. 39-46). New York: Plenum Press.

Buss, A.H., Iscoe, I., & Buss, E.H. (1979). The development of embarrassment. *Journal of Psychology, 103,* 227-230.

Carver, C.S., & Scheier, M.F. (1981). *Attention and self-regulation: A control theory approach to human behavior.* New York: Springer-Verlag.

Darwin, C. (1872). *The expression of the emotions in man and animals.* London: Murray.

Doyle, A.B., Connelly, J., & Rivest, L.P. (1980). The effect of playmate familiarity on the social interactions of young children. *Child Development, 51,* 217-223.

Edelmann, R.J. (1987). *The psychology of embarrassment.* Chichester: Wiley.

Elkind, D., & Bowen, R. (1979). Imaginary audience behavior in children and adolescence. *Developmental Psychology, 15,* 38-44.

Flavell, J.H., Botkin, P.T., Fry, C.L., Jr., Wright, J.W., & Jarvis, P.E. (1968). *The development of role-taking and communication skills in children.* New York: Wiley.

Fodor, J.A. (1985). *The modularity of mind.* Cambridge, MA: MIT Press.

Fowles, D.C. (1987). Application of a behavioral theory of motivation to the concepts of anxiety and impulsivity. *Journal of Research in Personality, 21,* 417-435.

Gallup, G.G., Jr., & Suarez, S.D. (1986). Self-awareness and the emergence of mind in humans and other primates. In J. Suls & A.G. Greenwald (Eds.), *Psychological perspectives on the self* (Vol.3, pp. 3-26). Hillsdale, NJ: Erlbaum.

Gottman, J.M. (1977). Toward a definition of social isolation in children. *Child Development, 48,* 513-517.

Gray, J.A. (1982a). *The neuropsychology of anxiety: An enquiry into the functions of the septo-hippocampal system.* Oxford: Oxford University Press.

Gray, J.A. (1982b). Précis of The neuropsychology of anxiety: An enquiry into the functions of the septo-hippocampal system. *Behavioral and Brain Sciences, 5,* 469-534.

Greenberg, M.T., & Marvin, R.S. (1982). Reactions of preschool children to an adult stranger: A behavioral systems approach. *Child Development, 53,* 481-490.

Horner, I.M. (1983). On the formation of personal space and self-boundary structures in early human development: The case of infant stranger reactivity. *Developmental Review, 3,* 148-177.

Kagan, J. (1981). *The second year. The emergence of self-awareness.* Cambridge: Cambridge University Press.

Kagan, J., Kearsley, R.B., & Zelazo, P.R. (1978). *Infancy: Its place in human development.* Cambridge, MA: Harvard University Press.

Kaltenbach, K., Weinraub, M., & Fullard, W. (1980). Infant wariness toward strangers reconsidered: Infants' and mothers' reactions to unfamiliar persons. *Child Development*, *51*, 1197-1202.

Lewis, M., & Brooks-Gunn, J. (1979). *Social cognition and the acquisition of self.* New York: Plenum Press.

Lewis, M., Sullivan, M.W., Stanger, C., & Weiss, M. (1989). Self development and self-conscious emotions. *Child Development*, *60*, 146-156.

Mackintosh, N.J. (1974). *The psychology of animal learning.* New York: Academic Press.

Miller, J.G. (1978). *Living systems.* New York: McGraw-Hill.

Monson, T.C., Hesley, J.W., & Chernick, L. (1982). Specifying when personality traits can and cannot predict behavior: An alternative to abandoning the attempt to predict single-act criteria. *Journal of Personality and Social Psychology*, *43*, 385-399.

Öhman, A. (1986). Face the beast and fear the face: Animal and social fears as prototypes for evolutionary analyses of emotion. *Psychophysiology*, *23*, 123-145.

Öhman, A., & Dimberg, U. (1984). An evolutionary perspective on human social behavior. In W.M. Waid (Ed.), *Sociophysiology* (pp. 47-86). New York: Springer-Verlag.

Parten, M.B. (1932). Social participation among preschool children. *Journal of Abnormal and Social Psychology*, *27*, 243-269.

Sameroff, A.J. (1983). Developmental systems: Contexts and evolution. In P.H. Mussen (Ed.), *Handbook of child psychology: Vol.1. History, theory, and methods* (pp. 237-294). New York: Wiley.

Scherer, K.R. (1984). On the nature and function of emotion: A component process approach. In K.R. Scherer & P. Ekman (Eds.), *Approaches to emotion* (pp. 293-317). Hillsdale, NJ: Erlbaum.

Schlenker, B.R., & Leary, M.R. (1982). Social anxiety and self-presentation: A conceptualization and model. *Psychological Bulletin*, *92*, 641-669.

Schwarz, J.C. (1972). Effects of peer familiarity on the behavior of preschoolers in a novel situation. *Journal of Personality and Social Psychology*, *24*, 276-284.

Simmons, R., Rosenberg, F., & Rosenberg, M. (1973). Disturbance in the self-image at adolescence. *American Sociological Review*, *38*, 553-568.

Spitz, R. (1965). *The first year of life.* New York: International Universities Press.

Sroufe, L.A. (1977). Wariness of strangers and the study of infant development. *Child Development*, *48*, 731-746.

Sroufe, L.A. (1979). Socioemotional development. In J.D. Osofsky (Ed.), *Handbook of infant development* (pp. 462-516). New York: Wiley.

Thelen, E. (1989). Self-organization in developmental processes: Can system approaches work? In M.R. Gunnar & E. Thelen (Eds.), *Minnesota symposia on child psychology: Vol.22. Systems and development* (pp. 77-117). Hillsdale, NJ: Erlbaum.

Waters, E., Matas, L., & Sroufe, L.A. (1975). Infants' reactions to an approaching stranger: Description, validation, and functional significance of wariness. *Child Development, 46*, 348-356.

Zajonc, R.B. (1980). Feeling and thinking: Preferences need no inferences. *American Psychologist, 35*, 151-175.

Zimbardo, P.G. (1977). *Shyness.* Reading, MA: Addison-Wesley.

Zimbardo, P.G., Pilkonis, P.A., & Norwood, R.M. (1974). *The silent prison of shyness* (ONR Techn. Rep. Z-17). Stanford, CA: Stanford University.

Acknowledgements: This work was supported by NATO grant 0467/86 for international collaboration in research to the author and Kenneth H. Rubin.

Overcoming Inhibition:
Rethinking the Roles of Personality, Cognition, and Social Behavior

JAMES W. PENNEBAKER

When individuals inhibit their thoughts and feelings, they increase their chances of succumbing to physical and mental health problems. Evidence for this observation is primarily based on correlational data. Individuals low in emotional expressiveness are more likely to suffer from asthma (see the chapter by Florin, Fiegenbaum, Herrmanns, Winter, Schobinger, & Jenkins in this volume), headache (see Traue & Michael's chapter), early death due to cancer (see Temoshok's chapter), and complications related to heart disease (see Huber & Gramer's chapter). Other studies indicate that the failure to talk about psychologically threatening events is related to a broad range of health problems (e.g., Pennebaker, 1989, 1990).

Although the inhibition-health correlation has been established, very few causal mechanisms have been identified. The purpose of this chapter is twofold. First, I wish to explore the toxic as well as the benign dimensions of inhibition. In the following pages, the multiple components of inhibition are first discussed. As will be seen, inhibition can be insidious for reasons other than the overcontrol of emotion. Rather, inhibition can reflect – rather than cause – genetic proclivities to be hypersensitive to novel stimuli. On a situational level, processes of inhibition can impede the normal cognitive changes that help individuals naturally cope with upsetting experiences. In addition, inhibition processes can completely disrupt normal social interaction resulting in further isolation by the traumatized individual. The second purpose of this chapter is to discuss approaches that have been adopted that can aid individuals in overcoming inhibition and its components.

The Good, Bad, and Ugly Dimensions of Inhibition

In reviewing the psychosomatic literature, one comes to the inescapable conclusion that the inhibition of thoughts and feelings is potentially toxic. Closer inspection, however, reveals that this is a gross oversimplification. In many, if not most cases, the processes of inhibition are beneficial for the individual and adaptive for society.

Consider the forms of inhibition in the natural world. Beginning around age 2, we learn to inhibit and control our bowels and bladder. Soon, most of us have acquired the ability to restrain our impulses to harm others. Throughout our lives, our self-restraint promotes our health by checking our drinking and drug-taking, channeling our urges for participating in dangerous sporting activities, and controlling our desires for wanton sex and violence.

Inhibition, then, is not inherently unhealthy. Indeed, in the grand scheme of things, it actually may contribute to a nation's health rather than diminish it. Despite its positive attributes, however, some rather insidious dimensions to inhibition exist. In the remainder of this section, I explore some facets of inhibition that are most likely to undermine physical health.

Biological Correlates of Childhood Inhibition

Other chapters in this book persuasively argue that people who fail to express their emotions and thoughts suffer from a variety of health risks. Those who chronically inhibit emotional expression have variously been categorized as repressive copers, alexithymics, Type-C personalities, or individuals high in the traits of constraint, socialization, self-control, or inhibition. Why are these chronic inhibitors at risk? In order to begin to answer this question, it is imperative to explore the possible genetic/biological bases of inhibition that manifest themselves, in part, by early childhood.

The tendency to inhibit one's thoughts and feelings undoubtedly has a genetic basis. Recent studies by researchers at the University of Minnesota on identical and fraternal twins separated, on average, 3 months after birth indicate that personality markers of contraint have remarkably high heritability coefficients (Bouchard, Lykken, McGue, Segal, & Tellegen, 1990; Tellegen, Lykken, Bouchard, Wilcox, Segal, & Rich, 1988). Using the constraint dimension of the *Multiple Personality Questionnaire*, Tellegen and his colleagues (1988) reported that the intraclass correlations among identical twins reared apart ($r = .57$) were no different from those of identical twins reared together ($r = .58$). Fraternal twins, who share only half of their genes, exhibited far lower relationships ($r = .25$ for twins reared together versus $r = .04$ for twins reared apart). The Minnesota project is impressive in that the 44 identical and 27 fraternal twin pairs had been separated, on average, 33.8 years prior to the study.

Although traits associated with the expression and inhibition of emotion apparently exist, adult twin studies have not identified *how* self-report markers of constraint can be tied to health or physiology. That is, in what manner can inhibitory processes result in illness? Recent developmental work by Jerome Kagan and his colleagues (e.g., Kagan, Reznick, & Snidman, 1988) offers some important insights into the biological mediators of inhibition.

Drawing from an original population of 400 children, Kagan selected 54 inhibited and 53 uninhibited 2- and 5-year olds. Inhibition was defined by observing children in social situations with adults and other children. Those classified as inhibited were least likely to initiate an interaction, were consistently shy, quiet, and timid. The uninhibited children were generally sociable, talkative, and spontaneous when they met unfamiliar people. Across the 5-year longitudinal study, those classified as inhibited exhibited significantly higher heart rates in the laboratory and when asleep. More striking was that the inhibited children had markedly higher levels of urinary norepinephrine and salivary cortisol in comparison to the more outgoing uninhibited participants. Indeed, stress markers such as these have long been known to be predictors of illness episodes. In fact, we have found that 3-year old children enrolled in nursery schools who were rated as shy by parents and/or teachers were absent from school for illness more than other children (Pennebaker, Hendler, Durrett, & Richards, 1981).

The work by the University of Minnesota researchers together with Kagan's indicates that health-relevant correlates of inhibition begin to surface at birth (or, more accurately, at conception). Of particular significance are the findings that young children who exhibit signs of behavioral inhibition also demonstrate generalized higher sympathetic nervous system activation. In many ways, the early childhood findings suggest an even more complicated link between inhibition and illness: Specifically, do children who are naturally inhibited and who work to hold back their emotions become stressed in the process? Conversely, do the biological indicators of stress cause the child to become more inhibited?

A particularly likely scenario is that children predisposed towards inhibition may have lower pain thresholds and may be hypersensitive to novel stimuli. Indeed, research with inhibited versus disinhibited adults supports these observations both in terms of differential pain threshold and central nervous system responsivity (e.g., Zuckerman, 1990). This hypersensitivity channels the child's behavior into an inhibitory, overcontrolled style. The potentially sickly, hypersensitive infant, then, becomes an inhibited, emotionally expressionless youngster. Rather than claiming that the inhibition of emotional expression causes illness, we could just as well argue that illness-proclivity causes inhibition (see also the chapter by Asendorpf).

At this point, we are only able to conclude that the correlation between potential health problems and the inhibition of behavior and emotional expression is seen by the time that the individual is 2 years old. It is reasonable to assume that inhibition as a personality trait predicts illness episodes with some regularity. But this is only part of the picture. A large number of individuals who are not innately inhibited are sometimes thrust into situations where they must restrain their thoughts, emotions, or behaviors. In situations such as these, do most individuals exhibit adverse health problems?

Beyond Personality: The Cognitive Correlates of Inhibition

Consider what happens when we are forced to suppress a powerful emotion, thought, or behavior. Think back in your own life, for example, to the death of a loved one, the breakup of a relationship, or an unexpected trauma. In the hours, days, or weeks after the event, images or thoughts of the event probably ran through your mind with some frequency. Most individuals report that these thought intrusions are painful and disjointed (e.g., Horowitz, 1976). Further, most people occasionally attempt to suppress these thoughts and associated feelings.

When people attempt to suppress or inhibit their thoughts and feelings surrounding a significant personal event, a number of problems soon emerge. Dan Wegner (1989), for example, has demonstrated that individuals are quite poor at suppressing even the most common thoughts. When students are asked to not think of a white bear for 5 minutes, they tend to think of it almost as frequently as control subjects who are asked to actively think of the bear. In his work, Wegner found that attempts to suppress thoughts – especially emotion-laden thoughts – are doomed to failure. One reason is that each time we try to distract ourselves away from the forbidden thought, the distraction stimulus itself becomes linked with the unwanted thought. Over time, repeated attempts at distraction merely increase the number of stimuli that remind us of the forbidden thought. In short, when individuals face a trauma and subsequently try to put the trauma out of their minds, trauma-relevant thoughts can increase in frequency rather than decrease.

Another problem associated with the inhibition of thoughts and emotions is that suppression attempts require physiological work. Some of the early work for this idea evolved from the theorizing of Jeffrey Gray (1975) who posited the existence of two independent behavior control systems: the behavioral activation system (BAS) and the behavioral inhibition system (BIS). The BAS and BIS were assumed to be represented independently in the brain. Initial research on the BIS, for example, indicated that major inhibitory centers exist in the hippocampus/septum area and in the frontal cortex (Gray, 1975; Luria, 1980).

In extending Gray's work, Don Fowles (1980) suggested that the action of the BAS and BIS were separately represented in the autonomic nervous system. In summarizing dozens of studies, Fowles demonstrated that most standard cardiovascular measures (e.g., heart rate, blood pressure, finger temperature) reliably tapped the action of the BAS. Inhibition, however, was most closely linked to measures of electrodermal activity (e.g., skin conductance level, GSR). Fowles's review has served as an important building block in allowing inhibition researchers to better know when the short-term "work" of inhibition was in progress.

Measures of electrodermal activity now point to additional problems of attempts at thought and emotion suppression. Wegner and his colleagues (e.g.,

Wegner, Shortt, Blake, & Page, 1990; Wenzlaff, Wegner, & Klein, 1991) found, for example, that subjects who attempt to suppress embarrassing or threatening thoughts exhibit as great or greater autonomic activity as when they are required to talk about them. Similarly, in our own research, we find that high disclosive subjects who are told to avoid talking about traumatic experiences exhibit higher skin conductance levels than when they are asked to actively talk about the experiences (Pennebaker, Hughes, & O'Heeron, 1987). These and related studies (see the chapter by Buck) suggest that short term attempts at thought or emotion suppression are doomed to failure and, at the same time, are causally linked to heightened physiological activity.

Perhaps the most insidious cognitive problem associated with inhibition is that it interferes with the natural ways that we process information. Typically, when individuals face an upheaval, they think and talk about it many times each day. For example, random telephone surveys on San Francisco resident's reactions to the 1989 Loma Prieta Earthquake indicated that people were still discussing the quake over eight times per day one week after its occurrence (Pennebaker & Harber, 1990). Recent analyses of Dallas, Texas, residents' reactions to the 1991 Persian Gulf War were similar. On the day following the beginning of the war, the average Dallas adult reported talking about the war 14 times. After 5 weeks of the 6-week war, residents continued to talk about it over seven times per day.

Talking with others is a normal and healthy way to cope with an upheaval. By talking about an event, people learn more about the event as well as their own personal reactions to it. Further, talking allows people to express their deepest thoughts and feelings about the experience. Finally, putting the upheaval into words undoubtedly changes the way that it is represented in memory (Harber & Pennebaker, in press). That is, once an experience is talked or written about, it goes from being represented only in image format to becoming linguistically coded. Once a massive emotional experience is put into words, then, it should be easier to organize and assimilate.

Almost by definition, inhibiting the expression of a personal experience will limit the degree to which the experience is put into words and, ultimately, assimilated. Inhibition, then, is potentially dangerous in blocking the cognitive processes that normally occur during and following traumas. In short, when people try not to talk about the event or express their feelings about it, they inadvertently cause the trauma to live on in their minds longer than it would have otherwise.

The Social Causes and Consequences of Inhibition

What is so toxic about inhibition? So far, two components of inhibition have been identified that clearly contribute to health problems associated with the psychological state of holding back: longstanding personality processes and, when inhibition results from situational pressures, the cognitive prolonging of a trauma. A third noxious correlate of inhibition occurs within the social realm. Specifically, individuals who face traumas often promote undesirable changes in their social worlds which, in turn, bring about increased inhibition and further deleterious social changes.

The social dilemma of trauma is best seen with an example. In 1990, my mother died following a long illness. Although her death was not unexpected, it was quite painful for me. Most people in my department – who were between the ages of 30 and 45 – had not yet faced a parental death. Whereas virtually everyone was extremely nice and supportive immediately after hearing about the death, it was evident that many did not know what to say or how to respond. Indeed, some good friends began to actively avoid me or, if that was impossible, they would nervously initiate a discussion about the weather or other superficial topics in order to avoid the topic of death. I also noticed in myself a gradual disengagement from several of my awkward friends. It was simply too unpleasant to interact with them.

Compared to most of the traumas that I have studied, my experience was almost trivial. Imagine how my social world would have been affected if I had unexpectedly faced the death of a child, wrongly (or rightly for that matter) been arrested for prostitution, or had been raped. In the case of a truly massive trauma, I would have needed to talk about the experience to a far greater degree. Further, the social effects of talking about these traumas would have been much greater than I experienced with the death of my mother. Indeed, several recent studies support these predictions.

Recently, we asked 66 college students to observe one of 33 videotapes of Holocaust survivors recounting their experiences in Germany and Poland during World War II. The original Holocaust interviews had been made in our laboratory 1-4 years earlier (from Pennebaker, Barger, & Tiebout, 1989). Each interview lasted 1-2 hours and the survivor's autonomic nervous system levels (skin conductance and heart rate) were continuously measured. In the follow-up study, we were able to monitor the same autonomic channels on the students who viewed the videotapes. We were then able to correlate the survivors' and listeners' skin conductance levels for each person on a minute-by-minute basis (see Shortt & Pennebaker, in press, for details of the methods and results).

The most interesting effect of the study was the emergence of a weak but significant negative correlation between the Holocaust survivors' and the listeners' skin conductance levels. That is, when the survivors were disclosing deeply personal and traumatic experiences, their skin conductance levels were dropping. At the same point, the listeners' levels were increasing. In other words, hearing another's trauma can be stressful for the listener.

If listening to another's problems is potentially stressful, it is clear why people often avoid others who are in distress. It may be good for you to talk about your problems but, at the same time, it may be bad for my health to listen to you. In fact, there is some fascinating corroborating evidence for this idea from the social support literature. It is well-known, for example, that having a social support network during stressful times can help buffer the physical and psychological effects of the stressors (Cohen & McKay, 1984; House, Landis, & Umberson, 1988). Less publicized, however, is the observation that those who provide social support to another person in distress suffer significantly higher physical and mental illness rates than they would have otherwise (Belle, 1982; Coyne, Kessler, Tal, Turnbull, Wortman, & Greden, 1987; Kessler, McLeod, & Wethington, 1985).

One can begin to appreciate the social dilemma that can evolve when individuals face a trauma. If Person A experiences an overwhelming trauma, Person A's friends may soon begin to avoid Person A in order to protect their own health. The more massive and psychologically threatening Person A's trauma, the more Person A will want and need to talk about it and, at the same time, the more that Person A's friends will be motivated not to talk about it. This painful social dance will ultimately force Person A to inhibit his or her urges to discuss the event. Through subtle social forces, then, Person A must actively inhibit his/her emotions and behaviors in order to maintain any semblance of a friendship network (see Pennebaker, in press, for discussion).

We are currently gathering evidence for this social constraint process from a variety of sources. In studying the social psychological responses to the Loma Prieta Earthquake, we have found that approximately 3 weeks after the quake people stopped talking about the earthquake abruptly even though most continued thinking about it at a high rate. Closer examination of the data reveals that at the 3 week point, people reported that they would still like to tell others about their earthquake experiences but didn't want to hear other people tell theirs. Ironically, about a month after the earthquake, T-shirts began appearing in the earthquake-damaged area that announced, "Thank you for not sharing your earthquake experience" (Pennebaker & Harber, 1990).

Summary

In order to understand the many facets of inhibition, it is important to realize that the constraint of many behaviors, thoughts, and feelings is both healthy and adaptive for the individual as well as society. There are times, however, when inhibition can result in physical illness. One difficulty in understanding the potential risk of inhibition is that there are several independent dimensions to inhibition. Whereas inhibition *per se* may be stressful, the self-restraint of thoughts, emotions, and behaviors can trigger ancillary problems which themselves can exacerbate stress.

In this section, three major stress-relevant correlates of inhibition have been identified. Inhibition can be viewed as a personality trait that predisposes the child to illness. One explanation for this early inhibition-illness pattern may be that inhibition-prone infants are hypersensitive to novel stimuli and/or exhibit lower pain thresholds. Beginning at a very early age, these hypersensitive children learn that they must be cautious and generally inhibited to survive in novel situations. This hypersensitivity, in turn, results in overall higher autonomic and central nervous system arousal, thus placing the child at greater risk for stress-related disease. One dimension of inhibition, then, may reflect hypersensitivity and, by extension, illness-proneness rather than vice versa.

Two other correlates of inhibition go beyond personality and focus on problems surrounding the situational responses to traumatic experience. The inhibition of emotions, thoughts, and behaviors often occurs during times of severe stress. A natural outgrowth of trauma is the occurrence of repeated unwanted thoughts and the urge to talk about them. Talking or putting the traumas into words helps to organize complex and painful experiences. When people try to suppress thoughts of a trauma, they are usually unsuccessful and, at the same time, fail to resolve the trauma. Cognitively, then, the inhibition of thoughts can inadvertently block the natural coping process.

Finally, traumatic experiences can often set up an inhibition-relevant social trap. Whereas talking about a trauma may be healthy, listening to others' traumas can be stressful. Consequently, a personally traumatic experience may inadvertently drive away one's friends – thus resulting in social isolation.

Overcoming Inhibition and Its Correlates

From a prevention or treatment perspective, changing the degree to which individuals inhibit their behaviors can pose a number of problems. In this section, three general strategies are suggested for altering the potentially deleterious dimensions of inhibition. After briefly discussing possible biochemical interventions, a more detailed analysis of cognitive methods that have been successfully used in our laboratory to overcome problems of inhibition will be introduced. Finally, possible methods to deal with the social causes and effects of trauma will be discussed.

Biochemical Treatments Related to Chronic Inhibition

As noted in the first part of this paper, the proclivity to inhibit behaviors has a genetic component with manifestations apparent by early childhood. Biological markers of hypersensitivity and low pain thresholds hint that inhibition may be in part a reflection of brain neurochemistry. Assuming that an individual is constitutionally inhibited (i.e., the inhibition does not stem from a depressive episode), what biochemical treatments could modulate inhibition? This turns out to be a difficult question to ask since someone who exhibits signs of chronic inhibition would normally be diagnosed with a personality disorder – an Axis-II diagnosis according to *DSM-III-R*. By definition, the American psychiatric community does not typically treat personality disorders. Despite this general rule, occasional studies have examined the efficacy of specific drugs on behavior patterns that are closely related to inhibition-related personality dimensions.

In considering young children, heightened states of inhibition are most often manifested by extreme shyness, also referred to as avoidant disorder (Wanlass & Prinz, 1982). Children as young as 2.5 years old who are diagnosed with avoidant disorder are hypersensitive to rejection or criticism and typically avoid social interaction and novel settings. Although various social skills training techniques are occasionally effective (Conger & Keane, 1981), there is some evidence that certain central nervous system agents may reduce the avoidant child's maladaptive fears and behaviors. Studies with young monkeys as well as children who suffer from severe separation anxiety have found that imiprimine – which increases the levels of the neurotransmitters serotonin and norepinephrine – reduces many of the behavioral manifestations of anxiety (Fyer, 1987). Interestingly, childhood separation anxiety is a predictor of school phobias and, in adults, panic attacks and agoraphobia.

In adults, biochemical studies have been conducted that relate to two classes of inhibition-relevant personality disorders: anxious-fearful traits and obsessive compulsive disorders. Among individuals who are classified as avoidant and socially anxious/phobic, several pharmacologic treatments have been attempted. Standard antidepressants such as imiprimine appear to reduce avoidant behaviors to some degree (Fyer, 1987). Similarly, drugs that block sympathetic nervous system activation (e.g., beta-blockers) appear to reduce many of the manifestations of anxiety as well (Soloff, 1990). Alcohol, too, has been demonstrated to be a powerful disinhibitor – both in humans and animals. Indeed, some of the earliest work on the neurochemistry of inhibition demonstrated that rats treated with alcohol or sodium amytal exhibited significantly less frustration, fear, anxiety, and persistence than controls (Gray, 1971).

Obsessive-compulsive disorder (OCD) is a fascinating example of an extreme case of inhibition. As a group, OCD patients actively attempt to suppress unwanted thoughts and to control their behaviors according to rigid self-imposed rules. Although anxiety has been hypothesized as the underlying cause of the disorder, numerous studies have found that standard antianxiety agents such as beta-blockers do not reliably reduce OCD symptoms (e.g., Rabavilas, Boulougouris, Perissaki, & Stefanis, 1979). More intriguing are studies suggesting that serotonin levels are related to OCD. This hypothesis is based on the findings that clomipramine (an antidepressant that affects both brain norepinephrine and serotonin levels) and other serotonergic antidepressants reduce reports of obsessional thoughts (Marks, 1982).

Interestingly, psychosurgery has also been used successfully in the treatment of OCD. Of the various methods, the most promising appears to be leucotomies – a relatively simple technique of severing the fibers that connect the frontal cortex with the limbic system. Across several studies with relatively small sample sizes, between 50% and 75% of OCD patients are significantly improved following surgery compared with controls (see Turner, Beidel, & Nathan, 1985, for review). Although leucotomies are controversial and not standard treatment methods for OCD, they further point to the role of brain mechanisms in our understanding of the causes and treatments of chronic inhibition.

Treating the Cognitive Effects of Inhibition

As discussed in the first half of the paper, one of the most serious problems associated with traumatic experiences is that individuals often avoid talking about the trauma. The failure to put a personal upheaval into words greatly impedes the entire healing process. Over the last decade, we have conducted several studies that focus on the cognitive and health changes that result when we require people to talk or write about personal traumas. In this section, a brief review of the general disclosure paradigm and its basic health and psychological effects are introduced. The probable cognitive mechanisms underlying inhibition and disinhibition that help explain the healing power of confiding are then explored.

Over the years, my students, colleagues, and I have adopted two disclosure paradigms. The first, which requires individuals to talk briefly into a microphone about each of two topics, taps the immediate psychophysiological effects of confiding. The second technique encourages participants to write about either the most traumatic experiences of their lives or about superficial topics for 15-20 minutes per day for 3-4 consecutive days. The writing studies differ from the talking studies in that the primary measures are changes in longterm health and immune function.

Studies in our lab and elsewhere (e.g., Murray, Lamnin, & Carver, 1989) find that participants readily open up and disclose deeply personal experiences – many of which they have never divulged before. Typically, students feel somewhat anxious or depressed immediately after initially disclosing their traumas. These negative feelings, however, quickly dissipate by the end of the experiment and follow-up surveys completed several days and/or weeks later (see Pennebaker, 1989, 1990, for details). Psychophysiologically, subjects who are judged to be especially high disclosers evidence significant drops in skin conductance levels while talking about traumas compared to superficial topics. Immediately following their traumatic disclosures, highly disclosive subjects also demonstrate drops in blood pressure (Pennebaker, Hughes, & O'Heeron, 1987).

Particularly striking are the results from our longterm writing studies. Overall, students who have been randomly assigned to write about the most traumatic experiences of their lives have consistently evidenced significant drops in physician visits for illness in the 2-6 months after the study in comparison with control subjects (Pennebaker & Beall, 1986; Pennebaker, Colder, & Sharp, 1990; Pennebaker, Kiecolt-Glaser & Glaser, 1988). In an experiment wherein serum immune markers were assayed before the study, after the fourth day of writing, and again 6 weeks after the study, Pennebaker, Kiecolt-Glaser, and Glaser (1988) found an enhancement in T-lymphocyte function for the experimental subjects compared to the controls from before to after the writing period (using a blastogenesis method using PHA as the mitogen).

Why does writing about a traumatic experience for 15 minutes a day for 4 days affect objective indicators of health as well as self-reports of well-being? The answer goes far beyond the release of inhibitions. True, not talking about their traumas probably set many of our participants up for illness. However, the health of the trauma writers was improved simply by writing without any feedback on the part of the experimenters.

In analyzing the essays that our participants have written, it is apparent that writing forces people to stand back and reorganize their thoughts and feelings about significant experiences. For example, independent judges evaluated each essay on the degree to which it was well-organized with a clear beginning, middle, and end. Overall, the more organized subjects' essays <u>and</u> the more that subjects' essays became organized over the 4 days of writing, the more their immune function improved (Harber & Pennebaker, in press). Note that conceptually similar findings have been reported by Esterling, Antoni, Kumar, and Schneiderman (1990).

Interestingly, subjects seem to be aware of the importance of standing back and evaluating their thoughts and feelings themselves. In each of our studies, we ask participants to evaluate the experiment several months after its completion. Virtually all of the participants in our trauma conditions report that the studies have been worthwhile and meaningful. More important is that over 75% describe the long-term benefits in insight terms such as: "... it made me think things out ...", "... it helped me look at myself from the outside," "... it was a chance to sort out my thoughts." Only about 10% used venting or abreaction/catharsis terms to describe the value of writing about traumas such as: "I purged some of my feelings." Indeed, those who have used venting terms have rarely evidenced improvements in their health as a function of the study.

Although the specific cognitive changes that result from writing about traumas have not yet been pinpointed, it is becoming increasingly clear that putting upsetting experiences into words changes the nature of the trauma itself. Whereas situational processes of inhibition may cause people to suppress their thoughts and emotions about an upsetting event, much of the healing can be accomplished by disclosing the event on paper.

Altering the Social Dynamics that Exacerbate Inhibition

Personal traumas have the potential to completely disrupt one's social world. As noted earlier, if I have a major upheaval in my life, it will affect how I interact with my friends and how they deal with me. A trauma, then, can be devastating on multiple levels. The trauma itself may bring about intense feelings of loss, anger, and depression. At the same time, however, it may result in the victim's becoming more socially isolated. Through subtle social processes, the victim may be forced to inhibit his or her thoughts and feelings so as not to adversely affect future interactions with friends.

What can be done to maximize the benefits of social support without undermining friendships? Based on our research with the Mt. St. Helens volcanic eruption in 1980 (Pennebaker & Newtson, 1983), the Loma Prieta Earthquake (Pennebaker & Harber, 1990), and the Persian Gulf War, any understanding or intervention concerning social dynamics must take into account the natural social changes that occur over time. In our research, we are finding three social stages that occur during the first year of the trauma (e.g., Pennebaker, 1992; Pennebaker & Harber, 1990).

During the first 2-3 weeks after a major emotional event, people feel free to actively talk and think about the event. During this emergency phase, individuals are drawn together by the common bond of the trauma. Beginning about 3 weeks after the event, the social dynamics shift. At this point, people enter the inhibition phase of the trauma. It is during this period that individuals continue to think about the trauma a great deal but greatly curtail their talking about it. The inhibition phase lasts about 4-8 weeks. It is during this period that individuals report dreaming about the trauma, getting into fights (e.g., assault rates increase), and reporting an increased number of health problems. Indeed, in the 3 to 8 weeks following the Loma Prieta quake, San Francisco residents evidenced a 10% increase in aggravated assaults from the previous year. During the first 2 weeks after the quake and after 9 weeks following the quake, assault rates returned to their normal rates (see Pennebaker, 1992, for discussion). Finally, about 8 weeks after the trauma, people move into the adaptation phase wherein they greatly reduce their thinking about the trauma as well as their talking. At this point, people's lives begin to return to normal.

The three social phases of a disaster are important in pointing to the problem period of 3-8 weeks after the trauma's occurrence. As humans, we tend to look for simple cause-effect relationships that span seconds, minutes, or, at most, days. If an earthquake occurs or our best friend dies, we tend to look for social or psychological indicators of problems immediately afterwards. It is also at this time that we provide and receive the bulk of social support. All of our evidence suggests that the real problems do not surface until the emergency phase passes. It is during the inhibition phase in which groups that may provide social services should actively intervene.

Finally, in interviews with a variety of individuals and groups who have faced overwhelming traumas, I have been struck with the difficult day-to-day social problems that they face. One difficulty in our traditionless society is that there are no explicit social rules to define how we should interact with someone in grief or pain. Over the years, I have found it helpful to provide brief social skills training for traumatized individuals. In this informal training, people are taught how to introduce the topic of the trauma in conversation and to make others at ease. By the same token, those who are in pain must also learn how to read and interpret others' awkward behaviors around them (see also the chapter by Hufnagel, Steimer-Krause, Wagner, & Krause in this volume).

Summary and Conclusions

Actively inhibiting our emotions and behaviors is associated with a variety of health problems. We must be cautious, however, in our criticisms of inhibition in the real world. It is a mistake to assume that inhibition is inherently unhealthy. Indeed, there is good reason to believe that, on balance, inhibitory processes are highly adaptive for both the individual and society.

By the same token, we must be precise in defining what aspects or correlates of inhibition may serve as health risks. In this chapter, three significant correlates of inhibition have been discussed. Each correlate can be viewed as a separate stressor that may occasionally result from or be independent of inhibition. Genetic and early childhood research, for example, indicates that inhibition is partially heritable. Several lines of work suggest that hypersensitivity to novel stimulation and/or low pain thresholds evident in early childhood may ultimately cause both inhibited personality styles and illness proclivity. From a strict personality perspective, then, inhibition may be a byproduct of emotional expressivity and illness rather than a cause.

Particular emphasis has been placed on situational instances of inhibition. Most toxic instances have been associated with traumatic experiences wherein individuals have not freely talked about their thoughts and feelings surrounding the upheaval. Two significant outgrowths of this form of inhibition include cognitive and social dilemmas. Specifically, not putting an upsetting event into words can impede the natural coping process and prolong both mental and physical suffering brought on by the trauma. By the same token, a major personal or shared upheaval can profoundly affect one's social relationships. Whereas talking about a trauma may be beneficial for the victim, hearing about it may be unhealthy.

Whereas the inhibition of emotions, thoughts, and behaviors may cause health problems, intervention strategies should go beyond techniques that encourage the open expression of thoughts and feelings. Rather, we should focus on prevention or intervention methods that also affect the deleterious correlates of inhibition. Some evidence supports the use of central nervous system medication and psychosurgery in altering extreme cases of inhibited personalities. Writing or talking about traumatic experiences has been shown to improve physical health and affect the cognitive processes that may result from inhibition. Finally, preliminary work pointing to possible social interventions has been discussed.

References

Belle, D. (1982). The stress of caring: Women as providers of social support. In L. Goldberger & S. Breznitx (Eds.), *Handbook of stress: Theoretical and clinical aspects* (pp. 497-505). New York: Free Press.

Bouchard, T.J., Lykken, D.T., McGue, M., Segal, N.L., & Tellegen, A. (1990). Sources of human psychological differences: The Minnesota study of twins reared apart. *Science, 250*, 223-228.

Cohen, S. & McKay, G. (1984). Social support, stress, and the buffering hypothesis. A theoretical analysis. In A. Baum, S. E. Taylor, & J.E. Singer (Eds.), *Handbook of psychology and health: Vol.4. Social psychological aspects of health* (pp. 253-268). New Jersey: Erlbaum.

Conger, J.C. & Keane, S.P. (1981). Social skills intervention in the treatment of isolated or withdrawn children. *Psychological Bulletin, 90*, 478-495.

Coyne, J.C., Kessler, R.C., Tal, M., Turnbull, J., Wortman, C.B., & Greden, J.F. (1987). Living with a depressed person. *Journal of Consulting and Clinical Psychology, 55*, 347-352.

Esterling, B.A., Antoni, M.H., Kumar, M., & Schneiderman, N. (1990). Emotional repression, stress disclosure responses, and Epstein-Barr viral capsid antigen titers. *Psychosomatic Medicine, 52*, 397-410.

Fowles, D. C. (1980). The three arousal model: Implications of Gray's two-factor learning theory for heart rate, electrodermal activity, and psychopathy. *Psychophysiology, 17*, 87-104.

Fyer, A.J. (1987). Agoraphobia. *Modern problems in pharmacopsychiatry, 22*, 91-126.

Gray, J. (1971). *The psychology of fear and stress.* New York: McGraw- Hill.

Gray, J. (1975). *Elements of a two-factor theory of learning.* New York: Academic.

Harber, K.D. & Pennebaker, J.W. (in press). Overcoming traumatic memories. In S.A. Christianson (Ed.), *The handbook of emotion and memory.* New York: Guilford.

Horowitz, M.J. (1976). *Stress responses syndromes.* New York: Jacob Aronson.

House, J.S., Landis, K.R., & Umberson, D. (1988). Social relationships and health. *Science, 241*, 540-545.

Kagan, J., Reznick, J.S., & Snidman, N. (1988). Biological bases of childhood shyness. *Science, 240*, 167-171.

Kessler, R. C., McLeod, J. D., & Wethington, E. (1985). The costs of caring: A perspective on the relationship between sex and psychological distress. In I.G. Sarason & B.R. Sarason (Eds), *Social support: Theory, research, and applications* (pp. 491-506). Dordrecht: Martinus Nyhoff Publishers.

Luria, A.R. (1980). *Higher cortical functions in man* (2nd edition). New York: Basic Books.

Marks, I. (1982). Are there anticompulsive or antiphobic drugs?: Review of the evidence. *Psychopharmacology Bulletin, 18,* 78-84.

Murray, E.J., Lamnin, A.D., & Carver, C.S. (1989). Emotional expression in written essays and psychotherapy. *Journal of Social and Clinical Psychology, 8,* 414-429.

Pennebaker, J.W. (1989). Confession, inhibition, and disease. In L. Berkowitz (Ed.), *Advances in Experimental Social Psychology, vol 22* (pages 211-244). New York: Academic.

Pennebaker, J.W. (1990). *Opening up: The healing power of confiding in others.* New York: Morrow.

Pennebaker, J.W. (1992). Inhibition as the linchpin of health. In H. Friedman (Ed.), *Hostility, health, and coping.* Washington: American Psychological Association.

Pennebaker, J.W. (in press). Mechanisms of social constraint. In D. Wegner and J.W. Pennebaker (Eds.), *Handbook of mental control.* New York: Plenum.

Pennebaker, J. W., Barger, S. D., & Tiebout, J. (1989). Disclosure of traumas and health among Holocaust survivors. *Psychosomatic Medicine, 51,* 577-589.

Pennebaker, J.W. & Beall, S.K. (1986). Confronting a traumatic event: Toward an understanding of inhibition and disease. *Journal of Abnormal Psychology, 95,* 274-281.

Pennebaker, J.W., Colder, M., & Sharp, L.K. (1990). Accelerating the coping process. *Journal of Personality and Social Psychology, 58,* 528-537.

Pennebaker, J.W. & Harber, K.D. (1990). The psychological effects of the Loma Prieta Earthquake: A preliminary report. Unpublished manuscript. Dallas: Southern Methodist University.

Pennebaker, J.W., Hendler, C.S., Durrett, M.E., & Richards, P. (1981). Social factors influencing absenteeism due to illness. *Child Development, 52,* 692-700.

Pennebaker, J.W., Hughes, C.F., & O'Heeron, R.C. (1987). The psychophysiology of confession: Linking inhibitory and psychosomatic processes. *Journal of Personality and Social Psychology, 52,* 781-793.

Pennebaker, J.W., Kiecolt-Glaser, J.K., & Glaser, R. (1988). Disclosure of traumas and immune function: Health implications for psychotherapy. *Journal of Consulting and Clinical Psychology, 56,* 239-245.

Pennebaker, J.W., & Newtson, D. (1983). Observation of a unique event: The psychological impact of Mt. St. Helens volcano. In H. Reis (Ed.), *Naturalistic approaches to studying social interaction* (pp. 93-109). San Francisco: Josey-Bass.

Rabavilas, A.D., Boulougouris, J.C., Perissaki, C., & Stefanis, C. (1979). The effect of peripheral beta-blockade on psychophysiologic responses in obsessional neurotics. *Comprehensive Psychiatry, 20*, 378-383.

Selye, H. (1976). *The stress of life*. New York: McGraw-Hill.

Shortt, J.W., & Pennebaker, J.W. (in press). Talking versus hearing about Holocaust experiences. *Basic and Applied Social Psychology*.

Soloff, P.H. (1990). What's new in personality disorders?: An update on pharmacological treatment. *Journal of Personality Disorders, 4*, 233- 243.

Tellegen, A., Lykken, D.T., Bouchard, T.J., Wilcox, K.J., Segal, N.L., & Rich, S. (1988). Personality similarities of identical twins reared apart and together. *Journal of Personality and Social Psychology, 54*, 1031-1039.

Turner, S.M., Beidel, D.C., & Nathan, R.S. (1985). Biological factors in obsessive-compulsive disorders. *Psychological Bulletin, 97*, 430-450.

Wanlass, R.L. & Prinz, R.J. (1981). Methodological issues in conceptualizing and treating childhood social isolation. *Psychological Bulletin, 92*, 39-55.

Wegner, D.M. (1989). *White bears and other unwanted thoughts*. New York: Viking.

Wegner, D.M., Shortt, J.W., Blake, A.W., & Page, M.S. (1990). The suppression of exciting thoughts. *Journal of Personality and Social Psychology, 58*, 409-418.

Wenzlaff, R.M., Wegner, D.M., & Klein, S.B. (1991). The role of thought suppression in the bonding of thought and moods. *Journal of Personality and Social Psychology, 60*, 500-508.

Zuckerman, M. (1990). The psychophysiology of sensation seeking. *Journal of Personality, 58*, 313-345.

Acknowledgements: This paper was written with the help of grants from the National Science Foundation, BNS 9021518 and BNS 9001615

Gendered Health:
Differences Between Men and Women in the Relation Between Physical Symptoms and Emotion Expression Behaviors

CAROL Z. MALATESTA AND CLAYTON CULVER

Health is not gender-neutral although in many ways it tends to be treated as such. Obviously, certain medical conditions are considered specific to men and women as a function of their reproductive differences – cystytis, breast cancer, and endometriosis are conditions that only affect women, whereas prostate cancer, low sperm count, and male pattern baldness are conditions that are specific to men. However, beyond the obligatory recognition that health varies as a function of reproductive status, there has been little consideration of the broader way in which health is affected by gender. This gender astigmatism skews our vision with respect to health issues, with multiple consequences for research and health care in this country.

Let us consider a somewhat prototypical example. One of the most intensively researched health problems in modern times is cardiovascular disease, a condition that has been, and continues to be, the leading cause of death in the United States (Houston, 1988). Although cardiovascular disease incapacitates and/or kills more men than women (Eaker & Castelli, 1988) and begins afflicting men at an earlier age than it does women, it is also the chief cause of death in women. Despite this, almost all of the major longitudinal studies tracing the origins and course of the disease over time have relied exclusively on male·subjects (the Framingham heart study is a notable exception); then, quite often, and without justification, results are interpreted as applicable to all adults. For example, in 1978 a panel of leading scientists, called together by the National Heart, Lung, and Blood Institute to evaluate the contribution of Type A Behavior Pattern (TABP) to heart disease, concluded that,

> "Type A behavior … is associated with an increased risk of clinically apparent coronary heart disease in employed, *middle-aged U.S. citizens.* This risk is greater than that imposed by age, elevated values of systolic blood pressure and serum cholesterol, or smoking, and appears to be of the same order of magnitude as the relative risk associated with the latter three of these factors" (Cooper, Detre, & Weiss, 1981, p. 1200).

The above implies that the risk applies equally to men and women; however, in the two decades of Type A investigations before 1978, the bulk of research linking coronary heart disease (CHD) with TABP was with men; in fact, there have been no prospective studies employing the Structured Interview (SI) as the typing device (the best predictor of heart disease) with women. Thoresen and Low's (1990) most recent review of the literature indicates that our understanding of the Type A construct remains primarily limited to male, middle-class men.

Another example of the aversion of researchers to the use of women as subjects in medical research is found in a study of the relation between obesity and the development of cancer in breasts or uterine lining, conducted at Rockefeller University. Pilot subjects for the study were all men; while explanations for resorting to men in this study have been given, they are not completely convincing (Jaschik, 1990). More recently, the lack of attention to gender in medical research has become an issue of some concern; indeed, in July of 1989 the National Institutes of Health issued a set of guidelines for authors of grant application aimed at encouraging greater inclusion of women in studies.

The issue of gender is particularly germane to the present volume because the volume addresses the role of emotional expressivity (or inhibition) as a factor in health and illness. While human emotions are biologically rooted – there are but a limited set of basic or "primary" emotions (Izard, 1971, 1977) – subserved by neurological "command circuits" (Panksepp, 1986) and accompanied by organized patterns of facial expressions that can be recognized cross-culturally (Ekman, 1973), it is also readily acknowledged that considerable differences exist in the activation and display of emotions across individuals and that certain features of emotion expression are shaped by cultural and familial forces (Scherer, 1988).

The expression of emotion in Western culture is also highly constrained by gender roles (Scherer, 1990). Studies of early infant development demonstrate that parental tuition in gender-appropriate "display rules" is already underway as early as the first few months of life (Malatesta, Culver, Tesman, Lamb, & Shepard, 1989; Malatesta, Grigoryev, Lamb, Albin, & Culver, 1986; Malatesta & Haviland, 1982). However, socialization factors are not the only contributors to gender differentiated expressive behavior. Subtle morphological and constitutional differences between male and female infants are probably at least partially responsible for the differential emotion socialization patterns practiced by parents. For example, male infants are more irritable, more emotionally labile in general, and less able to sustain protracted eye contact than female infants (Haviland & Malatesta, 1981). Structural properties of the face, including a lower brow line in males, may make male infants appear more guarded and less social than females, which could conceivably elicit different patterns of interaction with caregivers and therefore produce different kinds of emotional experience for young boys and girls.

Although the observed gender differences in emotional expressivity during infancy are not large, and gender differences interact with a number of other important individual difference variables (Malatesta et al., 1989), the impact is apparently considerable over time. By adulthood, men and women in at least Western culture, are seen as polarized with respect to emotion expression patterns and sensitivities. In general, women are seen as more nurturant, affectionate, more emotionally labile, more prone to shame and depression, more emotionally false and conflicted, more accurate in reading others' emotions, and generally more neurotic than men. Men are viewed as more stoical, aggressive, angry, more emotionally inhibited, and less sensitive to the emotional cues of others. To a certain extent these popular cultural stereotypes are empirically supported in one form or another. For example, with respect to anger, although Averill's (1982) large-scale survey study did not find significant gender differences for this emotion by self-report, more naturalistic data provide a compelling argument for considering men as more prone to anger and aggression; crimes of violence, whether they involve children, women, or men as victims, are far and away disproportionately committed by men. In terms of the more tender sentiments and behaviors, for whatever set of complex biological and social reasons, women have been, and continue to be, even today, the primary nurturers of children. Empirical research also indicates that women experience more emotional conflict or ambivalence than men (King & Emmons, 1990), and that they engage in more expressive "masking" or dissimulation (Bugental, Love, & Gianetto, 1971; Malatesta, Jonas, Shepard, & Culver, in preparation). In terms of mental illness, women's emotional disturbances more often take the form of depression, while men's take the form of "acting out". In empirical studies of emotion decoding, girls and women of all ages are better at the task than boys and men (Hall, 1978), and thus they appear more interpersonally sensitive.

The emotional dimorphism noted above would seem to make it axiomatic that any consideration of the relation between emotional expressivity and health take special note of gender differences. And yet, all too frequently, gender is simply not considered, or, if it is taken into account, it is either "controlled" by eliminating one of the two genders (usually women), "balanced" in the experimental design and ignored, treated as a nuisance variable and co-varied out in regression analysis, or if differences are examined and found, reported as "anomalous" gender differences. Because of this, there are few systematic data on whether the expressive differences observed between the genders constitute anything more than superficial social conventions ("display rules") devoid of physical correlates or consequences, or whether, in fact, there are differential health benefits and penalties for different kinds of expressive patterns.

Part of the reason that gender has been ignored in the past in health research relates to the general neglect of personality and individual difference variables. Until fairly recently, studies of the etiology and course of disease employed mathematical risk models that treated an assortment of biological and environmental factors but excluded behavior and personality. With the advent of behavioral medicine and health psychology, questions of mind/body interaction – once the province of psychosomatic medicine and largely discredited due to imprecision of theory and measurement, are being pursued anew. The present volume presents a range of new perspectives on an old problem, all organized around the premise that emotion and its manner of expression may be intimately connected with the disease process.

The choice of emotion as a critical personality variable around which to examine behavior/health linkages is an especially promising one for two reasons. First, because emotions have a direct bearing on physiology – and not just in terms of "general arousal" or "mass action" as older models of emotion would have it (Cannon, 1927) – but in terms of emotion-specific patterns of physiological activity (Ekman, Levenson, & Friesen, 1983; Levenson & Carstensen, in press; Schwartz, Weinberger, & Singer, 1981). Secondly, the linkage between particular kinds of emotional distress – repeatedly experienced or repeatedly inhibited – and particular patterns of disease, is specifically predicted by discrete emotions theory (Izard, 1971, 1977; Tomkins, 1962, 1963, 1982). Although investigations in this area have only begun to scratch the surface of what promises to be a very rich vein of research, the initial studies have provided encouraging results.

Others in this volume will have much to offer in this regard. In the present chapter we raise the particular issue of gender as it engages the link between emotion expressivity and illness. The research we report upon was gathered in the course of a study that was designed specifically to consider the emotion expression profiles of Type A (and B) behavior pattern using behavioral measures of expressivity and a discrete emotions component analysis (Malatesta et al., in preparation); in addition, unlike most research on Type A behavior pattern our study included equal numbers of men and women. Although the study was not originally designed to examine emotion/illness linkages per se, one measure that was included in the battery of tests – the *Cornell Medical Index,* a self-report measure of illness and physical symptoms – provides an opportunity to explore just that issue. Despite the admitted limitations of self-report measures of symptoms, and the concurrent nature of the measures of expressivity and symptoms – which preclude drawing inferences about causality – the data set was large and unique enough to encourage an examination of the association between expressive patterns and symptomatology. We begin with a brief introduction to the methods and procedures of the study and then proceed to an examination of symptom/emotion linkages.

Methods
Subjects and Procedures

Two hundred and forty subjects were recruited for a study of "emotions across the lifespan." The study was specifically focused on generating emotion profiles of the "coronary prone" Type A Behavior Pattern. Subjects filled out a number of personality measures, underwent a videotaped mood induction procedure, and participated in the *Structured Interview* (SI), which is the standard assessment procedure for identifying TABP.

The Structured Interview

The SI is an approximately 20 minute long interview designed to elicit reactivity in persons prone to impatience and irritation. When faced with the deliberate provocation of the interview, Type A individuals typically show features of hostility and impatience – especially evident in voice stylistics. On the basis of their performance in the SI, subjects are classified as A1, A2, B1 or B2, depending on the relative salience of Type A features, although most studies base their analyses on a breakdown only by major type – A versus B. A fifth category, X, is reserved for cases that do not readily fall into either of the two Type A or Type B categories, and is used relatively infrequently. In our sample of 240 subjects, only 4 were identified as Type X. For most of our analysis (Malatesta et al., in preparation) we restricted the sample to 160 subjects so as to balance for two levels of each of three factors: Type (A vs. B) gender (male, female), and age (< 50, > 50). There were thus 20 subjects per cell.

The present investigation is focused exclusively on the relation between emotional expressivity and symptoms in men and women. For all analyses, then, there were 80 males and 80 females, balanced for age and type. The mean age for the female sample was 48.42 years (*SD* = 22.46); the mean age of the males was 48.92 years (*SD* = 21.68).

Emotion Induction Procedure

This procedure (Malatesta & Izard, 1984) is designed to produce behavioral expression of emotion in subjects under conditions of authentic emotional arousal; sessions are videotaped so that they can be subjected to analysis via validated emotion coding procedures. In essence, subjects recollect and recount emotionally charged events from the recent past; instructions and training are such that subjects are usually successful at accessing personally meaningful and highly charged events that then result in considerable facial expressivity. Details of the training procedure can be found in Malatesta and Izard (1984). In the present study subjects were asked to recollect and recount events that produced strong feelings of anger, sadness, fear, and interest/excitement. At the end of each induction episode, they also rated the intensity of their emotional experiences using Izard's (1972) *Differential Emotions Scale* (DES), which was used both as a manipulation check on the induction's effectiveness (all inductions were effective, and differentially so) as well as in assessing the degree of concordance between felt emotion (as rated on the DES) and expressed emotion (as measured by MAX coding of facial expressive behavior). An analysis of the degree of difference between the ratings was used as one means of assessing emotion inhibition. In the ensuing report we refer to emotion variables computed in this way as "suppression" variables.

Self-Report Measures

Symptoms: The presence of illness and disease was measured by the *Cornell Medical Inventory* (CMI), a self-report instrument which has been found to show good convergent validity with independent clinical evaluations and has shown strong predictive validity for future health status, including mortality (Daly & Tyroler, 1972; Weaver, Ko, Alexander, Pao, & Ting, 1980). It consists of items in separate sections dealing with different organ systems such as the cardiovascular, respiratory, gastrointestinal, muscle, bone and joint, skin, and a cluster of items involving the eye, ear, head, and mouth. In the present study the instrument was modified slightly to enhance its sensitivity. We converted the individual items from a yes/no format to a scaled version that allowed respondents to indicate the presence and extent of symptoms on a four-point-scale.

The items were subjected to a principal components factor analysis to determine if the items in the various syndrome groups aggregated in a face valid way and by groupings within the inventory. The procedure produced a 22 factor solution using an eigenvalue requirement of > 1; these clusters of symptom items cohered in a meaningful and reasonable way and were subsequently rotated to varimax criteria. Of the 22 factors, 11 produced sufficient category coherence and face validity to retain for subsequent analysis. Table 1 displays the highest loading items for each factor. These symptom clusters formed the basis for our analysis of the relation between symptoms and facial expressivity. Each cluster of items was summed across the highest loading items so as to achieve an aggregate score for each of the 11 clusters. These summed scores constituted the "symptom variables" in all subsequent analyses. The symptom clusters/variables are referred to in the tables and text as: Respiratory I (Colds), Respiratory II (general respiratory symptoms), High Blood Pressure, Cardiovascular I (see items), Cardiovascular II (see items), Joints, Gastrointestinal, Skin I (general dermatological symptoms), Skin II (eczema), Skin III (skin growths), and Headaches.

Personality Measures: Most previous attempts to measure the relation between disease and emotional dispositions have employed personality inventories (see Friedman & Booth-Kewley, 1987, for a review of the literature). The most extensively used measures appear to be those that tap the personality dimensions or emotion traits of anxiety, depression, and anger/hostility and/or aggression. Unfortunately, individual studies rarely employ more than one or two dimensions of personality related to emotionality; consequently, it has been difficult to determine whether or not there is merely a general, stress-responsive "disease-prone" personality (Friedman & Booth-Kewley, 1987), a general neuroticism factor, or alternatively, whether symptoms relate to emotional patterns in a symptom-specific, emotion-specific manner (Malatesta, 1988). Moreover, we know little about how patterns of disease/emotion linkage are moderated by gender.

Table 1:   Highest Loading Items of Principal Components Analysis of the Cornell Medical Index

Factor	Loadings
Respiratory I (Colds)	
Item 20 (Do you catch severe colds?)	.71
Respiratory II (General)	
Item 14 (Do you have to clear your throat a lot?)	.80
Item 15 (Do you feel a choking lump in your throat?)	.59
Item 16 (Are you troubled with bad spells of sneezing?)	.47
Item 17 (Do you suffer from a running or stuffed-up nose?)	.34
Item 21 (Do you get hay fever?)	.30
Item 22 (Do you suffer from asthma?)	.36
Item 23 (Are you troubled by constant coughing?)	.73
High Blood Pressure	
Item 28 (Do you have high blood pressure?)	.82
Cardiovascular I	
Item 27 (Do you have low blood pressure?)	.30
Item 29 (Do you get pains in the heart or chest?)	.30
Item 30 (Are you bothered by thumping of the heart?)	.62
Item 31 (Does your heart beat faster than usual?)	.80
Item 32 (Can you feel your heart beating fast?)	.78
Item 33 (Do your ankles swell?)	.40
Item 36 (Do you suffer from cramps in your legs?)	.39
Item 38 (Do you have hot or cold spells?)	.30
Cardiovascular II	
Item 25 (Do you get out of breath easily?)	.55
Item 29 (Do you get pains in the heart or chest?)	.75
Item 30 (Are you bothered by thumping of the heart?)	.46
Joints (Arthritis)	
Item 33 (Do your ankles swell?)	.31
Item 57 (Do you suffer from stiffness, swelling, or pains in joints?)	.79
Item 58 (Do you have trouble with severe rheumatism [arthritis]?)	.78
Item 60 (Are you bothered by neck and back pains?)	.60
Gastrointestinal	
Item 46 (Do you gulp your food in a hurry?)	.63
Item 47 (Are you bothered by stomach pains or indigestion?)	.64
Item 48 (Do you feel bloated after eating?)	.73
Item 49 (Do you belch a lot after eating?)	.69
Item 52 (Do you suffer from loose bowel movements?)	.39

Skin I (General)
Item 63 (Is your skin very sensitive or tender?)	.63
Item 65 (Do cuts in your skin usually stay open a long time?)	.57
Item 66 (Do you get hives?)	.49
Item 67 (Does your face get hot and blushes?)	.34
Item 69 (Are you bothered by severe itching?)	.36
Item 70 (Do you get warts?)	.31
Item 71 (Does your skin break out in a rash?)	.68

Skin II (Eczema)
Item 64 (Do you get eczema?)	.73
Item 69 (Are you bothered by severe itching?)	.67

Skin III (Skin growths)
Item 70 (Do you get warts?)	.42
Item 74 (Do you have problems with skin growths of any kind?)	.73

Headache
Item 10 (Do you suffer from severe headaches?)	.60
Item 11 (Do you have pressure headaches [e.g., sinus]?)	.33

In the present study we administered several personality measures that purport to tap emotional dispositions and analyzed the results by gender. The self-report inventories employed in this investigation were: 1) Spielberger's *State-Trait Anxiety Inventory* (STAI); 2) Beck's *Depression Inventory*; 3) the *Cook-Medley Scale* from the *MMPI* for the measurement of hostility; 4) Spielberger's *Anger Expression Scale* (AX/EX), which yields separate scores for anger-in and anger-out (related to the concept of anger inhibition versus expression), as well as total anger proneness; and 5) the trait scale from Spielberger's *State/Trait Aggression Inventory*. Subject's scores on these scales became variables in subsequent analysis of the relation between emotion traits and illness. The seven variables derived from these measures will be referred to by the following abbreviated terms as the personality traits of: Anxiety, depression, hostility, anger proneness (total AX/EX score), anger-in, anger-out, and aggression.

Behavioral Measures

Our behavioral index of emotionality relied on the coding of facial expressive patterns obtained during the four emotion induction episodes (anger, fear, interest, sadness). Facial expressions were coded with the adult-modified version (Malatesta & Izard, 1984) of Izard's (1979) *Maximally Discriminative Facial*

Movement Coding System, better known as MAX. The MAX system is a theoreti-cally-based, anatomically-linked component facial action coding system that codes muscle movement changes in three grand regions of the face. Originally designed for use with infants and children, it has also been employed in studies of adults, with some adjustments to the system to accommodate special features of adult expressivity. For example, in infants and young children, emotion is ty-pically expressed in two or three regions of the face at once, rather than in only one region. Adults however, tend to use miniaturized versions of emotion ex-pression, usually involving one region of the face or, less frequently, 2 regions. Involvement of all three regions of the face is very limited, being largely re-stricted to extreme episodes of emotional arousal. Older children and adults also employ "emotion regulators" (Malatesta & Izard, 1984; Malatesta et al., 1989); these are expressive gestures that serve to restrict or curtail emotion that is either currently being expressed or which threatens to break out.

Material to be Coded

Each emotion induction episode consisted of the subject's recounting of the specific event (called the emotion episode) and a summary by the subject imme-diately following the narration of the episode in which the subject was asked to summarize "in a sentence or two" how the event "really made you feel." The lat-ter, called the "peak" was designed to provide a condensed and intense encapsu-lation of the emotional experience just narrated. The emotion episodes were too variable and sometimes too long for complete MAX coding. Instead, we used the last 20 seconds of the episode and the complete peak as the material to be coded for our facial expressivity analysis. This amounted to about 30 to 50 se-conds of facial expressive behavior for each subject which was deemed sufficient to characterize the nature of the subject's expressive patterns. Since the amount of material coded per subject varied somewhat due to unequal length of seg-ments, all data were subsequently proportionalized.

The Facial Coding System

Video records from the emotion induction procedures were coded for the pres-ence of, and changes in, muscle movement patterns related to emotion on a second-to-second basis. Almost all codes used in this study derive from Izard's (1979) MAX system; the remainder constitute a set of emotion regulators that have been found to be more characteristic of older children and adults. The va-rious classes of emotion, emotion blends, emotion regulators, and other facial signals examined in this study, and their corresponding MAX codes, are presen-ted in Table 2.

Table 2:   MAX Facial Codes and Affect Regulators

Positive Emotions

Interest
    I-1   (one component interest expression): Code 20 or 30 or 68 alone
    I-2   (two component expression): Codes 20 + 30 or 20 + 68 or 30 + 68
    I-3   (three component expression): Codes 20 + 30 + 68

Joy: Code 52

Surprise
    SP-1: Code 50
    SP-2: Codes 50 + 20 or 50 + 30 or 50 + 31
    SP-3: Codes 50 + 20 + 30 or 50 + 20 + 31

Negative Emotions

Fear
    F-1:   Code 53
    F-2:   Code 53 with any eye code, i.e., 30, 31, or 20
    F-3:   Codes 59 + 20 + 30 or 55 + 20 + 31
    F-S: Code 64 (suppressed fear)

Code 64 involves a sucking in of the lower and sometimes also upper lip; this is one of the "emotion regulators" that appears to function as a means of dampening intense negative affect, in this case fear. Note that Izard included this code in the formula for shame configurations. However, it has been our observation that in adults it is more related to fear regulation. Factor analysis (see Tables 2 – 5) confirms that it is intercorrelated with other fear codes.

Sad
    SD-1: Code 56 or 23
    SD-2: Codes 56 + 23 or 56 + 75 or 23 + 75
    SD-3: Codes 56 + 23 + 75

Contempt
    C-1:   Code 61 or 21
    C-2:   Codes 61 + 21 or 61 + 39 or 23 + 39
    C-3:   Codes 61 + 21 + 39

Disgust
    D-1:   59b or 42
    D-2:   59 + 42

Shame

Sh: Code 36 if it occurs alone, and in combination with Code 75 (Code 75 does not appear in the MAX system, but was empirically validated as a shame component in subsequent research (Malatesta & Izard, 1984). Code 75, if it occurs alone, is not counted as a shame code, since it sometime combines with Sad codes (see above).

Anger

A-R   (Anger, rage – i.e., strong, unmodulated form): Code 54 and/or 25.

A-I   (Anger, irritation): Codes 33 (narrowed, staring eyes) or 55 (open tense mouth that appears as a slightly modified version of Code 54)

A-S1:   Code 67, suppressed anger (consists of compressed lips – a "regulator" code not found in the original MAX system; appears to function as an anger inhibitor, as found in a study by Malatesta et al., 1989)

A-S2:   Inadequately suppressed anger; i.e., Code 67 in *conjunction* with any other anger code.

Special Codes: These are codes that index facial signals whose immediate emotional relevance is not as well understood as the emotion codes above.

BF: Brow-flash, Code 20-0 (Regular MAX Code 20, but which occurs as only a brief flicker and which has been described by Eibl-Eibesfeldt (1989) as a universal signal of greeting and/or agreement).

KB: Knit brow. Code 24. This code occurs predominantly as a non-specific negative affect signal which is thought to be an alternative means of encoding the specific negative affective states of anger, fear and sadness (Malatesta & Izard, 1984). It also can, at times, co-occur with interest (Izard, 1979; Oster, 1978).

Blend Expressions

+B1:   Positive blend. Co-occurrence of Codes 52 + 20

-B1:   Negative blend. Any two negative codes (e.g., codes involving sadness and anger expressions).

+/-B1:   Positive/negative blend. Co-occurrence of a positive and negative code.

When the facial coding was complete, frequency counts were made for all of the separate codes and their distributions were examined. If a particular code occurred very frequently, or displayed too little variance, it was either deleted or combined with other codes in the same emotion category. Twenty-one codes were retained after this deletion and aggregation procedure, as follows:

SP: Surprise, 1-, 2-, and/or 3-component expressions
I-1:   Interest, one component
I-2,3:   Interest, consisting of 2- and/or 3-component expressions
J: Joy
F1:   Fear, 1-component
F-2,3:   Fear, 2- and/or 3-component expressions
F-S: Fear, suppressed
SD: Sad, 1-, 2-, and/or 3-component expressions
C1:   Contempt, 1-component expressions
C-2,3:   Contempt, 2- and/or 3-component expressions
DG: Disgust, 1-, 2-, and/or 3-component expressions
SH: Shame
A-R: Anger/rage (the strong form of anger emotion)
A-I: Anger/irritation (a less intense form of anger emotion)
A-S1:   Anger, suppressed
A-S2:   Anger, inadequately suppressed
+B1:   Positive blend
-B1:   Negative blend
+/-B1:   Positive/Negative blend
BF: Brow-flash
KB: Knit brow

Note that 2-3 component expressions are considered to be the more intense, unmodulated versions of each emotion type, whereas 1-component expressions are considered "miniaturized" (Tomkins, 1963) versions.

How do the Various MAX Codes Relate to One Another?

Before proceeding further, we checked to see that assumptions we made about emotion regulators were warranted. We also wanted to determine if our assumption about the categorical membership of 2-3 component expressions and 1-component expressions were justified. To these ends we performed a principal components factor analysis on the 21 emotion code categories (N = 160); four separate analyses were conducted, one for each emotion induction condition. Tables 3 to 6 display the results of the factor analyses. The data indicate that our assumptions about emotion regulators and 1- and 2-3 component expressions were for the most part justified. They also indicated that certain codes joined one another in slightly different ways under the four separate induction conditions. This latter finding suggested to us that we should retain the 21 codes rather than use factor scores in our examination of the relation between expressive behavior and symptoms; nevertheless, the factor analyses were helpful in subsequent interpretation of the data.

Table 3:   Rotated Factor Pattern for MAX Facial Codes

Anger Induction

Factor	Loading
Mixed Emotion	+.87
Positive/negative blend	+.73
Anger S1	-.40
Masking	
Joy	+.73
Positive blend	+.80
Anger-S1	+.21
Contempt/Disgust	
Contempt -1	+.84
Contempt -2,3	+.55
Disgust	+.32
Surprise	
Surprise	+.62
Brow flash	+.72
Anger-W	-.51
Fear	
Fear -2,3	+.74
Fear-S	+.81
Anger, irritation	
Knit brow	+.82
Anger-S2	+.78
Anger, rage	
Anger-R	+.55
Negative blend	+.80
Sad	
Sad	+.58
Fear-1	+.79
Interested, Accepting	
Interest-2,3	+.90
Disgust	-.31
Shame	
Shame	+.90

Table 4: Rotated Factor Pattern for MAX Facial Codes

Fear Induction

Factor	Loadings
Mixed Emotion	
Interest-1	+.72
Interest-2,3	+.68
Positive/negative blend	+.71
Fear, Mixed	
Fear-2,3	+.73
Negative blind	+.72
Disgust	
Disgust	+.72
Anger-I	+.76
Fear, Unexpectancy	
Fear-1	+.77
Surprise	+.81
Anger, Strong	
Anger-R	+.72
Anger-S2	+.78
Masking	
Joy	+.78
Positive blend	+.76
Contempt	
Contempt-1	+.77
Contempt-2,3	+.72
Anger, suppressed	
Anger-S1	+.82
Sad	-.34
Brow flash	-.39
Fear	
Fear-S	+.56
Knit brow	+.66

Table 5:   Rotated Factor Pattern for MAX Facial Codes

Interest Induction

Factor	Loadings
Enjoyment	
Joy	+.82
Positive blend	+.78
Contempt, dislike	
Contempt-2,3	+.87
Negative blend	+.78
Anger	
Knit brow	+.76
Anger-S2	+.76
Anxious Anger	
Fear-S	+.70
Anger-R	+.51
Anger-S1	+.70
Rejection	
Disgust	+.74
Anger-I	+.77
Surprised/ashamed	
Surprise	+.67
Shame	+.84
Sad	
Sad	+.82
Fear	
Fear-2,3	+.87
Fear-S	+.35
Ambivalent Interest	
Interest-1	+.83
Positive/negative blend	+.45
Interest, Agreement	
Interest-2,3	+.64
Brow flash	+.74

Table 6:   Rotated Factor Pattern for MAX Facial Codes

Sad Induction

Factor	Loadings
Anger	
Anger-S2	+.87
Knit brow	+.83
Masking	
Surprise	+.73
Joy	+.50
Positive blend	+.83
Angry, Upset	
Anger-C	+.77
Negative blend	+.83
Fear	
Fear-2,3	+.63
Fear-S	+.79
Interest, Mixed	
Interest-1	+.78
Interest-2,3	+.47
Positive/negative blind	+.38
Anger, Weakly articulated	
Anger-I	+.72
Anger-S1	+.59
Brow flash	-.46
Sad	
Sad	+.66
Fear-1	+.61
Contempt	
Contempt-1	+.72
Contempt-2,3	+.73
Disgust	
Disgust	+.80
Brow flash	-.50

Analysis and Discussion of the Data
Relation between Symptom Clusters and Personality Variables.

We examined the pattern of intercorrelation between symptoms and personality traits first since almost all previous studies that examined such relationships had relied on similar measures (Friedman & Booth-Kewley, 1987). The present study departs from earlier investigations that used these instruments in that it includes *several* measures of emotion traits with the *same* population of subjects and examines the relation between several types of symptom clusters with respect to these measures.

The significant correlation between our CMI symptom clusters and the various personality measures are presented in Table 7. (Alpha was set at .01 rather than .05 to reduce the chance of Type I error, and scatterplots were inspected to detect and eliminate variables that violated assumptions of linearity; associations that appeared spurious are not presented in the Table.)

Table 7:   Correlation Between CMI Symptom Clusters and Personality Variables (* Designates correlations that are <.01)

	r	
	Females N = 80	Males N = 80
Personality Variables		
Hostility (MMPI Ho Scale)		
Cardiovascular I	.34*	.25
Gastrointestinal	.16	.29*
Anger Out (Spielberger AX-EX Scale)		
Respiratory II (general)	.18	.28*
Cariovascular I	.30*	.12
Gastrointestinal	.10	.28*
Anger In (Spielberger AX-EX Scale)		
Cardiovascular I	.31*	.20
Gastrointestinal	.31*	.20
Overall Anger (Spielberger AX-EX Scale)		
Cardiovascular II	.28*	.16
Gastrointestinal	.25 .	30*
Joints (arthritis)	.04 .	39*
Depression (Beck Depression Inventory)		
Respiratory II (general)	.20	.29*

Anxiety (STAI)
    Respiratory I (colds)   .39 *   -.05
    Respiratory II (general)   .37 *   .11
    Cardiovascular I   .33 *   .09
    Cardiovascular II   .33 *   .12
    Gastrointestinal   .33 *   .26
    Skin I (general)   .37 *   .25
    Headache   .28 *   .24 *

Aggression
    Gastrointestinal   .22   .46
    Skin I (general)   .32 *   .28 *

As indicated in the table, only 7 of the symptom clusters showed any significant degree of association with the 7 personality variables, and these are among those that come closest to those diseases that are most commonly considered as especially stress-responsive or have a psychosomatic component (Friedman & Booth-Kewley, 1987).

We can summarize the results in terms of patterns specific to men and women as follows:

	Females	Males
Symptoms	Associated Emotion Traits	
Respir I (colds)	Anxiety	None
Respir II	Anxiety	Anger-out and depression
High BP	None	None
Cardio I	Hostility, anger-out, anxiety	None
Cardio II	Anger-in, overall anger, anxiety	None
Joints	None	Overall anger
GI	Anger-in and anxiety	Hostility, anger-out, overall anger
Sk I (general)	Anxiety and aggression	None
Sk II (eczema)	None	Aggression
Sk III (growths)	None	None
Headaches	Anxiety	Anxiety

The above results indicate that there is a greater number of associations between emotion traits and symptom clusters in women than in men (13 versus 8). We also note that 75% (6 out of 8) significant correlations are related to anger and aggression in men, but only 46% (6 out of 13) are related to these traits in women. Instead, the majority of associations in women – 54% (7 out of 13) – are related to anxiety; in men only 25% (2 out of 8) of the symptom linkages are with emotions other than anger (one instance of anxiety, one instance of depression).

This pattern of results suggests several possibilities. One is that the data reflect gender-related differences in reporting style, such that women are more likely to acknowledge anxiety, whereas men are more likely to acknowledge anger and aggression. Or the data could reflect differential interpretation of emotional distress such that when men are emotionally aroused they interpret their distress as anger, whereas when women are upset, they interpret their distress as anxiety. Yet another possibility is that men and women experience differential amounts of anger and anxiety in their daily lives, an hypothesis entertained by Tomkins and McCarter (1964). In fact, although not statistically significant, there was a trend for women to report more trait anxiety than men ($p = .09$, and men to score marginally higher on trait hostility ($p = .13$), though not on the anger or aggression measures. Thus, it is conceivable that greater hostility is what takes a health penalty in men and that a greater predisposition to anxiety is what takes more of a health toll in women.

Only one symptom cluster showed a similar association with an emotion trait in both men and women – that between headaches and anxiety – and there are several other striking differences in the pattern of correlations between disease and emotion traits in men versus women. First, the relation between anger and joint disease, long claimed in the clinical literature (Achterberg-Lawlins, 1982), holds only for men, at least using self-report measures. Second, in terms of gastrointestinal symptoms, in men they are associated with anger-out, whereas in women they are associated with anger-in. Third, in the case of respiratory problems, these symptoms are linked to anxiety in women, but anger and depression in men. Fourth, in women, several symptom clusters are linked to two emotion traits (see Cardiovascular I, Cardiovascular II, headaches, colds, gastrointestinal and skin I). In men, only respiratory symptoms are associated with more than one emotion trait. Finally, it is interesting to note that there was an association between anger and cardiovascular symptoms in women but not in men. The findings with respect to women are in accord with other investigations, for example, prospectively in the Framingham longitudinal study of women (Eaker & Castelli, 1988) – which also found a linkage with anxiety, as we do here; however, the lack of significant association between anger and cardiac symptoms in our sample of men is out of step with the bulk of research showing a significant association between anger/hostility and aggression and heart disease and high blood pressure. Part of the explanation may reside in the present study's application of exclusionary criteria. Because we wished to avoid the influence of knowledge of cardiac disease on dependent measures, we excluded any subject who had a known history of cardiac disease, although subjects might experience and report symptoms that unbeknownst to them related to CHD. Of course, this does not rule out heart disease but it would attenuate or obviate any real association. (We should also note for the record that since we wanted to recruit an older sample we did *not* rule out those with high blood pressure since this condition is fairly common in older people; we accepted subjects with high blood pressure, as long as the condition was being pharmacologically controlled.)

The above pattern of results is not entirely in accord with the findings of Friedman and Booth-Kewley's (1987) meta-analysis. They found that CHD, asthma, arthritis, ulcers and headaches all showed associations with anxiety, anger/hostility and depression. Our categories of symptoms are not as specific as those mentioned in this review but they appear to involve a good deal of overlap in underlying symptomatology; nevertheless, our data do not indicate a generic "emotionality" configuration, but rather symptom-specific/emotion-specific linkages. The lack of concordance between the Friedman and Booth-Kewley meta-analysis and the results of our own study may be due to the fact that the former authors did not break down the various samples by gender as we have. Thus direct comparisons may not be warranted; moreover, most studies cited in the Friedman and Booth-Kewley review did not use multiple measures or examine multiple symptoms, or if they did, could not be treated due to limitations of meta-analysis (Malatesta, 1988). The above data, as well as the studies reviewed by Friedman and Booth-Kewley (1987) are all based on self-report measures. We turn now to an alternative means of examining the relation between emotion traits or dispositions and symptoms.

Relation Between Symptom Clusters and Facial Expressions

A total of 25 variables based on expression codes were used in this analysis – the 21 individual MAX and regulator codes, and four "suppression" variables. The suppression variables were derived in the following way. First MAX ratios (amount of expressive behavior) and DES scores (subjects' ratings of the intensity of emotional experience following each induction) were converted to z scores. These scores were then converted to cumulative probabilities on the normal curve. Finally, each subject's score on the DES cumulative probability was subtracted from his/her score on the MAX ratio cumulative probability. Suppression score variables with a minus sign would indicate that the subject experienced greater emotion than he/she expressed and the coefficient was interpreted as an index of the amount of suppression. The suppression variables included "Suppression of A-R," "Suppression of A-I," (no suppression variable was created for A-S1 or A-S2 because theoretically these codes already index suppression), suppressed fear under the fear induction, and suppressed sadness under the sadness induction.

Pearson r correlations were run on the 25 expression variables noted above and the 11 symptom clusters; correlations were calculated separately for each induction condition and by gender. We used an alpha of .01 rather than .05 to reduce the chance of Type I error, and we carefully screened scatterplots to detect violations of assumptions of linearity; with this alpha level, there were 62 significant correlations. Inspection of the scatterplots and conservative criteria caused us to eliminate 41 of the correlations as potentially spurious, leaving a total of 21 correlations. Table 8 presents these correlations organized by symptom category.

Table 8: Correlations Between Symptom Clusters and Expressed or Inhibited[a] Facial Expressions of Emotion

	r	
	Females (N = 80)	Males (N = 80)
Respiratory I (Colds)		
Suppressed fear, fear induction (dampened fear [negative sign of correlation indicates suppression])	-.28 *	-.01
Respiratory II (General)		
Positive blend, fear induction (masking of fear)	+.32 *	-.09
Positive/negative blend in sad induction (conflict over sadness)	-.01	+.28 *
High Blood Pressure		
No reliable associations		
Cardiovascular I		
Knit brow, anger induction (expressed anger)	+.15	+.39 *
Cardiovascular 2		
Knit brow, anger induction (expressed anger)	-.04	+.46 ***
Anger-S1, anger induction (suppressed anger)	+.28 *	-.17
Fear-S, fear induction (suppressed fear)	+.31 *	+.07
Joints		
Anger-S2, anger induction (inadequately suppressed anger)	-.14	+.49 ***
Knit brow, fear induction (expressed fear)	+.40 **	+.04
Gastrointestinal		
Fear-S, fear induction (suppressed fear)	+.03	+.28 *
Knit brow, fear induction (expressed fear)	+.41 **	+.00
Positive/negative blend, sad induction (masking of sadness)	-.17	+.28 *

Skin I
  Anger-S2, anger induction (inadequately
  suppressed anger)   -.10   +.32 *

Skin II
  Contempt-1, anger induction (element of the
  hostile triad)   +.35 *   +.16
  Positive blend, fear induction (masking of fear)   +.38 **   +.05
  Anger-I, interest induction (expressed irritation) +.28 *   -.01
  Joy, sad induction (masking of sadness)   +.34 *   -.11

Skin III
  Knit brow, anger induction (expressed anger)   +.09   +.31 *
  Anger-I, anger induction (expressed irritation)   +.39 **   -.05
  Knit brow, fear induction (expressed fear)   +.02   +.28 *
  Positive/negative blend, fear induction
  (masking of fear)   +.09   +.28 *
  Positive/negative blend, sad induction
  (masking of sadness)   +.04   +.33 *
  Anger-I, sad induction (expressed irritation)   +.38 **   -.11

Headaches
  No reliable associations

a
  "Inhibited" emotion includes variables as suppressed, dampened, and masked.

    *   = $p < .01$
   **   = $p < .001$
  ***   = $p < .0001$

Interpretation of the Facial Data

Inhibition vs. Expression of Emotion: The data were interpreted in terms of what is known about the regulation of emotion in adults (Malatesta, in press; Malatest & Izard, 1984; Tomkins, 1962, 1963). Emotions can be either expressed or inhibited. In the present study, inhibition was indexed in several ways. As mentioned earlier, one means of assessing inhibition involved calculating the difference between experienced (DES rating) and expressed emotion (MAX codes). The four variables that were created in this way were referred to earlier as "suppression" scores for anger (two types – A-R, A-I), sadness, and fear, and can be regarded as instances of "dampened" emotionality. There were also the three emotion regulators identified in Table 2, referred to as suppression codes F-S, A-S1 and A-S2. In addition, we interpreted several other facial signals as indexing the suppression or inhibition of emotion, as described below.

Another emotion control mechanism is "masking." (Ekman & Friesen, 1975; Malatesta & Izard, 1984). Masking occurs when a person substitutes one emotion expression for that of another, for example smiling when what one really feels is anger. Masking is usually regarded as a means of preventing other people from having access to one's true feelings, but because masking involves the alteration of an expressive behavior, and since, according to discrete emotions theory and the doctrine of facial feedback (Izard, 1971, 1977) altering expressive behavior alters emotional experience, the individual's own emotion is subverted. Thus, one can regard masking as indexing submerged or inhibited emotion.

In the present study masking could occur in two forms. Given the elicitation of negative experience during the sadness, fear, and anger inductions, we infer that the appearance of positive affect codes signals that negative experience is being masked. Joy expressions, positive blend expressions (which were intercorrelated with joy expressions), and brow flash instances (which were intercorrelated with positive emotion) occurring during any of the three negative emotion inductions, then would constitute grounds for inferring affect inhibition. A second kind of masking involves the mixing of positive and negative expressions under the negative emotion induction condition, that is, the appearance of positive/negative blends during negative emotion inductions. The occurrence of positive/negative blends is also grounds for inferring conflict.

To summarize, emotions may either be expressed (facial expressions of joy, surprise, interest, sadness, anger, fear, disgust, shame, contempt, disgust) or inhibited in some form. Indices of inhibited emotion and/or conflict over expressed emotion in the present study can be summarized in the following way:

Types of Emotion Inhibition

Dampened emotion:
>   Fear suppression under interest induction (MAX – DES)
>   Sadness suppression under sadness induction (MAX – DES)
>   Anger suppression under anger induction (MAX – DES): A-R, A-I

Suppressed emotion:
>   Emotion regulators of F-S, A-S1, A-S2

Masked emotion:
>   Joy, positive blend, or brow flash under negative emotion induction

Ambivalent or conflicted emotion:
>   Positive/negative blends.

Gender differences and general trends: Returning to Table 8, we find that the single most striking finding related to these data is that there is not a single instance in which the pattern of correlation between symptom cluster and expression or inhibition of emotion holds for both men and women; the linkages appear to be highly gender specific. For example, the symptom cluster Respiratory II is positively associated with the masking of fear in women, but with conflict over sadness in men. Gastrointestinal complaints are associated with suppressed fear and masking of sadness in men, but expressed fear in women. We turn now to a further analysis of the patterns revealed in these data.

Table 9 summarizes the various correlations reported in Table 8 by gender, expressed versus inhibited emotion, and by affect type. As indicated, in general, symptom clusters are more closely associated with inhibited (inhibited / dampened / suppressed / masked / conflicted) emotion rather than expressed emotion (13 versus 10 instances, respectively). Of the three negative emotions associated with symptoms, the associations are strongest for inhibited fear and expressed anger (6 and 7 instances, respectively). There is a nearly equal number of significant associations between emotions and symptoms for men and women (11 and 12, and they are distributed fairly equally across expression and inhibition categories. While the pattern of associations across emotions for expressed emotion is similar for the two genders, it appears to be different for associations involving the inhibition of emotion, with women more likely to inhibit fear and men sadness. We do not want to make too much of this apparent difference since the numbers are relatively small.

Table 9:   Distribution of Inhibition and Expression Codes Related to Symptoms

	No. of Inhibition Code Associations			No. of Expression Code Associations			
	Female	Male	Total	Female	Male	Total	Gd Total
Emotion							
Sadness	1	3	4	0	0	0	4
Fear	4	2	6	2	1	3	9
Anger	1	2	3	4	3	7	10
Total	6	7	13	6	4	10	23

	Sadness	Fear	Anger	Total
Total Codes (Expression and Inhibition)				
Females	1	6	5	12
Males	3	3	5	11

In Table 10 we contrast the pattern of intercorrelation between emotional dispositions and symptoms obtained with self-report measures (personality scales) and via MAX coding of facial expressions under emotion induction conditions. Note that for the facial data (MAX Codes columns), we have collapsed across redundant emotion codes for each symptom category so as to categorize each symptom's association with a particular emotion constellation. The table also indicates where the distinction has been made in the personality measures and with respect to the facial codes, whether the data indicate a pattern of inhibition or expression.

Table 10:   Comparison of MAX-identified Emotion Constellations that are Linked with Symptoms with Those Identified by Self-Report

Personality Questionnaires

	Personality Measures		MAX Codes	
	Females	Males	Females	Males
Symptoms				
Respir I	Fear	None	Fear (I), Anger (I)	None
Respir II	Fear	Anger (E),	Fear (I)	Sad (I)
High BP	None	None	None	None
Cardio I	Fear, Anger (E)	None	None	Anger (E)
Cardio II	Fear, Anger (I)	None	Fear (I), Anger (I)	Anger (E)
Joints	None	Anger	Fear (E)	Anger (I)
G-I	Fear, Anger (I)	Anger (E)	Fear (E)	Fear (I), Sad (I)
Sk I	Fear, Anger	Anger	None	Anger (I)
Sk II	None	None	Anger (E), Fear (I) Sad (I)	None
Sk III	None	None	Anger (E)	Anger (E), Fear (E & I), Sad (I)
Headaches	Fear	Fear	None	None

There are two things that are particularly noteworthy concerning these comparisons. It is clear from both types of measures that the relation between symptoms and emotional traits varies as a function of gender. Second, although the patterns of association revealed by the two approaches differ to a certain extent, there is also considerable overlap with respect to certain configurations to allow us to conclude that both personality measures and behavioral measures have a degree of concurrent validity. For example, both personality measures and MAX codes indicate that respiratory symptoms are linked to fear (or anxiety) in women, and that joint symptoms are associated with anger in men. However, the Max codes appear to yield greater specificity as to whether linkages are with expressed or inhibited emotion; among the personality measures only the *Spielberger Anger Expression Scale* (with its anger-in and anger-out subscales) allows such a distinction.

Summary and Conclusion

To summarize, the present study found that gender was a significant individual difference variable in the association between symptoms and emotional traits. This was true in the case of the so-called "subjective" self-report measures of personality and the apparently more "objective" behavioral measures obtained during authentic emotional arousal. This suggests, then, that men and women may be differentially susceptible to the activation of different kinds of emotional states, as Tomkins and McCarter (1964) originally anticipated, and that the observed differences between symptoms and emotion traits are not merely a function of differences in the readiness with which men and women admit experiencing various emotions, or, if so, that it is accompanied by differential emotional expression, as the behavioral data indicate. These findings would seem to provide justification for the concerns, recently voiced by the media as well as by the federal government, that medical research that excludes women, or generalizes from men to women, or fails to conduct analyses appropriate to the detection of gender differences, is in serious jeopardy of missing or obfuscating gender-specific relationships.

The findings of the current study also suggest that behavioral assessment of emotion patterns may be a useful and clarifying adjunct in the study of emotion/illness linkages since patterns of *both* expression and inhibition are linked to symptoms, or at least the reporting of symptoms. Physical problems are thus apparently associated with excessive activation of certain emotions as well as excessive inhibition. The system of indexing various types of emotion inhibition that were developed in this investigation may be of special use to those convinced that the inhibition of emotion is at least as equally important in emotion/illness linkages as excessive activation, and provides more of a fine-grained level of analysis of different patterns of inhibition. It may be the case that only certain kinds of inhibition – complete suppression versus masking, e.g., are causally linked to the development of symptoms. Facial expressive data taken during emotion induction procedures appears to offer a promising means of assessing personality traits related to both the expression and inhibition of emotion. In the case of the self-report measures used in the present study, only the *Spielberger Anger Expression Scale* discriminates between expressed and inhibited emotion, and the test is limited to just one emotion.

As a concluding caveat we note that the data reported in this study are purely correlational, and moreover, opportunistic rather than driven by hypothesis testing. As such the data capitalize on chance and we thus eschew any kind of statements concerning causality. However, given that a number of prospective studies have found significant predictive validity for personality measures of emotion predicting health status (Eysenck, 1990; Friedman & Booth-Kewley, 1987), and given the moderate overlap between these kind of measures and behavioral measures in the present study, we are encouraged to think that behavioral measures of emotion might show predictive validity as well, and moreover, that they might even provide more robust and specific prediction. Prospective study using these measures is presently being planned.

References

Achterberg-Lawlis, J. (1982). The psychological dimensions of arthritis. *Journal of Consulting and Clinical Psychology, 50,* 984-992.

Averill, J. R. (1982). *Anger and aggression: An essay on emotion.* New York: Springer.

Bugental, D. E., Love, L. R., & Gianetto, R. M. (1971). Perfidious feminine faces. *Journal of Personality and Social Psychology, 17,* 314-318.

Cannon, W. B. (1927). The James-Lange theory of emotions: A critical examination and an alternative theory. *American Journal of Psychology, 39,* 106-124.

Cooper, T., Detre, T., & Weiss, S. M. (1981). Coronary prone behavior and coronary heart disease: A critical review. *Circulation, 63,* 1199-1215.

Daly, M. B., & Tyroler, H. A. (1972). Cornell Medical Index response as a predictor of mortality. *British Journal of Preventive Social Medicine, 26,* 159-164.

Eaker, E. D., & Castelli, W. P. (1988). Type A behavior and coronary heart disease in women: Fourteen-year incidence from the Framingham Study. In B. K. Houston & C. R. Snyder (Eds.), *Type A behavior pattern: Research, theory, and intervention* (pp. 83-97). New York: Wiley.

Eibl-Eibesfeldt, I. (1989). *Human ethology.* New York: Aldine de Gruyter.

Ekman, P. (Ed.). (1973). *Darwin and facial expression.* New York: Academic Press.

Ekman, P., & Friesen, W. V. (1975). *Unmasking the face.* Englewood Cliffs, NJ: Prentice-Hall.

Ekman, P., Levenson, R., & Friesen, W. V. (1983). Autonomic nervous system activity distinguishes among emotions. *Science, 221,* 1208-1210.

Eysenck, H. J. (1990). Type A behavior and coronary heart disease: The third stage. *Journal of Social Behavior and Personality, 5,* 25-44.

Friedman, H. S., & Booth-Kewley, S. (1987). The "disease-prone personality:" A meta-analytic view of the construct. *American Psychologist, 42,* 539-555.

Hall, J. A. (1978). Gender effects in decoding nonverbal cues. *Psychological Bulletin, 85,* 845-857.

Haviland, J. M., & Malatesta, C. Z. (1981). A description of the development of sex differences in nonverbal signals: Fantasies, fallacies, and facts. In C. Mayo & N. Henley (Eds.), *Gender and nonverbal behaviors* (pp. 183-208). New York: Springer-Verlag.

Houston, B. K. (1988). Introduction. In B. K. Houston & C. R. Snyder (Eds.), *Type A behavior pattern: Research, theory, and intervention.* New York: Wiley.

Izard, C. E. (1971). *The face of emotion.* New York: Appleton-Century-Crofts.

Izard, C. E. (1972). *Patterns of emotions: A new analysis of anxiety and depression.* New York: Academic.

Izard, C. E. (1977). *Human emotions.* New York: Plenum.

Izard, C. E. (1979). *The maximally discriminative facial movement coding system (Max).* Newark, DE: University of Delaware, Instructional Resources Center.

Jaschik, S. (1990). Report says NIH ignores own rules on including women in its research. *The Chronicle of Higher Education, 36*(41), 18.

King, L. A., & Emmons, R. A. (1990). Conflict over emotional expression: Psychological and physical correlates. *Journal of Personality and Social Psychology, 58,* 864-877.

Levenson, R. W., & Carstensen, L. (in press). Emotion during the later lifespan. *Psychology and Aging.*

Malatesta, C. Z. (1988). A second look at the illness/emotion specificity hypothesis: A response to Friedman and Booth-Kewley. *American Psychologist, 43,* 750-751.

Malatesta, C. Z. (in press). Emotion socialization and developmental psychopathology. In D. Cichetti & S. Toth (Eds.), *Rochester symposium on developmental psychopathology: Internalizing and externalizing expressions of dysfunction, Vol. 2.* Hillsdale, NJ: Erlbaum.

Malatesta, C. Z., Culver, C., Tesman, J., & Shepard, B. (1989). The development of emotion expression during the first two years of life. *Monographs of the Society for Research in Child Development* (pp. 1-104). Chicago: University of Chicago Press.

Malatesta, C. Z., Grigoryev, P., Lamb, C., Albin, M., & Culver, C. (1986). Emotion socialization and expressive development in preterm and fullterm infants. *Child Development, 57,* 316-330.

Malatesta, C. Z., & Haviland, J. M. (1982). Learning display rules: The socialization of emotion in infancy. *Child Development, 53,* 991-1003.

Malatesta, C. Z., & Izard, C. E. (1984). Facial expression of emotion in young, middle-aged, and older adults. In C. Z. Malatesta & C. E. Izard (Eds.), *Emotion in adult development.* Beverly Hills: Sage Publications.

Malatesta, C. Z., Jonas, R., Shepard, B., & Culver, C. (in preparation). Facial expressions of emotion in younger and older Type A's.

Oster, H. (1978). Facial expression and affect development. In M. Lewis & L. A. Rosenblum (Eds.), *The development of affect* (pp. 43-76). New York: Plenum.

Panksepp, J. (1986). The anatomy of emotions. In R. Plutchik & H. Kellerman (Eds.), *Emotion: Theory, research, and experience* (Vol. 3, pp. 91-124). New York: Academic Press.

Scherer, K. R. (Ed.). (1988). *Facets of emotion: Recent research:* Hillsdale, NJ: Lawrence Erlbaum Associates.

Scherer, K. R. (July, 1990). The role of gender in intercultural comparison of emotional experience. In C. Lutz (Chair), *Gender and emotion.* A symposium given at the International Society for Research on Emotion, New Brunswick, NJ.

Schwartz, G. E., Weinberger, D. A., & Singer, J. A. (1981). Cardiovascular differentiation of happiness, sadness, anger, and fear following imagery and experience. *Psychosomatic Medicine, 43,* 343-363.

Shields, S. A. (July, 1990). Paradoxes in the study of gender and emotion. In C. Lutz (Chair), *Gender and emotion.* A symposium given at the International Society for Research on Emotion, New Brunswick, NJ.

Thoresen, C. E., & Low, K. G. (1990). Women and the Type A behavior pattern. In M. J. Strube (Ed.), *Type A behavior.* [Special issue]. *Journal of Social Behavior and Personality, 5,* 117-133.

Tomkins, S. (1962). *Affect, imagery, consciousness: Vol. 1: The positive affects.* New York: Springer.

Tomkins, S. (1963). *Affect, imagery, consciousness, Vol. 2: The negative affects.* New York: Springer.

Tomkins, S. (1982). Affect theory. In P. Ekman (Ed.), *Emotion in the human face* (pp. 353-423). Cambridge: Cambridge University Press.

Tomkins, S. S., & McCarter, R. (1964). *Perceptual and Motor Skills, 18,* 119-158.

Weaver, C. A., Ko, A., Alexander, E. R., Pao, Y., & Ting, N. (1980). The Cornell Medical Index as a predictor of health in a prospective cardiovascular study in Taiwan. *American Journal of Epidemiology, 111,* 113-123.

PART B: THE CLINICAL DIMENSION

Inhibition and Psychosomatic Processes

J. W. PENNEBAKER AND H. C. TRAUE

Whereas psychophysiologists have examined the links between emotion and concurrent autonomic nervous activity, researchers in the field of psychosomatic medicine have been concerned with the long-term health effects of chronic emotions. Although the nature of emotional experience within different diseases has been of interest, a central thrust within psychosomatic medicine has been to investigate the problems associated with the inhibition or suppression of emotions. In this section, we briefly trace the history and development of emotional inhibition and its links to disease.

The Psychosomatic Tradition: Personality and Disease

The roots of modern-day psychosomatics were established by the publications of Helen Flanders Dunbar (e.g., 1935). In her initial books, Dunbar summarized hundreds of case studies by noting the close association between specific emotional states and illness. A recurring theme within her work was that the failure to openly express powerful emotions appeared to be a health risk. Soon after the publication of Dunbar's books, several thinkers who had been influenced by Freud began to systematically study various chronic illnesses and their relations to emotional expression and suppression. The underlying idea behind these studies was that chronic emotions served as a form of wear-and-tear on the body, thus making individuals prone to specific diseases. Indeed, William James (1890) had noted this assumption half a century earlier.

By the early 1940s, Harold G. Wolff and his colleagues (e.g., Wolf, Cardon, Shepard, & Wolff, 1955; Wolff, 1948, 1953) had embarked on a fascinating research career wherein psychosomatic patients suffering from a variety of disorders, such as asthma, headaches, ulcers or hypertension were tested individually in the laboratory. As part of a stress interview, Wolff would ask a given patient about a number of psychologically threatening issues and, at the same time, measure illness-relevant physiological activity. Muscle tension measures, for example, would be monitored when studying headache patients (Traue, 1989a). Two important findings evolved from this work. First, specific emotions were related to specific chronic health problems. Second, health problems were more likely to be evident if the relevant emotions were not openly expressed and/or acknowledged by the patient (for an excellent summary, see Wolf & Goodell, 1968).

Other findings surrounding the health risks of suppressed emotions soon followed. Ruesch (1948) noted that individuals who suffered from various communication deficits (i.e., those who could not freely express their emotions) were over-represented among psychosomatic patients. In Ruesch's terminology, these patients evidenced infantile personality structures with deficient communicative behavior and inappropriate social communication. Stokvis (1953) described suppressed aggressive emotions as a characteristic sign of psychosomatic patients. In an intercultural, comparative study, Wittkower and Lipowski (1966) concluded that the high rate of psychosomatic illnesses in women in Kuwait resulted from their having very little freedom to emotionally express themselves within the culture.

In elaborating his psychoanalytic model of psychosomatics, Franz Alexander (1950) described the controlled emotional tension between submission and dominance towards a close personal object as the primary cause of several health problems such as rheumatic arthritis (RA). RA, in his view, expressed itself as a state of inhibited hostility. Accordingly, increased muscle tension was viewed as a correlate of inhibited aggression and blocked behavior. Inhibition, then, can be understood as an active motorical process by which an unwanted or forbidden behavior is suppressed. Interestingly, Moos and Solomon (1965) examined a sample of women suffering from rheumatic arthritis and their healthy identical twin sisters. Overall, they found that the arthritic sisters were more likely to describe themselves as shy, emotionally inhibited, and socially inactive. When asked about particular happenings during which they reacted with open aggression, the patients could only describe events of long ago, whereas their healthy sisters described events of the immediate past. During a psychodrama following the interview, the healthy women were more self-assured than their rheumatic sisters.

The Specificity Hypothesis within Psychosomatics

An assumption common to Dunbar, Wolff, and Alexander was that specific emotions were related to specific health problems. As noted earlier in the book, this specificity assumption has surfaced within the psychophysiological realm as well. That is, some researchers argue that electrodermal activity is related to inhibition whereas brief cardiovascular changes reflect behavioral activation (Fowles, 1980). The specificity hypothesis within psychosomatic medicine is more broad-ranging and controversial. In its most extreme form, the specificity hypothesis suggests that individuals who often experience and/or fail to express specific emotions will ultimately succumb to specific emotion-related diseases (Alexander, 1950). Note that this is a straightforward causal argument. Anger, for example, is thought to cause heart disease. Cancer reflects suppressed positive and/or negative emotions. As we discuss below, the evidence for the specificity hypothesis is interesting but far from conclusive. In the remainder of this section, we focus on three of the most studied areas within psychosomatic medicine: asthma, heart disease, and cancer.

Emotion and Emotional Expressiveness Related to Asthma.

Alexander (1950) assumed that asthma patients were unable to express anger and hostility due to strong dependency wishes and fears of loss. He argued that the inhibited outward aggression turned inward and caused "vegetative agitation," thereby exacerbating an asthma attack. Unfortunately, most of the psychological links hypothesized by Alexander could never be isolated (Gauthier et al., 1977). The one exception was the finding that asthma patients displayed a deficit in emotionally expressive behavior. In an intriguing experiment employing mental and social stressors, Hahn and Clark (1967) reported that asthmatics were far less likely to make aggressive remarks than controls. In a comparable experiment, Mathé and Knapp (1971) found that stress caused a disturbance of the respiratory system of the asthmatic patients during tense days even though they evidenced less expression of anger and aggression following the experiment compared to controls.

Hollaender and Florin (1983) investigated children with bronchial asthma and a comparable control group during a laboratory test wherein the test person was aggravated by another child playing with him. Overall, the asthma patients showed less anger, less pleasure, and less surprise (assessed by the FACS-system from Ekman & Friesen 1978) compared to a control group. The respiratory function was on the average reduced by 11.3% in asthmatic children compared to a reduction of only 1.3% among controls. The correlation between the reduction of respiratory function and duration of emotional expression was $r = -.50$ ($p < .03$) and the frequency of emotional expression $r = -.33$ (trend). The correlations within the control group were insignificant.

In a related study by Florin and her colleagues (1985), asthmatic and healthy control children underwent the social stress experiment but were also given the opportunity to view a comical movie. As in the first experiment, asthmatic children displayed fewer negative emotions than controls during the stress portion of the procedure. During the comic film, however, asthmatics and controls did not differ in terms of overt emotional behaviors. Interestingly, during both the stressful period and comic movie asthmatics evidenced respiratory disturbances relative to baseline and in relation to controls. Finally, the correlations between expressive behaviors and physiological indexes were negative but not significant in either group.

What are the underlying causes for the reduced expressiveness of asthmatics in stressful situations? Only recently have investigators begun to address this question. One hypothesis is that mothers of asthmatics would express more negative emotions than mothers of non-asthmatic children. The one study that tested this idea used interaction measures of mother-children communication. During a problem discussion the mothers of asthmatic children made more critical remarks and had more critical attitudes than the controls' mothers (Herrmanns et al. 1989, see Florin et al. in this volume). Somewhat broader family systems models have focused on openness and family dynamics in explaining childhood asthma episodes. Minuchin et al. (1975), for example, reported evidence that asthmatics use their physical symptoms as a family signal for distress. That is, whenever family conflict arises, the child develops asthma which then reduces the social conflict. Asthmatic symptoms, then, function as a form of emotional expression.

Anger and Hostility as Predictors of Heart Disease.

Perhaps the most tested hypothesis in psychosomatic medicine is that anger is a contributing cause of coronary heart disease (CHD). Although most psychosomatic investigators agree that there is a solid empirical link between anger and CHD, considerable controversy exists concerning which dimensions, definitions, and measures of anger are most predictive. Currently, a particularly important debate is being addressed that seeks to determine the relative danger of anger versus the suppression of anger in the etiology of CHD.

Perhaps the most systematic work on anger and heart disease evolved from research on Type A behavior (Friedman & Rosenman, 1974; Glass, 1977). As originally conceived, the Type A individual was defined as a person who was hard driving, had a sense of time urgency, and exhibited occasional aggression or hostility. Although these Type A traits were typically correlated, later studies indicated that only the anger/hostility dimension predicted heart disease (Matthews et al., 1977). The obvious questions raised by these initial studies concerned the degree to which anger expression directly contributed to cardiovascular problems.

On the surface, then, the description of Type A as a predictor of coronary heart disease contradicts the general psychosomatic hypothesis of emotional inhibition. Recent studies into the nature of the Type A's emotional expressiveness paint a very different picture. Indeed, work pre-dating the Type A construct noted that the development of CHD was associated with "repressed hostility, inward expression of emotion, and a tendency to suffer in silence" (Gildea, 1949).

Laboratory experiments have shown that Type A's do not generally show aggressive and hostile emotions but do so in situations of challenge – such as during the standardized interview pioneered by Friedman and Rosenman (1974) to identify the Type A behavior pattern. When challenged, Type A's evidence elevations in blood pressure, heart rate, and catecholamine levels (Glass et al., 1980). Independent evidence suggests that there is a link between suppression of hostility, Type A, and susceptibility to heart disease (Haynes et al., 1980). Comparable data with a modified MMPI-scale "repressed hostility" was found by Kantor & Robertson (1977).

An interesting new direction to explain the problem of anger expression in Type A's has been adopted by Howard Friedman and his colleagues (1985; Friedman & Booth-Kewley, 1987). Using meta-analytic strategies, the correlation between measures of Type A and various biological markers of CHD averages +.17. The quite low but highly significant relationship indicates that many Type A's never evidence CHD, and a high number of Type B's do, in fact, suffer from cardiovascular problems. Using a sample of 60 adult males from the Multiple Risk Factor Intervention Trial (MRFIT) who were assumed to be at risk for CHD, Friedman et al. (1985) assessed each patient's degree of Type A and overall emotional expressiveness. Type A was measured by the *Jenkins Activity Survey* (JAS), a self-report instrument. Expressivity was measured in a variety of ways. Non-verbal competence was measured using the *Affective Communication Test* (ACT) – a short self-report scale (Friedman et al., 1980). Objective measures of nonverbal and emotional behavior were based on judges' ratings of a 4 minute videotaped interview. Finally, a variety of medical data were collected at the time of the study.

Using both a measure of Type A and the ACT, Friedman found that the Type A's with high ACT (healthy expressives) and the Type B's with low ACT (genuine type B) were rated healthier than the two other groups. Raters judged them to be more relaxed. Mimic and gestic behavior were factor-analyzed because of the many single scales. An important factor was "repression". Individuals loaded high on this factor when showing crossed legs, little hand movement, and many body-orientated gestures. The Type A's with high ACT loaded significantly lower on the repression factor than Type A's with low ACT. In other words, both healthy groups were less repressive than the two risk-groups. Overall positive correlations between medical health values and the behavior ratings in interview emerged. A comparison of transcripts of the interviews with voice-quality ratings indicated that the high ACT Type B's had verbal contents that were rated friendly and voice-qualities that were rated unfriendly.

Friedman's work indicates that an important difference between Type A and Type B individuals is the nature of their emotional expressivity. Type A may not be problematic *per se*. Rather, its hostile, ambitious form can be destructive if not accompanied by a more emotionally expressive style. This may also be true for Type B's. Only one part of this group is unlikely to develop CHD. Despite their self-reports as outgoing and emotionally expressive, a significant percentage of Type B's are not rated by judges that way. They are motivated to be the center of attention but have poor social skills, poor coping behaviors, and display nervous and inhibited characteristics that are ultimately stressful. Although their words sounded relatively friendly, their tone of voice sounded relatively less friendly (Friedman et al., 1985).

Perhaps the greatest difficulty in pursuing research on Type A is that Type A is not a *psychologically* meaningful construct. The construct was empirically derived from interviews taken from individuals in the months or years before they evidenced cardiovascular problems. The ultimate criterion in defining Type A, then, was CHD rather than emotion or emotion suppression. The Type A idea, although inherently meaningless theoretically, has been extremely worthwhile in pointing to some central health-relevant constructs.

A particularly promising direction has been forwarded by Spielberger and his colleagues (1985) in distinguishing between the expression and suppression of emotion. Using his Anger Expressiveness questionnaire, Spielberger finds that individuals who are high in both anger expressiveness and in supression are the ones most prone to CHD. Interestingly, several researchers now corroborate the link between people who score high on anger suppression, or Anger-In scales, and a variety of pursuasive measures of CHD (e.g. Dembroski, et al., 1985).

Other approaches have also found that various indexes of anger inhibition may place individuals at risk for CHD. Holroyd and co-workers (Appel et al., 1983) reported that a family history of high blood pressure as well as anger inhibition covaried with elevated blood pressure and heart rate reactions. During laboratory-induced stressful tasks using competition, subjects were arbitrarily shocked by the experimenter. The more the subjects expressed their anger, the lower their blood pressure and heart rate responses. These results were replicated with comparable groups using other manipulations of anger (Gorkin et al., 1983). Two longitudinal studies corroborated these effects. In a five-year prospective study of Israeli male public servants, Kahn et al. (1972) found that suppression of anger in social conflicts predicted high blood pressure. Similarly, McClelland (1979) found that measures of inhibited power motivation among males at age 30 predicted elevated blood pressure for the sample at age 50.

The evidence that inhibited anger is associated with CHD, then, is becoming persuasive (cf., Anderson, 1981; Appel, et al., 1983). Although somewhat more speculative, a small number of studies have suggested that anger expression may have potential healing effects. For example, McFarland and Cobb (1967) reported that patients with anger reactions had higher survival chances than patients who exibited little anger after they fell ill. High blood-pressure patients acted less self-assured in psychodrama (Kalis et al., 1957), more controlled and less overt during interviews (Handkins & Munz, 1978), and were less critical than normal persons (Matarazzo, 1954). Blood pressure patients appear to be less sensitive compared to healthy controls towards variations in frustation-free and frustrating interactions in film scenes.

We must be extremely careful in drawing a cause-effect relation in terms of any potential value of anger expression as therapy. Studies that have attempted to get hypertensives to openly express anger or other negative emotions have not found any straightforward cardiovascular benefits (see Lynch, 1977). Similarly, in our own work, we have found hypertensives to be resistant to expressing any moods or emotions either in the laboratory or in more naturalistic settings (Pennebaker, 1990; Pennebaker & Watson, 1988). Further, anger may well be a unique emotion from a psychosomatic perspective. A person who *expresses* anger may not be attuned to the fact that he or she is *feeling* emotion. In other words, the therapeutic value of emotional expressiveness may be in the self-reflection or awareness that one is angry rather than in acting on the anger (Pennebaker, 1989). In short, researchers must make the distinction between a patient's saying, "I feel angry" as opposed to "I am going to hit you in the nose." In a crude sense, both are examples of emotion expression. However, the first is probably beneficial whereas the second may be detrimental.

Interestingly, Tavris (1982) made a similar argument about the complex role that anger plays in the etiology of heart disease. In her view, the actual emotion of anger is less of a problem than the conflicts that may be aroused associated with the anger. When a person is conflicted (or, in our terms, inhibited) about expressing an emotion such as anger, the person should manifest more biological signs of stress. By reflecting on the feeling of emotion, the person can begin to resolve conflicts that may only be exacerbated by the blind expression of anger.

Emotional Expression and Immune Dysfunction

No chapter on inhibition and psychosomatics would be complete without a section on the quickly-advancing area of psychoneuroimmunology. Since the early 1980s, a number of exciting studies have been published that point to the role of emotions and stress in affecting immune function (e.g., Kiecolt-Glaser & Glaser, 1988). Particularly encouraging are a number of projects that note that measures of emotional inhibition or constraint are associated with compromised immune function and cancer.

Personality researchers have found that individual difference measures of constraint are linked to immune problems. Gary Schwartz and his colleagues, for example, have examined an inhibition-related construct that they call repressive coping style. In their initial experiment on this construct, it was found that repressive copers were physiologically responsive to anger-related stimuli (e.g., Weinberger, Schwartz, & Davidson, 1979). Repressive copers are defined as having high responses on the *Marlowe-Crowne Social Desirability Scale* (a constraint measure) and low on the *Taylor Manifest Anxiety Scale* (a negative affectivity marker). Interestingly, individuals who are identified as repressive copers have more disturbed white blood cell counts, including monocyte and eosinophile levels, than non-repressive copers (Jamner, Schwartz, & Leigh, 1988).

There are a number of reports that specifically focus on the role of anger inhibition on cancer. Morris and his collaborators (Greer & Morris, 1975; Morris et al., 1981) interviewed female patients with benign and malignant breast tumors. Those patients with breast cancer showed more signs of suppressing anger than of overt anger. Suppression of anger as an habitual personality characteristic correlated with higher immune globulin-A blood serums (Pettingale, 1977). Immunoglobulin-A serum has a correlation with spreading metastases in breast cancer. These findings in cancer diseases correlate with mortality rates of breast cancer patients.

In studies of patients with malignant melanomas, Temoshok (1985, 1987) reported that several tumor variables correlate with inhibited expressivity. In her first studies, there were differences between higher mitotic rates and less lymphocyte infiltration at tumor base in patients who, after therapy, showed no growth compared to patients with recurrent tumor growth. Both of these biological factors correlated with emotional expressivity which was documented by videotapes of initial interviews. Apparently, expressive persons have a better prognosis in the case of cancerous diseases of the skin.

In a prospective study by Derogatis et al. (1979), patients with longer duration of life after illness showed higher scores on negative emotion scales. Those patients who expressed more hostility, aggression, guilt, and depression survived longer than those patients who reported fewer negative emotions. Physicians rated the emotionally expressive women as being less adjusted and more aggressive toward clinic staff and treatment. Conceptually similar results have been reported for other breast cancer patients (Jensen, 1987) and overall cancer mortality among Western Electric Company employees (Persky et al., 1987). These findings related to cancer may generalize to measures of life expectancy in the elderly. Temoshok (1987) reported that the best psychological predictor of morbidity and mortality in the elderly were subjects' scores on a measure of passivity/aggressivity. The more passive the elderly subjects, the more probable were illness and death.

Finally, it is premature to note that only the inhibition of anger or aggression was linked to cancer and other immune disorders. Sandra Levy and her colleagues (1988) found that the expression of joy is associated with better prognosis once breast cancer is diagnosed than if the person does not express joy.

Beyond Specificity: The Generalized Health Risks of Inhibition

As the cancer research suggests, a specificity model within psychosomatics is probably incomplete. Indeed, a recent meta-analysis of specificity models within psychosomatics found weak evidence that only anger-related emotions specifically predicted CHD. For other disorders, such as ulcers, asthma, and headaches, all other negative emotions that were measured were equally correlated with the health problems (Friedman & Booth-Kewley, 1987).

A central question concerns the role of inhibition in exacerbating specific illnesses or disease. All available evidence suggests that chronic forms of inhibition may serve as a generalized stressor that can affect the cardiovascular system, immune function, autonomic activity, muscle activity and other bodily systems. Evidence for this generalized consequence for inhibition can be seen within the first few years of life. Jerome Kagan and his colleagues (1988), for example, found that children who are assessed as being socially inhibited by the age of 2 years evidence increased cortisol excretion, elevated heart rates, and other biological disturbances. Other studies have found that 3-year old nursery-school children and older children in primary school who are rated as shy or inhibited by their parents or teachers are more frequently absent from school for illness and report more physical symptoms than other children (Pennebaker, Hendler, Durrett, & Richards, 1981). In all studies, the illnesses and symptoms that are found among inhibited children are quite diverse.

Studies with college students and adults find comparable patterns. Emmons and King (1988) reported that generally healthy students who admit having goal conflicts and who inhibit a variety of emotions also suffer from a broad range of health problems. Similarly, studies with health care professionals as well as students by Larson (1990) have examined the personality domain of individuals who habitually keep secrets from others using the *Self-Concealment Scale*. Overall, the authors found that high self-concealers report more physical symptoms, mood disturbances, and health problems. Again, this approach to inhibition suggests that the chronic inhibition of thoughts may result in a variety of health problems.

All things considered, the specificity hypothesis has some validity. Its main value is in suggesting that specific conflicts associated with specific emotions may selectively affect different physiological indices. Research that has focused more on the nature of inhibition, however, has typically not found specificity-relevant effects. That is, the biological work of inhibition may serve as a generalized stressor and can be considered as a risk-factor for health (see Traue & Kraus, 1988). Consequently, psychosomatic researchers should be careful in distinguishing between the adverse health effects of specific emotions or of inhibitory processes related to the emotions. The expression of particular emotions *per se* may be tied to specific physiological changes whereas the inhibitory processes that may block their expression result in global stress responses (Traue, 1989a).

Situationally-Induced Inhibition: The Role of Traumatic Experiences

Historically, most of the work within the field of psychosomatic medicine has focused on chronic psychological and biological processes. Such a personality-based model of health inherently confounds the role of genetics, early experience, and even recent traumatic upheavals in the etiology of illness. Since the 1960s, a new psychosomatic tradition has been growing that points to the important role of particular events in the person's situation that can affect physical health. Although the first forrays into this area examined the events themselves, more recent studies have considered the role of inhibition.

It is now well-established that traumatic life events can increase the probability of disease irrespective of pre-existing individual differences (Holmes & Masuda, 1974). In general, the incidence of disease is a function of the number and severity of certain life events. In addition to the well-documented health correlates of major life events that have been found using the Holmes and Rahe (1967) *Schedule of Recent Experience*, comparable findings have been reported using scales that tap less traumatic daily hassle scales (e.g., Lazarus & Folkman, 1984).

A continuing debate within the literature on life events and daily hassles concerns the reason why these events correlate with health problems. One problem is that individuals high in negative affectivity, or NA, tend to over-report both unpleasant life experiences as well as health problems (Watson & Clark, 1984; Watson & Pennebaker, 1989). NA is defined as the general proclivity to notice and report psychological distress. Central measures of NA include the *Taylor Manifest Anxiety Scale*, Byrne's (1961) *Repression/Sensitization Scale*, and other measures of neuroticism (Costa & McCrae, 1985). When NA measures are used to statistically control for the relations between upsetting life experiences and health, the overall predictive power of the life events drops significantly (Watson & Pennebaker, 1989). Nevertheless, even when NA measures are partialled out, negative life events and daily hassles continue to reliably – albeit weakly – predict health problems.

Why, then, do negative life events correlate with health problems? Recent evidence points to the role of inhibition. A common reaction to personal upheavals is for individuals to talk with others about them. In many cases, however, people are not able to do so. Some life stressors are more difficult to openly discuss than others. Individuals are often reticent to discuss sexual assault, divorce, the death of a child, and personal shortcomings because the topics threaten their friends or they fear humiliation or punishment from others. Consequently, individuals often actively inhibit their desire to talk. Across several correlational studies, Pennebaker and his colleagues have found that people who have had major upheavals are far more likely to become ill if they have not talked about the traumas than if they did talk about them (e.g., Pennebaker, 1989; Pennebaker & Hoover, 1985). These effects hold even after controlling for social support, NA, sex, and demographic factors (e.g., Pennebaker & Susman, 1988). A significant difficulty of life events, then, is that people often actively hold back from discussing them with others. In short, inhibition, rather than the life events *per se*, predicts health difficulties (Pennebaker, 1990).

Comparable effects have been found among samples of people who have faced recent traumatic events. In one study, 19 individuals who had recently suffered the death of their spouses due to car accidents or suicide reported that they had more illness episodes in the year following the deaths if they had not talked with others about their spouses' deaths (Pennebaker & O'Heeron, 1984). These basic findings have been replicated with larger samples, controlling for a variety of potential confounding variables (Stroebe & Stroebe, 1988). In other words, actively avoiding discussions of traumatic experiences appears to pose a significant health risk (see Pennebaker's chapter in this volume for a more detailed discussion of these findings).

Although the inhibition of talking about a trauma is probably unhealthy in its own right, it also contributes to other insidious problems. Talking about a trauma helps individuals to understand and organize the event (Horowitz, 1976). When people are unable to come to terms with the event, they tend to obsess about it for a much longer period. Indeed, recent research suggests that uncontrolled ruminations about unresolved traumas are both psychologically and physically unhealthy (Nolen-Hoeksema, 1990; Pennebaker & O'Heeron, 1984). Viewed from another perspective, inhibition may be dangerous because it does not allow individuals to psychologically resolve their traumatic experiences.

Reversing the Adverse Effects of Inhibition Through Verbal Expression

A clear implication of the inhibition approach is that inducing individuals to express their thoughts and feelings should be associated with health improvements. Research findings from a variety of perspectives support this view.

In his research on dermatological patients, Seitz (1953, quoted from Katz et al., 1957) trained subjects to show their hostile feelings overtly during therapy sessions. He reported that about half of his patients did not follow his instructions. Those subjects who did not comply evidenced poorer dermatological prognosis than those who did. Similarly, Katz et al. (1957) examined exzema patients and measured their abilities to show aggressive emotions. Their expressivity rate predicted how patients would react to a histamine injection. Nine out of twelve expressive patients evidenced an enhanced histological reaction to a subsequent skin test compared with only one out of seven of the nòn-expressive patients.

As a part of the therapy plan for ulcer patients, Brooks and Richardson (1980) taught subjects to become more emotionally expressive as part of a social skills training in social abilities during which emotional expression was practiced. During the sessions, the patients learned how to express aggressive emotions. Overall, the ulcer patients demonstrated significantly less anxiety, fewer ulcer symptoms, and required less medication than a control group. Even in a follow-up 3 years later, the success of the therapy remained stable.

Another strategy that researchers have adopted has been to examine the health effects associated with general forms of psychotherapy. Perhaps the most impressive study within this domain was conducted with a sample of 86 advanced breast cancer patients. David Spiegel and his colleagues (Spiegel et al., 1989) at Stanford University Medical School randomly assigned half the women to weekly group therapy sessions. The therapy sessions encouraged the women to talk about their emotions, experiences, and coping methods with each other in a semi-structured manner. The control patients met with physicians but did not participate in therapy. Although indepth medical exams indicated that the two groups of women were comparable at the beginning of therapy, subsequently, those who participated in the therapy sessions lived, on average, one and a half years longer than controls.

Several epidemiological studies have also demonstrated that once individuals voluntarily begin psychotherapy, medical utilization drops. In an impressive review, Mumford et al. (1981) examined medical use of individuals within over a dozen Health Maintenance Organizations that began to offer psychotherapy. Those individuals who entered psychotherapy evidenced significant drops in medical use. According to the authors, the institution of psychotherapy was efficient and cost-effective.

There are a number of possible reasons that can explain why psychotherapy may have health benefits. In a series of studies, Pennebaker and his colleagues (e.g., Pennebaker & Beall, 1986) randomly assigned healthy college students to conditions in which they wrote either about their traumatic experiences or about superficial topics for 4 consecutive days. Although writing about traumas was associated with a brief increase in self-reported unhappiness, trauma subjects evidenced significant drops in physician use for up to 5 months following the study. Subsequent studies demonstrated that writing about traumatic experiences resulted in the enhancement of immune function as measured by a blastogenic procedure that taps T-lymphocyte response. Although immune function was enhanced on the last day of writing about traumas (as opposed to superficial topics in the control group), the effect tended to persist for up to 6 weeks after the writing sessions (Pennebaker et al., 1988).

According to participants in these and other writing studies, subjects define the psychological value of writing in cognitive terms. That is, they report that writing about traumas helped them to better understand themselves, their emotions, and the situations that they were in. In short, writing may be beneficial in helping individuals to organize and assimilate complex experiences (see Pennebaker, 1990; Pennebaker et al., 1990).

Summary

In this chapter, we have pointed to a variety of research findings that indicate the potential health risks of inhibition. The precise mechanisms that explain the dangers of inhibition are only now beginning to be understood. Although inhibition may be stressful in its own right, it is also associated with other psychological processes. For example, when individuals do not or cannot express their emotions and thoughts, they are also less likely to cognitively organize and resolve them. Indeed, the pure expression of emotions may not be a simple critical factor. If individuals can express their feelings, however, they can more easily relate to others, enhance their social support system, learn from their experiences, and adopt more healthy coping strategies in general.

References

Alexander, F. (1950). *Psychosomatic medicine. Its principles and applications.* New York: Norton.

Anderson, C. D. (1981). Expression of affect and physiological response in psychosomatic patients. *Journal of Psychosomatic Research, 25,* 143.

Appel, M. A., Holroyd, K. A., & Gorkin, L. (1983). Anger and the etiology and progression of physical illness. In L. Temoshok, C. van Dyke, & L. S. Zegans (Eds.), *Emotions in health and illness* (pp. 73-88). New York: Grune & Stratton.

Brooks, G. R., & Richardson, F. C. (1980). Emotional skills training: A Treatment program for duodenal ulcer. *Behavior Therapy, 11,* 198-207.

Byrne, D. (1961). The repression-sensitization scale. Rationale, reliabiltiy and validity. *Journal of Personality, 24,* 334-349.

Costa, P.T., Jr., & McCrae, R.R. (1985). Hypochondriasis, neuroticism, and aging: When are somatic complaints unfounded? *American Psychologist, 40,* 19-28.

Dembrowski, T. M., MacDougall, J. M., Williams, R. B., Haney T. L., & Blumenthal, J. A. (1985). Components of Type A, hostility and anger. In relationship to angiographic findings. *Psychosomatic Medicine, 47,* 219-233.

Derogatis, L. R., Abeloft, M. D., & Melisaratos, N. (1979). Psychological coping mechanisms and survival time in metastatic breast cancer. *JAMA, 242,* 1504-1508.

Dunbar, H. F. (1935). *Emotions and bodily changes.* New York: Columbia University Press.

Ekman, P., & Friesen, W. V. (1978). *Manual for the facial action code.* Palo Alto: Consulting Psychologist Press.

Emmons, R.A., & King, L.A. (1988). Personal striving conflict: Immediate and long-term implications for psychological and physical well-being. *Journal of Personality and Social Psychology, 54,* 1040-1048.

Florin, I., Freudenberg, G., & Hollaender, J. (1985). Facial expressions of emotion and physiological reactions in children with bronchial asthma. *Psychosomatic Medicine, 47 (3),* 354-364.

Fowles, D. C. (1980). The three arousal model: Implications of Gray's two factor theory for heart-rate, electrodermal activity and psychopathy. *Psychophysiology, 17,* 87-104.

Friedman, H. S., & Booth-Kewley, S. (1987). The disease-prone personality: A meta-analytic view of the construct. *American Psychologist, 42,* 539-555.

Friedman, H. S., Hall, J. A., & Harris, M. J. (1985). Type A behavior, nonverbal expressive style and health. *Journal of Personality and Social Psychology, 45,* Nr. 5, 1299-1315.

Friedman, H. S., Prince, L. M., Riggio, R. E., & DiMatteo, M. R. (1980). Understanding and assessing nonverbal expressiveness: The Affective Communication Test. *Journal of Personality and Social Psychology, 35,* 2, 333-351.

Friedman, M., & Rosenman, R. H. (1974). *Type A behavior and your heart.* New York: Knopf.

Gauthier, Y., Fortin, C., Drapeau, P. Breton, J., Gosselin, J., Quintal, L., Weisnagel, J., Tetreault, L., & Pinard, G. (1977). The mother-child relationship and the development of autonomy and self assertion in young (14-30 months) asthmatic children. *Journal of American Academic Child Psychiatry, 16,* 109-131.

Gildea, E. G. (1949). Special features of pesonality which are common to certain psychosomatic disorders. *Psychosomatic Medicine, 11,* 273-281.

Glass, D. C. (1977). *Behavior patterns, stress and coronary disease.* New York: Erlbaum, Hillsdale.

Glass, D. C., Krakoff, L. R., Contrada, R., Hilton, W. F., Kehoe, K., Mannuci, E. G., Collins, C., Snow, B., & Elting, E. (1980). Effects of harassment and competition upon cardiovascular and plasma catecholamine responses in Type A und Type B individuals. *Psychophysiology, 17,* 453-463.

Gorkin, L., Appel, M. A., Holroyd, K. A., Stander, L. J., Saab, P. G., & Upole, V. K. (1983). Family history of hypertension as a determinant of cardiovascular and self-report responding during anger provocation. Paper presented at the Behavioral Medicine Conference, Baltimore (May, 1983).

Greer, S., & Morris, T. (1975). Psychological attributes of women who develop breast cancer: A controlled study. *Journal of Psychosomatic Research, 19,* 147-153.

Hahn, W. W., & Clark, J. A. (1967). Psychophysiological reactivity of asthmatic children. *Psychosomatic Medicine, 24,* 526-536.

Handkins, R. E., & Munz, D. C. (1978). Essential hypertension and self-disclosure. *Journal of Clinical Psychology, 34,* 870-875.

Haynes, S. G., Feinleib, M., & Kannel, W. B. (1980). The relation of psychosocial factors to coronary heart disease in the Framingham Study: III. 8-year incidence of coronary heart desease. *American Journal of Epidemiology, 3,* 37-58.

Hermanns, J., Florin I., Dietrich, M. Rieger, C., & Hahlweg, K. (1989). Maternal criticism, mother-child interaction and bronchial asthma. *Journal of Psychosomatic Research, 33,* 469-476.

Hollaender, J., & Florin, I. (1983). Expressed emotion and airway conductance in children with bronchial asthma. *Journal of Psychosomatic Research, 27,* 4, 307-311.

Holmes, T. H., & Masuda, M. (1974). Life change and illness susceptibility. In B. S. Dohrenwend & B. P. Dohrenwend (Eds.), *Stressful life events: Their nature and effects.* New York: Wiley.

Holmes, T. H., & Rahe, R. H. (1967). *Schedule of recent experience.* University of Washington, Seattle: School of Medicine.

Horowitz, M.J. (1976). Stress responses syndromes. New York: Jacob Aronson.

James, W. (1890). *The principles of psychology* (Vol. 1). New York: Henry Holt.

Jamner, L.D., Schwartz, G.E., & Leigh, H. (1988). The relationship between repressive and defensive coping styles and monocyte, eosinophile, and serum glucose levels: Support for the opioid peptide hypothesis of represion. *Psychosomatic Medicine, 50,* 567-575.

Jensen, M. R. (1987). Psychobiological factors predicting the course of breast cancer. *Journal of Personality, 55,* 317-342.

Kagan, J., Reznick, J. S., & Snidman, N. (1988). Biological basis of childhood shyness. *Science, 240,* 167-171.

Kahn, H. A., Medalie, J. A., Neufeld, H. NM., Riss, E., & Goldbount, V. (1972). The incidence of hypertension and associated factors: The Israeli ischemic heart disease study. *American Heart Journal, 84,* 171-182.

Kalis, B. L., Harris, R. E., Sokolow, M., & Carpenter, L. G. (1957). Response to psychological stress in patients with essential hypertension. *American Heart Journal, 53,* 572-578.

Kantor, S., & Robertson, A. J. (1977). Repressed hostility and coronary heart disease: Reappraisal of a relationship in terms of a meaning-focusses approach to psychological measurement. *Social Science Medicine, 11,* 625-634.

Katz, F., Wittkower, E. D., Vavruska, G. W., Telner, P., & Ferguson, S. (1957). Studies on vascular skin responses in atopic dermatitis: The influence of psychological factors. *Journal of Investigative Dermatology, 29,* 67-78.

Kiecolt-Glaser, J. K., & Glaser, R. (1989). Behavioral influences on immune function: Evidence for the interplay between stress and health. In T. M. Field, P. McCabe, & N. Schneiderman (Eds.), *Stress and coping* (Vol 2). Hillsdale, NJ: Erlbaum.

Larson, D. G. (1990). Self-concealment: Conceptualization, measurement, and health implications. *Journal of Social and Clinical Psychology, 9,* 439-455.

Larson, D. G., & Chastain, R. L. (1988). *Self-concealment: Conceptualization, measurement, and health implications.* Unpublished manuscript, Santa Clara University.

Lazarus, R. S., & Folkman, S. (1984). *Stress, appraisal, and coping.* New York: Springer.

Levy, S. M., Lee, J., Bagley, C., & Lippman, M. (1988). Survival hazards analysis in first recurrent breast cancer patients: Seven-year follow-up. *Psychosomatic Medicine, 50,* 520-528.

Lynch, J. J. (1977). *The broken heart: The medical consequences of loneliness.* New York: Basic Books.

Matarazzo, J. D. (1954). An experimental study of aggression in the hypertensive patient. *Journal of Personality, 22*, 423-447.

Mathé, A. A., & Knapp, P. M. (1971). Emotional and adrenal reactions to stress in bronchial asthma. *Psychosomatic Medicine, 33*, 323-340.

Matthews, K. A., Glass, D. C., Rosenman, R. H., & Bortner, R. W. (1977). Competitive drive, pattern A, and coronary heart disease: A further analysis of some data from the Western Collaborative Group Study. *Journal of Chronic Disease, 30*, 489-498.

McClelland, D. C. (1979). Inhibited power motivation and high blood pressure in men. *Journal of Abnormal Psychology, 88*, 182-190.

McFarland, D. V., & Cobb, S. (1967). Causal interpretations from cross-sectional data: An examination of the stochastic processes involved in the relation between a personal characteristic and coronary heart disease. *Journal of Chronic Disease, 20*, 393-406.

Minuchin, S., Baker, L., Rosman, B., Liebman, R., Milman, L., & Todd, T. (1975). A conceptual model of psychosomatic illness in children. *Archives of General Psychiatry, 33*, 1031-1038.

Moos, R. H., & Solomon, G. F. (1965). Psychological comparisons between women with reumathoid arthritits and their nonarthritic sisters: I. Personality test and interview rating data. *Psychosomatic Medicine, 27*, 135-149.

Morris, T., Greer, S., Pettingale, K. W., & Watson, M. (1981). Pattern of expression of anger and their psychological correlates in women with breast cancer. *Journal of Psychosomatic Research, 25*, 111-117.

Mumford, E., Schlesinger, H. J., & Glass, G. V. (1981). Reducing medical costs through mental health treatment: Research problems and recommendations. In A. Broskowski, E. Marks, & S. H. Budman (Eds.), *Linking health and mental health* (pp. 257-273). Beverly Hills, CA: Sage.

Nolen-Hoeksema, S. (1990). *Sex differences in depression.* Stanford, CA: Stanford University Press.

Pennebaker, J. W. (1989). Confession, inhibition and disease. In: L. Berkowitz (Ed.), *Advances in Experimental Social Psychology, 22* (pp. 211-244). New York: Academic Press.

Pennebaker, J. W. (1990). *Opening up: The healing power of confiding in others.* New York: William Morrow.

Pennebaker, J. W., & Beall, S. K. (1986). Confronting a traumatic event: Toward an understanding of inhibition and disease. Journal of Abnormal Psychology, 95, 274-281.

Pennebaker, J. W., Colder, M., & Sharp, L. K. (1990). Accelerating the coping process. *Journal of Personality and Social Psychology, 58*, 528-537.

Pennebaker, J. W., Hendler, C. S., Durrett, M. E., & Richards, P. (1981). Social factors influencing absenteeism due to illness in nursery school children. *Child Development, 52*, 692-700.

Pennebaker, J. W. & Hoover, C. W. (1985). Inhibition and Cognition: toward an understanding of trauma and disease. In R. J. Davidson, G. F., Schwartz, & D. Shapiro (Eds.), *Consciousness and self-regualtion*, Vol. 4. New York: Plenum.

Pennebaker, J. W., Kiecolt-Glaser, J. K., & Glaser, R. (1988). Disclosure of traumas and immune function: Health implications for psychotherapy. *Journal of Consulting and Clinical Psychology, 56,* 239-245.

Pennebaker, J. W., & O'Heeron, R. (1984). Confiding in others and illness rates among spouses of suicide and accidental death victims. *Journal of Abnormal Psychology, 93,* 473-476.

Pennebaker, J. W., & Susman, J.R. (1988). Disclosure of traumas and psychosomatic processes. *Social Science and Medicine, 26,* 327-332.

Pennebaker, J. W., & Watson, D. (1988). Blood pressure estimation and beliefs among normotensives and hypertensives. *Health Psychology, 7,* 309-328.

Persky, V. W., Kempthorne-Rowe, J., & Shekelle, R. B. (1987). Personality risk of cancer: 20-year follow-up of the Western Electric Study. *Psychosomatic Medicine, 49,* 435-449.

Pettingale, K. W., Greer, S., & Tee, D.(Eds.) (1977). Serum IgA and emotional expression in breast cancer patients. *Journal of psychosomatic Research, 21,* 395-399.

Ruesch, S. (1948). The infantile personality – the core problem of psychsomatic medicine. *Psychosomatic Medicine, 10,* 134-144.

Spiegel, D., Bloom, J. R., Kraemer, H. C., & Gottheil, E. (1989). Effects of psychosocial treatment of patients with metastatic breast cancer. *Lancet, ii,* 888-891.

Spielberger, C. D., Johnson, E.H., Russell, S.F., Crane, R.J., Jacobs, G.A., & Worden, T.J. (1985). The experience and expression of anger: Construction and validation of an anger expression scale. In M.A. Chesney & R.H. Rosenman (Eds.), *Anger and hostility in cardiovascular and behavioral disorders.* Washington: Hemisphere Publishing.

Stokvis, B. (1953). Het probleem van de "specificiteit" in de psychsomatsiche geneeskunde, structur analytisch benadert.

Stroebe, W., & Stroebe, M.S. (1988). Bereavement and health: The psychological and physical consequences of partner loss. New York: Cambridge University Press.

Tavris, C. (1982). *Anger: The misunderstood emotion.* New York: Simon and Schuster.

Temoshok, L. (1983). Emotion, adaptation and disease: A multidimensional theory. In L. Temoshok, C. v. Dyke & L. S. Zegans (Eds.), *Emotions in health and illness.* New York: Grune & Stratton.

Temoshok, L. (1985). Biopsychosocial studies on cutaneous malignant melanoma: Psychosocial factors associated with prognostic indicators, progression, psychophysiology and tumor-host response. *Social Science and Medicine, 20,* 833-840.

Temoshok, L. (1987). Personality, coping style, emotion and cancer: Towards an integrated model. *Cancer Surveys, 6*, 545-567).

Traue, H. C. (1989a). Behavioral inhibition in stress disorders and myogenic pain. In C. Bischoff, H. C. Traue, & H. Zenz (Eds.). *Clinical perspectives on headache and low back pain.* Toronto: Hogrefe & Huber Publishers.

Traue, H. C. (1989b). *Gefühlsausdruck, Hemmung und Muskelspannung unter sozialem Streß.* Göttingen: Hogrefe Verlag.

Traue, H. C., & Kraus, W. (1988). Ausdruckshemmung als Risikofaktor: Eine verhaltensmedizinische Analyse. *Praxis der angewandten Verhaltensmedizin und Rehabilitation, 2*, 85-95.

Watson, D., & Clark, L.A. (1984). Negative affectivity: The disposition to experience aversive emotional states. *Psychological Bulletin, 96*, 465-490.

Watson, D., & Pennebaker, J.W. (1989). Health complaints, stress, and distress: Exploring the central role of negative affectivity. *Psychological Review, 96*, 234-254.

Weinberger, D. A., Schwartz, G. E., & Davidson, R. J. (1979). Low-anxious, high-anxious and repressive coping styles. Psychometric patterns and behavioral and physiological responses to stress. *Journal of Abnormal Psychology, 88*, 369-380.

Wittkower, E. D., & Lipowski, Z. J. (1966). Recent developments in psychosomatic medicine. *Psychosomatic Medicine, 28*, 722-737.

Wolf, S., Cardon, R., Shepard, E., & Wolff, H. G. (1955). *Life stress and essential hypertension.* Baltimore: Williams & Wilkins.

Wolf, S., & Goodell, H. (1968). *Harold G. Wolff's Stress and Disease.* Springfield, Illinois: Charles C. Thomas.

Wolff, H. G. (1937). Personality features and reactions of subject with migraine. *Archives of Neurology and Psychiatry, 37*, 895-921.

Wolff, H. G. (1948). *Headache and other headpain.* New York: Oxford.

Wolff, H. G. (1953). *Stress and disease.* Illinois: Ch. C. Thomas Springfield.

Facial Expression and Introspection
Within Different Groups of Mental Disturbances.

Hans Hufnagel, Evelyne Steimer-Krause, Günter Wagner and Rainer Krause

Our research group has been investigating whether there are specific forms of preconscious interaction strategies in mentally ill persons when they talk with healthy subjects whom they do not know. This investigation has been conducted by making films of 210 subjects involved in a discussion of politics. The group with mental disturbances included (a) 11 male stutterers who could control the audible part of the stuttering (which meant that their partners in the conversation in some cases could not realize that they were talking to a stutterer), (b) 16 male stutterers who openly stuttered, (c) 20 male schizophrenics who were either in- or outpatients (10 each), (d) 30 male and female patients suffering from two forms of psychosomatic diseases (10 women and 10 men had ulcerative colitis and 10 men functional vertebral complaints). The 60 control group subjects were healthy males and females from either Switzerland or southern or southwestern Germany. With but one exception the schizophrenics were diagnosed as paranoid hallucinatric (ICD 9 295.3). Details of the setting as well as of the medical characteristics of the patients were published in Krause (1982) and Krause, Steimer, Sänger-Alt & Wagner (1989). We wanted to simulate a situation in which an experienced clinician could find himself and thus we did not limit the observations made on the subjects to any one specific communication channel (such as facial expression, speech, gestures, body position, gaze patterns, sound/silence distribution, etc). On a theoretical basis we predicted specific forms of algorithms between the different channels depending on the disturbance (for details see again the literature cited above). The starting point of our analysis was always facial expression and successively included the other channels like gaze, on-off patterns, etc. (see for example Kettner, Villenave-Cremer & Krause, 1989, for a content analysis of the speech process).

Data on Facial Expression

A major thrust of this paper is the relationship between facial expression and introspective processes, and this section will only briefly outline the results on facial expression. The data of the stuttering patients were based on comprehensive FACS (Facial Action Coding System, Ekman & Friesen 1978) codings of speech and listener samples. All others were based on online recording and subsequent coding of a 20-minute-long interaction between two subjects, with the help of EMFACS, the "emotional facial coding system" developed by Friesen and Ekman (1984) and computerized by Wagner (1986). The methodology as well as the validity are described briefly in Steimer-Krause, Krause and Wagner, 1989b. The "emotional facial coding system" was designed to register "primary effects", including happiness, contempt, disgust, anger, sadness, or fear. It is important to note that within the healthy control group of men 5,149 facial movements were grouped by segmentation rules into 3,183 facial events. Only 25% of them could be categorized under these primary affects. 16% of our observations were relegated to the category of "unfelt happiness", which is not a genuine affect but consists of different forms of deliberate social smiles. 29% of the events which could not be interpreted by the EMFACS coding system had to be subsumed under "facial illustrators". These are unspecific affective movements of the face and usually of the hands accompanying excited speech but giving no information on the quality of the affect. So in the end only 24% of the facial behavior of the healthy subjects was "ideosyncratic".

The healthy women showed significantly more facial affect than the males (chi-square 245.06, df.=1, 0.1%). This was true for all affects besides anger, fear and surprise. Fear and surprise were too rare in both groups, and anger was shown significantly more frequently in males (chi-square 26.03, df=1, 0.1%). Both groups of schizophrenic patients, as well as the psychosomatic patients of the nonconversion type (ulcerative colitis), showed significant less total facial activity irrespective of gender. The corresponding values in order of frequency are: healthy women 716 affects, women with ulcerative colitis 638, men with functional spine disturbances 525, healthy men 304, outpatient schizophrenics 175, and inpatient schizophrenics 164. One affect proved especially prominent for each group: contempt was found prominent in the 20 schizophrenics with a percentage value of 46% vs 19% in healthy subjects, while disgust was especially apparent in all 20 colitis ulcerosa patients with 30% vs 5.3% in healthy subjects. The conversion type psychosomatic patients showed a significant level in facial activity as compared to the healthy male subjects (525 vs 304), which was related to the tremendous augmentation of fear (83 vs 2), sadness (50 vs 21) and disgust (159 vs 67) accompanied by a low frequency in anger (21 vs 41). The patients with functional spine disturbances showed more blending, that is, the synchronous innervation of two affects.

Interestingly, their healthy conversation partners adapted quantitatively to their partners' facial style. When healthy subjects conversed with likewise healthy persons, irrespective of gender, the most frequent primary affect was happiness (46%), followed by contempt (23%), disgust (18%), sadness (6.%), anger (4%) and fear and surprise (0.2% each).

Data on the Affect Ratings

Subjective ratings were performed by asking the subjects to rate themselves and their conversation partners on a 30 item scale checking the intensity of the emotions of disgust, contempt, fear, sadness, anger, surprise and happiness. The rating is based on a translation of Izard's Differential Emotion Scale (DES) (Izard, 1982) and allows for three items per affect which are rated on a five-point intensity scale. Since there were no data on using this scale in German speaking countries, we carried out an item analysis, checking the difficulty of the items as well as Cronbach's Alpha. Not surprisingly, the ratings for positive affects such as happiness, interest and surprise follow more or less a normal distribution whereas all negative affect ratings are skewed to the left, with disgust scaling to the extreme and fear being among the mildest. This distribution of ratings does not follow the frequency of facial activities: instead, the criteria of average strength of expression and frequency distribution both revealed a decrease in the degree of the rated affectivity from interest, over happiness, surprise, fear, to anger and then contempt, with disgust and sadness being extremely rare. It seems quite plausible that in a political discussion people might very well experience anger and emotions of anxiety without directly venting them, instead covering them up by smiling or somehow "changing" them into indications of contempt on the way to the periphery of the body. On the other hand there also seems to be considerable social repression on admitting to feelings of disgust, contempt and sadness within healthy subjects. When self-ratings of all groups are compared with one another using the Kruskal-Wallis-Test, there are significant differences for fear ($p = 0.03$); sadness and surprise just narrowly missed reaching significance ($p = 0.8$, $p = 0.9$). The schizophrenics always demonstrated the highest value, the control group the lowest. Comparing the patients' ratings of their healthy partners, the difference for a combined measure of fear, sadness, and anger is significant ($p = 0.05$) with conversion and schizophrenic patients ranking highest and the control group lowest. Sadness again is significantly different in the same sequence. Healthy subjects interacting with the inpatient schizophrenics rated themselves highest in anhedonia.

The inpatient schizophrenics influenced their partners in the most consistently negative way. This occurred in spite of the fact that the healthy subjects did not realize that they were talking to a diagnosed schizophrenic since none of the latter acted in an openly psychotic way. In a clinical interview which took place with each subject after the discussion, some of the subjects did comment on their partners being "strange" or that they in fact felt anger at the experimenter for having brought them together with such people for such a task. But no subject ever mentioned the concept of a mental disturbance to explain the behavior of his partner in the dyad. The negative self-representation was internalized by the healthy subjects who then felt helpless and insecure, and this congruence in self-description made the two partners appear very similar in the analysis of their comments, despite the fact that the group of inpatients did give the worst description of themselves.

The dynamics of verbal influence have been described elsewhere (Kettner, Villenave-Cremer & Krause, 1979), but before discussing the data on facial display and its relation to introspection, a brief summary of our findings on these dynamics is appropriate. The colitis and schizophrenic patients talked less than their partners, while stutterers engaged more in talking than their partners did, irrespective of whether they stuttered openly or not.

Among dyads consisting of two healthy persons there was a negative correlation between the amount of words that one partner spoke compared to the amount spoken by the other (r= -.89), indicating that as a group there is a law within healthy subjects that the more one partner speaks, the less the other one engages in the conversation. This tendency towards splitting the roles between either talking or listening was reduced in the dyads consisting of a healthy person and a schizophrenic outpatient (-.54) but nevertheless present, which means that usually the schizophrenic patient was able to "seduce" his partner into talking more. For the stutterers and their partners as a group this was not the case (.02), indicating a less homogenous pattern of mutual influence among these groups. This is plausibly related to the fact that the healthy subjects as a group responded in at least two different ways to the stuttering. For example, some healthy partners of stutterers tried to hold up a talk despite the fact that they were massively hindered by the stutterers' speech behavior, while the others soon gave up these attempts.

In a later section we will discuss the data for speech behavior being strongly regulated through non-verbal behavior and for facial behavior being tightly woven into the speech-regulation system. At the present we will treat the results of the face/introspection interaction in the different groups.

Face Introspection Interaction

Since the data structure is extremely complicated we will only report some of the results. Firstly, we will compare male ulcerative colitis patients with inpatient schizophrenics and the normal control group. Secondly we will give details of our analysis of the happiness and anger "systems", with "system" designating an analysis in which codings of the facial expressions of both interacters are used as a starting point for correlational studies. Of course, the facial expressions themselves cannot yet be considered as the source of influence, and thus the correlations do not clarify questions of causal influence. The correlations with all other affect ratings are included here, since facial affect can be related to the experience of an assumed antagonistic emotion. Table 1 gives a listing of 12 possible interactions between facial expressions, and tenders preliminary explanations.

Table 1:   Possible relations between facial expression and affect experience in a dyadic interaction.

1.	mimic I	mimic II	contagion
2.	mimic I	rating I s	selfcongruence
2.	mimic I	rating I o	projection
3.	mimic I	rating II s	identification
4.	mimic I	rating II o	decoding ability II
5.	mimic II	rating II s	selfcongruence
6.	mimic II	rating II o	projection
7.	mimic II	rating I s	identification
8.	mimic II	rating I o	decoding ability
9.	rating I s	rating I o	resemblence I
10.	rating II s	rating II o	resemblence II
11.	rating I o	rating II s	validity of judement I
12.	rating I s	rating II o	validity of judement II

explanations: s = self
o = object
I = interaction partner I
II = interaction partner II

Some of the relations empirically supported by our data base are not included since the schema would be too complex. For the sake of simplicity, denial can serve as an introduction because here a signal such as the angry face is detected and in a lawful fashion interpreted as something else. The most important mechanism, namely the attribution of an affect either to one's self or to the other, is a superordinate mechanism, since two contradictory reactions, such as denial and, for example, projection, can both exist at the same time (Suppes & Warren, 1975). For a good number of possible relations we do not yet have a terminology and of course this kind of nomenclature would have to be validated. The listing is thus meant only as a starting point to understand and describe the hypothetical processes. The analysis of the data was conducted in such a way that the frequency with which every person facially expressed a primary affect was correlated with all his and his partner's affective facial expressions as well as with the ratings of all primary affects concerning the self as well as the other person. For the sake of uniformity we will talk about "self" and "object representations" for describing the data. This entailed developing a 42 x 42 matrix, which was calculated using Kendall's tau because of the above mentioned distribution of the data, which follows neither a normal distribution nor an interval scale. In addition, close inspection of the frequency distribution of answers reveals that the psychological difference between "no disgust" (Value 0) and "a little bit of disgust" (Value 1) was in fact higher than that between "a little bit of disgust"

and "disgusted" (Value 2), which may be related to the possibility that acknow-
ledging negative affect at all seems to imply a qualitative jump. (For this reason
some of the data were dichotomized and, instead of Kendall's tau, phi-co-
efficients for fourfold tables were computed categorizing the subjects according
to their expressivity [for example "high anger"] and their rating for intensity
[high or low], and thus all correlations were higher with that method.) So we
assumed that Kendall's tau is less prone to statistical artifacts. If 40 dyads of
healthy and schizophrenic as well as psychosomtic patients are analyzed together
no significant correlations between facial expression and affect ratings can be
found. This would not be unexpected if we assumed that every group of dyads
has antagonistic rules of associating facial affective behavior and introspective
ratings together, which could well balance out to correlations of zero after aver-
aging. What proved to be quite stable among healthy males talking to one another is the significant relation between the self- and the object ratings. The resemblance ratings for all affects except fear (-0.03) are all above .55 which
means that they are significantly different from zero on a 1% level. Quite apparently, in such a situation healthy males generally tend to augment the experienced degree of resemblance between their self- and their object-ratings with the
exception of situations described as involving fear. The high level of perceived
resemblance between disgust and sadness is related to the fact that both affects
were regularly rated as not being present in both the self and the healthy partner.
Women's ratings seem to be much more differentiated. There is a high degree of
resemblance in fear (.65**) and happiness (.78**), but only a low degree in anger (.31) and sadness (.23).

In order to simplify the complicated relations, we will always start with the
simplest possible analysis for the above mentioned three groups for one affect,
then proceed to the most complicated level for the same affect and then use the
same routine for the other affects.

The Happiness System

Healthy males showed a mild but reliable tendency to induce mutual facial happiness. Facial happiness, as defined in the correlation matrix, was based solely
on expressions of happiness actually felt, excluding all zygomaticus major activities during which additional facial or temporal cues for such an attribution are
missing. This made up 23% of the facial activity. So, for example, "smiling because of feeling miserable" was not included. Facial expression did not correlate
with self rated happiness, whereas self and object representations regarding happiness did correlate highly as already mentioned. Within the groups in which
the male inpatient schizoprenic patients were involved, no mutual induction of
facial happiness could be found. Within the group of the patient's healthy partners, facial happiness and self rating were negatively correlated (-.17), which fits

the negative correlation between facial happiness and the rating for the sick partner (-.43). The more the healthy partner smiles, the unhappier he considers the other, and vice versa. Thus the usual correlation between self and object representation disappears. Within the schizophrenic group resemblance can still be found; however it is only very low (.45). Within the male dyads with ulcerative colitis patients there was substantial mutual induction of facial happiness (.64*). The self and object representations concerning happiness have substantially high correlates on the side of the patients (0.54), but are low on the side of their partners (.29). There is a moderate "self congruence happiness" on the side of the partner (.41) and a negative one on the side of the colitis patients (.13). There is a very high negative correlation (-.25) between the partners' rating of the patients' happiness and the self rating of the patient. In addition there is a high negative correlation between the partner's self rating and the patient's self rating (-.07). This means that the patient's assumption of resemblance in happiness is not shared by their partners. On the contrary, the more the patient describes himself as feeling happy the less his partner attributes this state to him, or the other way round. This can be interpreted in different ways. In any case the patients make themselves pseudohappy by denying that their partners do not share their self-concepts and their phantasies about their being really happy. We will only go into a detailed explanation for this after discussing the results of the network of relations between happiness and the other affects.

Within the control group we find not only the mild, contagious mutual induction of smiling, but also 12 substantially negative correlations for situations during which smiling suppresses the rating for negative primary affect, the most influential ones being for anger object representations (-.45, -57) and self representations (-.57, -.40). There are negative correlations for self rating of sadness, disgust and object contempt ratings. Thus, despite the fact that there is no direct relationship between rated and facial happiness there is a powerful suppression of negative affect rating, both in the self and in the object representation through felt happiness expressions. This influence could be functioning either through attribution of benevolent motives to the other or directly as a form of happiness antidote. However, this system does not work so smoothly at all for the inpatient schizophrenics and their partners. The more the patient showed a happy face, the less he attributed sadness (-.64), fear (-.48), anger or disgust to the self structure. The other person's happy face was, however, positively correlated with the disgust (.46), contempt (.37) and anger (.46) ratings for the partner. This means that somehow the patients felt that the other was not laughing with but at him. The happiness system within the dyads consisting of patients with colitis again works quite differently.

Whereas finding a facial expression of happiness in the healthy partner still functioned as a suppressor for feeling sadness, and for reporting anger in reports on self attribution, and likewise suppressed sadness in the object attribution, a positive relation was found between contempt and happiness in the partner's self structure and fear in his attribution to the patient. For the patients the only evidence of a suppressive function of smiling is the partner's facial happiness on the patient's self rating for sadness and the patient's facial happiness on his self representation of anger. In all other cases the attribution of negative affects such as disgust, contempt, sadness and anger towards the object representation was positively correlated with the patients' happy faces. This means that, depending on the amount of their own happy expressions, the attribution rules of the other person's expression were changed in a negative direction. There is a marked dissimilarity in the happiness ratings of the two partners. The more one person attributes having a feeling of happiness in himself, the less the other follows suit. Since the group of patients assumed similarity in the self and the object rating of happiness, this might reflect a consequence of the well known denial of aggressive feelings as a defense mechanism which has been described as being specific for these patients (Sandweg, 1989). Whether this is the case can only be answered after analyzing the anger system in the same way.

The Anger System

Again there was a high level of resemblance between the self and the object attributions within the ratings of the two healthy groups when interacting with each other (.55), which is reflected in the similarity of the self representations (.60). Between facial anger and self representations slight negative correlations were observed (-.23 and -.21). The correlation between anger expression of the two interactands was practically zero.

In the dyads with schizophrenic patients quite a substantial mutual contagion of anger was observed: .56. Facial anger was reflected in the self attribution of each of the partners (.46) and negatively correlated with the patient's self attribution (-.41), which means the more often the schizophrenic patient made an angry face, the less he thought he was angry and vice versa. The other person's face functioned as a strong stimulus for the patient (-.35). Again there was considerable dissimilarity in the ratings on self structures (-28), but a mild congruence towards the ratings on the partner, which was unusual in dyads with healthy partners in the anger system. The patients with ulcerative colitis and their partners showed a negative correlation of facial anger (-.72). Self and object representations of anger by the patients were positively correlated with the partners' angry face. Self attribution of anger in the partner was negatively correlated with the patient's rating of his partner's anger (-.31). Again there is a negative correlation between the face expressing anger and the self attribution of anger (-.52), but in addition the attribution of anger to other persons was also governed by this process (-.38). Again there was the feeling of experiencing a high degree of resemblence on the part of the patient (.67) and none on the part of one's partner, and likewise the partners displayed a similar tendency towards observing facial anger and then describing their own self attribution (.29). Within healthy dyads anger expression was negatively related to the attribution of fear towards the partner (-.51, -.36), which fits in nicely with the observation that facial anger is correlated with mutual attribution of feelings of happiness to the self and the other. Apparently the men seemed to be enjoying their conversational "fights" and the associated feelings of fearlessness, which is also seen in the fact that these "fighting dyads" had the most productive outcome in the content of the discussions. Within the dyads with schizophrenic patients anger expression had a different function. For the patient's self rating, his own anger expression had a benevolent function and was negatively related to all negative affects of the self representation and positively related to happiness. For his partner it was just the opposite: Besides the negative correlation with fear (-.34), angry faces were positively correlated with feeling disgust (.45), contempt (.27) and attributing anger (.57) to the self and sadness to the object. The patient correctly attributed anger to the other person according to its frequency of occurrence (.54), while vice versa the patient's probability for admitting fear was related to his and his partners' having an angry face (.51 and .45).

Within the dyads of patients with colitis the situation, once again, was different. Expressing anger had no positive relation to the patients' own self attributions. Instead, their anger expression was correlated with the attribution of anger (.49) and was highly significantly correlated with sadness (.73*) in self ratings. The other person's angry face had "dire" consequences for these patients: First, there was a substantial negative correlation (-.72) between both subjects in anger expression, which was significantly different from that of both the schizophrenics and the healthy subjects. The patients felt anxious (.56) and assumed that the other was full of contempt (.55) and anger (.70) depending on the partner's frequency of anger expression. Anger expression was negatively correlated to contempt expression in the other person (-.48) and positively correlated to the patient's own feelings of having contempt (.51). The healthy subjects attributed contempt (.54), and disgust (.54) to their partner depending on their expressing anger, and in fact disgust and contempt expression within the healthy partners correlated quite substantially (.71**).

Discussion

The results of this work are preliminary and have to be replicated. With the small number of subjects included in the groups only very high correlations could be considered as significantly different from zero (the null hypothesis). In many cases the hypothesis is not different from zero but the difference between the partners is interesting, such as the negative correlation between face and self attribution within the schizophrenic group (-.41) as opposed to the positive correlation (.46) evidenced in their partners. In addition low or zero correlations are important elements in preliminary heuristic research. Nevertheless the following interpretation can only be considered tentative. It relies heavily on the knowledge we have gathered already on interaction processes (Krause, 1981; Krause, Steimer & Wagner, 1989; Steimer-Krause, Krause, & Wagner, 1989) and the clinical interviews we made with each subject after completion of the empirical part of the experiment.

It is quite evident that there is a high degree of attribution of resemblance within healthy dyads for anger and happiness accompanied by only low direct influence on the self and object representation. This is plausibly due to the fact that the generation of affect in healthy dyads is not so much a consequence of the social (facial, mimic-based) relation but of the content of the discussion, indicating that in such a theme-centered conversation the two partners might become mutually angry at, for example, politicians who allow pollution or airplane maneuvers at low altitudes. This anger must be distinguished from the feelings directly attributed to the self or the other person in the talk and involves a third common subject which in the process of social interaction generates common feelings which can differ substantially from those prompted by the talkers for each other. In such a case it is not surprising when anger (at the topic) correlates with happiness (due to the conversational partner's reactions) since it is often relieving to have a "common enemy" and very often it keeps the ongoing process devoid of friction. That implies that the self structure, in trying to solve the task, is not genuinely afflicted. But precisely this, apparently, is rarely the case in the dyads with the patients. The task of conducting a conversation on a political topic in one way or another directly affects the self structure, which means that the feelings shown or only subjectively deduced about the other person are much more relevant for the experience of one's self and the other person. The fundamental problem with the signalling of affect is that there is no information within the signal itself to which it uniquely "belongs", in a one-to-one fashion. From research in therapeutic interactions we know that a negative facial affect such as disgust might for example be shown when a patient is telling about her father's despiteful actions and attitudes towards her as a little girl, at the same time that she denies to herself any conscious awareness of his rejection of her. Frequently these patients are not able to develop empathetic feelings for themselves as the victims, since they act in identification with the former aggressor or so repress the events of a trauma that they absolutely fail to recognize these warnings signs when a similar victimizing situation starts developing (for a cogent study of the victims' tendencies to such revictimization, see especially Kluft, 1992). In doing so, they create a social situation whereby the social partner, for example the therapist, may experience the affect of the victim when he attributes the facial display of disgust to himself, which is ironically correct, and unconsciously effective, in that following a putative compulsion to repetition, the patients may repeatedly create the same situations, exchanging active and passive roles. This usually includes an exchange of self and object representation in relation to the visible affective signs (Krause & Lütolf, 1988).

If we consider the whole interaction as a cybernetic system, then at least for healthy subjects we have no congruence between facial expression and the rating for the self representation regarding the expressed affect. For the negative affects the relation is usually reversed. So the idea that the signalling of experienced affect is correlated to mental health cannot be deduced from our data. This seemingly self congruent behavior in an anger system could plausibly be interpreted as just being impolite and rude to the other (see Krause, 1979), since it excludes the influence of the other person's facial signalling. Since we usally do not see our own face but only that of our partner's, facial expression is an ideal signal system for blurring or misunderstanding one's own self and object representations, which is of course necessary for empathetic understanding.

The ability to monitor one's own facial affect is less developed than that of monitoring the voice since there is no equivalent to the listening process in which a speaker hears his own voice while talking. There can of course be too much empathy in that the other person's signalling of affect governs one's own experiences to the exclusion of the ability to identify self-processed feelings. This seems to be the case for the relations which are described as "narcissistic symbiotic", which rather well covers the above mentioned fact that for some persons, in whatever interaction they are involved in, their self system is directly afflicted by the other person's expressed feelings, and every affective sign from the conversational partner has to be checked to see whether it is related, not so much to the topics of a conversation, but to one's own person. Understandably, this can be a highly exacting state of affairs since even minute segments of an interaction can exert a tremendous influence on the self structure. This might prompt a self-defence in the form of forced trials to reduce the other person's influence in different ways. But we have to offer a caveat here: The kind of data which we have presented does not reflect the full degree of the factual influence of facial signalling in the dyad. A detailed temporal analysis of all channels which we can observe in dyads shows that the highly organized intertwining of speaking, gaze and facial behavior of both partners which we find in healthy dyads seems to be somehow disturbed in a dyad with schizophrenic patients. For example, in conversations within normal dyads the person listening up to a particular moment produces a burst of facial activity in the moment the speaker interrupts his vocalization process and looks at his auditor, and this interruptive gazing behavior, which did not take place during the talking phase, dictates a brief moment of mutual gaze, looking, signalling and silence (Jablonsky, 1989). This is one of the moments which can be considered as a form of parallel processing whereby the evaluation of the content of the speech and the social situation is monitored at the same time. Within schizophrenic dyads, on the other hand, gazing, thinking pauses, and facial signalling are not organized around this dyadic congruence. On the contrary, they seem to smile when the other person cannot see it, and they avoid smiling as a response to the other person's smiling. Again this seems to be a consequence of the inability to process content and self presentation in a condensed action. Despite the lack of direct influence of facial expression in the self representation in the healthy dyads, facial signalling has a profound influence on self and object ratings but in a more indirect way, by suppressing seemingly antagonistic experiences, such as anger and fear or happiness and anger, etc. If two interactands do not share these implicit rules about affective antagonisms the dyad obviously runs into great difficulties. For example, as in the schizophrenic patients, it does not make much sense in a conversation to display a maximum of facial happiness, if the other person's happiness is attributed to "Schadenfreude": this is a German term meaning being happy when others are in difficulties; literately translated it means "harmjoy". It seems to be the fundament of a lot of laughter in comical, "slapstick" movies (like the ones with Jerry Lewis: see Keßler & Schubert, 1989). It involves some form of splitting in the service of the ego, whereby the helpless parts of the self structure are attributed to the victim to be laughed at. These processes are not necessarily aggressive in nature, since laughter at the same time supresses the augmentation of negative affect.

For the schizophrenic patient the facial display of anger has approximately the same function for self experience as the happiness system has for the healthy person: It suppresses negative attributions of the self structure. Literature on the relation between the security and autonomy systems which are related to binding and aggressive behavior (Bischof, 1985) makes this interpretation intriguing, since the induction of mutually positive states of feeling creates a high risk to the coherence of the self structure of the patient. Our results are in favor of Kernberg's idea that reversing the function of the happiness and anger systems in the patients serves a defensive purpose (Kernberg, 1975).

Obviously the signals are decoded in a coherent way, but their meaning is changed depending on who is showing the signal. Thus, one's own facial anger is systematically decoded as non-anger in the self system, which means that there is a systematic rupture in the self structure within the colitic patients as well as the schizophrenic patients. Both groups tend to be deeply influenced by their partner's direct facial signalling, which opens up the interesting idea that from a cybernetic point of view the partner and parts of the patient constitute a "system" in which some subsystems of the patient are literally split off. The hallmark difference is that facial signalling of anger follows a positive feedback loop in the schizophrenic dyad and a negative one in the colitic dyad. From clinical reports as well as research on expressed emotion (Goldstein, Hand & Hahlweg, 1986) we know that very rapid escalations of negative affect can occur within families, escalations which are never experienced in such an intensity in other families. This may well result from the facts (a) that the families feel intuitively that their smiling no longer binds them together or soothes them, but (b) that they cannot feel aggressive at this situation or at that time. On the contrary, in our patients, the signalling of anger seems to soothe negative affect in the self structure, probably by augmenting the autonomy of the patient. In addition the patients correctly interpret the other person's angry face, but not their own. This is a form of defense mechanism based on denial and on an endless loop of positive feedback of anger which cannot be monitored by the patient since self representation is reversed in signalling. The latter is true for the colitic patients also, but here the feedback system is negative: The more one signals anger the less the other does. This may be due to their not having a common cause for anger about something else, as in healthy dyads, and instead the anger is decoded as being relevant to the self structure. Since the angry face of the other person is decoded correctly the defense is not in the perception system but in the interpretation of that person. One's own anger signalling is thus reversed in its meaning. The angry face of the other acts as an inhibitor for the patient's signalling. This strategy leads to appeasement and denial which opens up the door for fear and in fact for being seen with contempt by the partner.

Summary

107 dyads discussing politics 20 minutes long were requested to rate the facial expressions as well as affectivity in themselves and their partner. 27 were male stutterers, who either were able to control their speech disturbance (11) or openly stuttered (16), twenty of the subjects were male schizophrenics in either out- or inpatient treatment (10 each); 30 others had a psychosomatic disease, either ulcerative colitis (20) or a functional spinal disturbance of a conversion type (10). Ten of the colitic patients were female, the others male. 30 healthy subjects talking to another, similarly healthy person (30 subjects) served as a control group; 20 were female and 40 male. There were no mixed sex dyads. The healthy partners of the patients were naive as to the diagnosis of their confederates. Data on the alterations in facial expression of both patients and their partners have already been published (Krause, Steimer, Sänger-Alt & Wagner, 1989; Steimer-Krause, Krause & Wagner, 1990). Here we report on the relations between introspective as well as expressive data within the different groups and show that the induction of feeling in one's conversational partner through facial signaling varies according to whether one of the partners has a diagnosis of schizophrenia or ulcerative colitis or is a healthy subject.

References

Anstadt, T., & Krause, R. (1989). The expression of primary affects in portraits drawn by schizophrenics. *Psychiatry, 52*, 13-24.

Bischof, N. (1985). *Das Rätsel Ödipus.* München: Piper.

Friesen, W.F., & Ekman, P. (1984). *EMFACS-7: Emotional Facial Action Coding System, Version 7.* Unpublished manuscript.

Goldstein, M.J., Hand, I., & Hahlweg, K. (Eds.) (1986). *Treatment of schizophrenia.* New York: Springer.

Izard, C.E. (1977). *Human emotions.* New York: Plenum.

Jablonsky, D. (1989). *Zwei dyadische Interaktionen: Versuch einer differentiellen, "multikanalen" Analyse.* Thesis, University of Saarland, Saarbrücken, Germany.

Kernberg, O. (1975). *Borderline conditions and pathological narcissism.* New York: Aronson.

Keßler, B.H., & Schubert, H.J. *Mimische Reaktionen auf Filme mit aggressivem Humor: Medienpsychologie.*

Kluft, R.P. (1992). Dissociation and subsequent vulnerability and revictimization: Implications for the facilitation of psychotherapy with hypnosis. In W. Bongartz, B. Bongartz, & V. Gheorghiu (Eds.), *Hypnosis: 175 years after Mesmer: Recent developments in theory and application.* Konstanz (Germany): Universitätsverlag.

Krause, R. (1979). Zusammenhänge zwischen psychischer Gesundheit, Sozialisation und Kreativität. *Zeitschrift für klinische Psychologie und Psychotherapie, 27*, 49-74.

Krause, R. (1982). A social psychological approach to the study of stuttering. In: C. Fraser and K.R. Scherer (Eds.), *Advances in the social psychology of language.* Cambridge: University Press, 77-122.

Krause, R., & Lütolf, P. (1988). Facial indicators of transference processes within psychoanalytic treatment. In: H. Dahl and H. Kächele (Eds.), *Psychoanalytic process research strategies.* Heidelberg: Springer, 257-272.

Krause, R., Steimer, E., Sänger-Alt, C., & Wagner, G. (1989). Facial expression of schizophrenic patients and their interaction partners. *Psychiatry, 52*, 1-12.

Sandweg, R. (1989). Zur Psychodynamik und Therapie chronisch-entzündlicher Darmerkrankungen. *Praxis der Psychotherapie und Psychosomatik, 34*, 1-9.

Steimer-Krause, E., Krause, R., & Wagner, G. (1990). Interaction regulations used by schizophrenic and psychosomatic patients. Studies on facial behavior in dyadic interactions. *Psychiatry, 53*, 209-228.

Suppes, P., & Warren, H. (1975). On the generation and classification of neurotic defense mechanisms. *International Journal of Psychoanalysis, 56*, 405-414.

Villenave-Cremer, S., Kettner, M., & Krause, R. (1989). Verbale Interaktionen von Schizophrenen und ihren Gesprächspartnern. *Zeitschrift für klinische Psychologie und Psychotherapie, 37*, 401-421.

Wagner, G. (1986). *Entwicklung eines automatisierten Verfahrens zur Affektinterpretation*. Final thesis, University of Saarland, Saarbrücken, Germany.

Acknowledgements: This project was sponsered by the German Research Foundation under the titles "Dyadic interactive behavior of schizophrenics" and "Alexithymia" headed by Rainer Krause.

Emotional Expressiveness, Psychophysiological Reactivity and Mother-Child Interaction with Asthmatic Children

Irmela Florin, Wolfgang Fiegenbaum, Jutta Hermanns,
Heike Winter, Rudolf Schöbinger, and Melissa Jenkins

Asthma is an obstructive disease of the bronchial airways characterized by a tendency of the bronchial tree to respond by bronchoconstriction (narrowing of the airways), edema, and excessive secretion to a variety of stimuli (Holman & Muschenheim, 1972). A hallmark of bronchial asthma is that the generalized airway obstruction during an asthmatic attack totally or partially reverses either spontaneously or with treatment (McFadden, 1980). Asthma is one of the most common chronic diseases of childhood. According to a review by Weiner (1977), about 5% of children below the age of 15 suffer at some time from a form of asthma or allergic rhinitis. Extended epidemiological studies are scarce. It seems, however, that prevalence rates vary considerably across regions. As early as 1954, Kraepelin found that bronchial asthma was twice as prevalent in Stockholm as in the overall Swedish population. In addition, the disorder is about twice as common in boys as in girls. Traditionally, bronchial asthma has been considered one of the major psychosomatic diseases. It appears, however, that many other factors may initiate attacks of bronchial asthma. The major variables that can trigger asthma attacks in children are as follows:

(1) allergens such as pollen, dusts, animals, feathers, food constituents, molds
(2) a large variety of irritants: Cigarette smoke, air and environmental pollution, pharmaceutical and industrial agents (these seem to be most prominent)
(3) various medications, in particular aspirin and other pain remedies containing acetaminophen, and, to a lesser degree, drugs with iboprofen as an ingredient
(4) respiratory infections caused by viruses
(5) vigorous exercise
(6) inhaling dry, cold air
(7) crying and laughing
(8) emotional arousal.

This enumeration of potential precipitants, which is by far not complete, indicates that psychological factors in many cases may not play the primary role in childhood asthma.

Etiopathology of Childhood Asthma

The Medical View

From a medical viewpoint, two main factors are thought to precipitate paroxysmal dyspnoea and wheezing (Steptoe, 1984). The first factor is an allergic bronchial constriction: The allergen binds IgE to the receptors of mast cells which then release humoral mediators of anaphylaxis. These in turn act on bronchial smooth muscle cells to induce muscular contraction and the production of mucus (Steptoe, 1984, p.8). The second factor is bronchial hyperreactivity: The bronchial system of the patient responds with exaggerated constriction to stimulation from a broad range of stimuli. It appears that the parasympathetic nervous system is involved in the narrowing of the airways since bronchospasm is blocked by atropine (Boushey et al., 1980; Mc Fadden et al., 1969). Confusingly, it appears that sympathetic activity, as reflected in heart rate (HR) acceleration, may also be increased in situations in which bronchoconstriction is observed (Florin et al., 1985; Hahn & Clark, 1967; Tal & Miklich, 1976). On the other hand, the use of beta-adrenergic sympathomimetics or adrenaline is beneficial for patients during acute asthma attacks. The mechanism underlying these phenomena is not clear (for a review see Steptoe, 1984). The two factors, allergy and bronchial hyperreactivity, have to be considered as overlapping phenomena contributing to different extents to the manifestation of asthma in different individuals (Steptoe, 1984).

The Psychosomatic View

Alexander's Etiopathological Model
From a psychosomatic viewpoint, psychological factors have been discussed as core variables in the pathogenesis of asthma for decades. The expression of emotions played a major role in these conceptualisations. Typically, the asthmatic patient was thought of as a person who holds back certain kinds of emotion because of a special relationship with the mother. In this context, Alexander's (1950) psychobiological theory of psychosomatic disease is of general and, as it relates to asthma, of particular interest. Alexander emphasized that in psychosomatic diseases there is a predominance of either the sympathetic or the parasympathetic nervous system. According to that theory, the sympathetic nervous system prepares the individual for fight or flight responses while the parasympathetic nervous system serves the maintenance of the body and the building up of the body's anabolic system. While sympathetic activity implies an orientation toward external demands, parasympathetic activity implies withdrawal from external demands. In asthmatic individuals, the parasympathetic activity is assumed to be predominant. The individuals are characterized by a specific conflict, namely a strong infantile dependency of the individual upon the mother which

is repressed because it is not in line with societal demands. The asthmatic individual will, therefore, hold back expressions of the need for dependency, protection, affection, etc., because of the fear of separation from the mother or mother substitute. In this sense, asthmatic attacks are speculated to be "suppressed cries for the mother" (Weiss, 1922, in Weiner, 1977). When these feelings are held back, according to Alexander, no release of emotional tension is achieved: parasympathetic activity will be increased and may thus initiate an asthma attack. One complication of Alexander's theory is that bronchoconstriction in asthmatics may not only be elicited by situations in which the expression of dependency needs is held back, but also by conditions in which the individual wants to express such feelings as anger, hostility, and aggression. These feelings will also threaten the dependency relationship and induce separation anxiety. Consequently, expressions of these negative emotions will also have to be held back. In such cases, according to Alexander, the sympathetic nervous system is activated. For asthmatics, this would mean that in addition to frequent overactivity of the parasympathetic nervous system, there are also instances where sympathetic arousal is maintained over rather long periods. This results from tension, induced by feelings such as anger and hostility, which are not released due to the lack of expressiveness.

The Alexithymia Concept
Another influential theoretical consideration concerning the expression of emotions in psychosomatic patients is the concept of alexithymia. In this model psychosomatic patients are assumed to have an incapacity to express their feelings. Although Sifneos (1973) emphasized the inability of psychosomatic patients to verbally express their emotions (as reflected in the term alexithymia = no words for feelings) his concept was actually broader in that he also stated more globally that their experiencing of emotions is markedly constricted. Deficits in the expression of emotions should, therefore, be visible in communication channels other than the verbal. This consideration fits in well with the description of the typical psychosomatic patient given by Nemiah et al. (1976): The patients are "often stiff and wooden in their manner. They sit rigidly, move their bodies sparingly, use few gestures when they talk and maintain a near expressionless face. Their restricted behavior in combination with the lack of emotional colour in their speech ... often makes such individuals appear dull and boring to the examiner" (p. 433). Later authors, in line with these anecdotal observations, mainly referred to alexithymia in the sense of a profound overall deficit in the expression of emotion. As in Alexander's theory, the concept of alexithymia assumes that due to the lack of expressiveness, emotional tension cannot be released, and the somatic component of the emotion is possibly intensified, ultimately resulting in the manifestation of a psychosomatic disorder (Nemiah et al., 1977). From empirically based research, it is not clear whether alexithymia is characteristic of psychosomatic patients (for review see Gerhards, 1988). It is also not

clear whether the deficits in expressiveness actually exist as implied by Alexander's theory for the specific diagnostic subgroups of psychosomatic patients.

Beyond the mechanism of tension release, as postulated by the alexithymia and Alexander theories, it seems plausible that deficits in emotional expressiveness may increase vulnerability to psychophysiologic disorders. The expression of emotion has a communicative function. The expressions signalize to others which situations are distressing and which ones are pleasurable to the individual. Thereby, the expressions of emotion provide the premise for others to help eliminate or prevent distressing situations, and to support and help in the coping processes in those situations where the distress cannot be prevented. In addition, pleasurable conditions cannot easily be cared for which may counterbalance such distressing experiences. In this sense, emotional communication is crucial in the formation of a social support network that may buffer the adverse effects of various stressors on bodily function (Kamarck et al, 1990; Kiecolt-Glaser et al., 1984; Levy et al., 1990). It seems important, therefore, to further investigate whether deficits in emotional expressiveness are characteristic of patients with psychophysiologic disease. To overcome some of the shortcomings of previous research, it seems necessary to be more specific concerning the diagnostic groups, the situations in which the expressions of emotions are assessed, the emotions themselves, and the channels through which the emotions are expressed.

Empirical Studies of the Expressions of Emotions in Asthmatic Children

The present review focuses specifically on the expressions of emotions in one psychophysiologic disorder: childhood asthma. Reports on studies in childhood asthma were not intermixed with studies involving adult asthma for the following reasons: Asthmatic children suffer more frequently from extrinsic (allergic) asthma than adults. In a study of more than 11,000 cases, Ford (1969) found that 60% of the asthmatic children below the age of 14 had extrinsic asthma, while this was true for only 20% of the asthmatics between ages 15-44. In addition, childhood asthma is twice to three times as prevalent in boys as in girls whereas in adulthood asthma prevalence rates are about equal in women and in men. It is likely, therefore, that differences between childhood and adulthood asthma also exist with respect to pathogenesis and etiology (Richter & Dahme, 1982). To the authors' knowledge, only two studies dealing with the expression of affect/emotion and psychophysiological responding in asthmatic children were published prior to the commencement of the studies to be reported below. The first study was reported by Hahn and Clark (1967). He subjected asthmatic children and controls to various situations, namely tone, shock, problem solving tasks, and problem solving under criticism. Among others, heart rate (HR) and respiration rates were assessed, post hoc subjective ratings of affects during problem solving under criticism were collected, and information on the feelings regarding the test situation was obtained from a post-stress interview. During the tone and shock situations, HR responses and respiratory responses were similar for both asthmatics and non-asthmatics. The asthmatics, however, continued to show increasing HR as compard to controls during problem solving under criticism. At the same time they showed a curtailment of respiration rate increments. In addition, the asthmatic children responded to the criticism with a significantly greater increase in negative affect. Although more negative affect was felt, these children reacted to the criticism with less aggressiveness. Similar findings were obtained in college students (Mathé & Knapp, 1971) when respiratory rates and self reports on aggressiveness were studied under stressful conditions, one of which was a mental achievement task to be performed under criticism. The certainty with which conclusions can be drawn from these findings is, however, restricted due to the fact that the information on the expression of emotion consisted of post hoc and subjective ratings.

Straker and Tamerin (1974) investigated the relationship between the severity of asthmatic symptomatology and aggressive behavioral expression in children attending a summer camp for children with perennial asthma. It appeared that those children who had significantly lower air flow values and/or needed treatment (steroids, epinephrine, or hospitalization), were found to have significantly lower scores of aggressive behavior as rated by their counselors. It remains, however, unclear whether the counselors' ratings also covered the phases when the children were in need of treatment. During such periods, the children are likely to be tired and may be too weak to act out aggressive behavior.

Tal and Miklich (1976) investigated pulmonary flow rates in asthmatic children prior to and after the recall of incidents of intense anger and fear. Although the expression of emotion was not taken into account in this study, the physiological results are of interest: HR measures indicated that in both recall situations emotional arousal occurred. At the same time, the forced expiratory volume after 1 second (FEV_1) decreased, signifying that bronchoconstriction occurred. Curtailments of FEV_1 were positively correlated with FEV_1 increases under relaxation.

Overall, in the above studies the observational basis for the emotional expressiveness was quite narrow. In addition, the reliability is questioned since the data were assessed on either post hoc subjective ratings or on rather global ratings of others with no interrater reliability reported. It seems, therefore, necessary to employ objective and valid measures in assessing emotional expressiveness. In order to address this point, a series of laboratory studies with asthmatic children was performed at the University of Marburg.

Marburg Studies in the Facial Expressiveness of Asthmatic Children

Study 1

Asthmatic children and healthy controls, between the ages of 9 and 12, were studied in a frustrating achievement situation (Hollaender & Florin, 1983). The children had to solve a puzzle via a mirror image. Preceding this, a trained child accomplice of the experimenter completed the task while the asthmatic child watched. The children were given 5 minutes to put the puzzle together, too brief a period to complete the task. In addition, at the end of each minute, the child accomplice commented somewhat critically on the performance of the subject. Video recordings of the children's facial movements were taken throughout the experiment and analysed for expressions of emotion by use of Izard's (1979) *Maximally Discriminative Coding System*. The main finding in this study was a deficit in the facial expressiveness of the asthmatic children. They showed significantly less frequent and significantly shorter expression of emotions than their controls. These relative deficits were not restricted to the expression of anger; rather deficits were also shown in the expression of enjoyment and surprise. In addition to the facial expression of emotions, an indirect measure was taken of the children's airway conductance, namely the peak expiratory flow rate (PEFR) both before and after the stress inducing competitive achievement situation. The pre- and post-stress comparison of PEFR showed that the airway conductance was significantly reduced in the asthmatic children but not in the control children over the course of the stressing condition. Correlational analyses indicated a significant relationship between the mean individual expressions of emotions, and the extent to which the airway conductance decreased: The longer the expressions of emotions, the less pronounced the decrease in airway conductance.

Study 2

In an effort to replicate the above results and identify situational variables that may be crucial for the occurrence of a deficit in the facial expression of emotions, a second condition was introduced. Asthmatic children (ages 7-12) and healthy controls were exposed to both a stressful and a pleasurable condition. The stressful condition was nearly the same as in the first experiment, where the children needed to complete a puzzle under criticism and time pressure via a mirror image. The joyful condition consisted of a Walt Disney comic film. Facial expressions of emotions were recorded and pre- and posttest forced expiratory volume was assessed at 1 sec (FEV_1).

In the stressing condition, the asthmatic children once again showed significantly fewer expressions of emotion in several categories of negative and positive emotions, namely anger, comtempt, fear/anxiety, and interest. In contrast, during the pleasurable condition no significant differences between the asthmatic and the control children were found.

The asthmatic children's mean HR was significantly higher under both experimental conditions than during the preceding pauses. In contrast, the control group's mean did not significantly change from the pause to the stressful situation, but was significantly lower during the pleasurable situation. In accordance to the earlier findings (Hollaender & Florin, 1983), airway conductance of the asthmatic children was decreased by the stressful condition. This decrease was, however, not limited to the stress condition, but was also shown in the pleasurable condition. These findings lead to the assumption that airway conductance of asthmatic children is generally more affected by situations that evoke emotions, positive or negative. There was no significant correlation for either group between the expression of emotions and FEV_1 pre- to posttest differences or the respective differences in mean HR.

On the one hand, these results confirmed the earlier finding that in a stressful situation children with asthma show a deficit in their facial expression of emotions. On the other hand, data indicated that the asthmatic children do not show a general incapacity to express emotions. The deficit rather appeared to be dependent on the specific situation. The conditions under which a deficit in facial expressiveness had been visible so far was achievement related, stress inducing, with interactional properties, preprogrammed failure, and criticism. In order to further specify the conditions under which deficits in the expression of emotions are characteristic of asthmatic children, these conditions had to be varied.

Study 3
First, interactional properties of the situation were varied, while the achievement aspect and preprogrammed failure were held constant. The children once again had to solve puzzles via a mirror image. During one of the trials the children were by themselves, while in another trial the mothers joined them trying to help them by verbal guidance. Ekman and Friesen's (1978) *Facial Action Coding System* was used for analysis of the children's and the mothers' facial expressiveness. The previous measure, Izard's system, is used only for children and was, therefore, not appropriate in this study. HR was continuously recorded throughout the experimental phases. In addition, PEFR was assessed prior to and after each experimental phase (Linden, 1986; Marx, et al., 1986; Zöfel, 1986). No deficit in the emotional expressiveness was found for the asthmatic children in comparison to the control children in either condition. Both the total number of expressions and the numbers of emotions expressed in a specific category (anger, happiness, sadness) did not differ significantly between groups in the child and mother condition. On the contrary, in the "child alone" condition, the asthmatic children expressed more emotion, specifically anger and aggression, than the control children. HR significantly increased in both groups and in both conditions indicating that the experimental situations had in fact been stressful. No significant differences between groups were found with respect to the pre- to post changes in PEFR.

Study 4

Next, success and failure were varied. Mother and child were asked to play computer games. A cursor had to be carefully directed between two lines without crossing them. A turning knob was given to the mother as well as the child. They were sitting next to each other and had to cooperate in order to direct the cursor toward the goal. Under the condition of success, the goal was easy to achieve. Small movements of the knob had a small effect on the movement of the cursor. On the other hand under the failure condition, at irregular intervals, small movements of the knob had a large effect. In these instances, failure was highly probable.

Again no significant differences between the asthmatic children and the control children in the facial expression of emotion were shown in either the success or failure conditions. This held true for the frequency of emotions expressed in total and within the specific categories of emotions (joy, sadness, anger, surprise). In addition, FEV_1 pre-to post changes did not differ between groups under either condition (Bestmann-Seidel, 1985; Emde, 1986). In comparing the experimental conditions under which deficits in the expressiveness of the asthmatic children had occurred, two primary differences emerged. First, whenever a deficit was found, the interaction was rather direct and focussed on the target child, whereas when no deficit was found the communication was focussed on the task that had to be solved. Second, where a deficit was shown, criticism was used as a stressor, whereas no deficit was found under conditions where criticism was omitted. Criticism and more direct interaction with the focus on the child, therefore, appeared to be crucial variables in the expressiveness of the asthmatic children. In order to see whether this was the case, another condition was developed in which the mother and the child had to intensively interact.

Study 5

For ethical reasons, criticism was not systematically applied. Yet, a stressful situation was created which made it highly probable that criticism would be expressed by some of the mothers. It would, therefore, be possible to compare those children subjected to criticism to those who were not exposed to criticism (Auffermann, 1987). A city map was placed in front of the mother as well as the child. Mother had to verbally guide the child from a start to a goal. The maps of the mother and the child were not identical. Shortly after the start, there was a dead end in the child's map, but not in the mother's map. A stressful situation, therefore, arose.

Facial expressiveness of emotion, heart rate, and pre- and posttest FEV_1 were collected. No significant deficits were found in the asthmatic children's facial expressiveness as compared with the controls. On the contrary, during the stressful city map game, the asthmatic children showed more frequent expressions of emotions. Additionally, no significant differences emerged between those asthmatic children who were subjected to high criticism as opposed to those subjected to no criticism. Criticism, therefore, does not necessarily lead to a deficit in the facial expressiveness of emotionality.

The same children who participated in the stressful city map situation also took part in a pleasurable frog jumping game along with their mothers. The object of the game was to get colored plastic frogs into a water well by pressing on their tails. In that situation, no significant differences in the expresssion of emotions were found between groups. Mean HR during the stressful as well as the pleasurable situation did not differ between groups and proved independent of the asthmatic children's facial expressiveness. Changes in FEV_1 between pre- and posttest also did not differ between groups. While expression of emotionality was not systematically related to FEV_1 in the pleasurable situation, in the stressful situation there was a highly significant correlation indicating that the emotional expressiveness was inversely related to the changes in FEV_1: The more emotions expressed, the higher the probability that FEV_1 decreased. This finding contradicted the result of one of our initial studies (Florin et al., 1985) where the children's facial expressiveness was positively related to airway conductance.

Summary and Discussion
Facial expressions of emotions were observed in a total of nine situations. Deficits in emotional expression were found in only two of these situations. In another two, the asthmatic children showed, not fewer, but to the contrary, more facial expressions of emotion than their controls. In the remaining five situations no differences emerged between groups. In interpreting these findings, it appears that deficits in the facial expressiveness of asthmatic children, should they exist at all, are highly context-specific. The variations in the contexts chosen in these studies did not lead to the identification of situational characteristics that may be crucial for a deficit. So far, only facial expressions of emotions were observed. As a next step, two studies were performed by means of a coding system that takes into account both verbal and nonverbal aspects of behavior.

Marburg Studies of the Integrated Verbal and Nonverbal Expressiveness (Communicative Behavior) of Asthmatic Children in Parent-Child Interaction

Study 1
Asthmatic and healthy children, aged 7 to 13, and their respective mothers participated in the study (Hermanns et al., 1989a,b). First, mother and child were seen individually to find issues that had repeatedly led to conflict between them during the last weeks. Mother and child were then brought together and asked to discuss an issue that both had independently mentioned earlier as a mutual problem. Video recordings were taken throughout the discussion, which lasted between 5 and 8 minutes. The analysis of the negative communication between mother and child was assessed using a reliable coding system (categorial system

for partner interaction, KPI, Hahlweg et al., 1984) that was developed for the analysis of communicative behavior in dyadic interactions. The basic coding unit is a verbal response that is homogeneous in content without regard to its duration or syntactical structure (Hahlweg et al., 1989). Each coding of a verbal category is supplemented with a nonverbal qualification (+/-/0) which expresses whether a positive or negative affect is expressed in facial, vocal or postural terms. Specifically, criticism, justification, disagreement, and negative solution were measured.

No significant differences were found in any of the four categories or in the total amount of negative verbal behavior for the asthmatic children compared to the controls. Yet, in analysing the mothers' behavior, interestingly, it was found that mothers of the asthmatic children displayed significantly more critical communicative behavior than mothers of the control children. They did not significantly differ from their controls in justifications, disagreements, negative solutions and total amount of negative communicative behavior. One might conclude that the asthmatics did not differ from controls in the frequency of their negative communicative behavior although they were treated differently by their mothers than the control children were.

Further analyses, therefore, focussed on interactions between mother and child in addition to the child's behavior. Sequential analyses of the mother-child communication were performed by means of the K-Gramm-method (Revenstorf et al., 1984), which was explicitly designed for analysis of dyadic data. As the number of codings for the individual mother-child dyads was low, sequential analysis was based on data summed across mother-child dyads in each group. As indicated in Figure 1, the asthmatic group compared with the control group shows a negative escalation pattern, that is, a particularly long sequence of negative communications.

Data combined in this way cannot be statistically evaluated for group differences, but can only be described (Revenstorf et al., 1984). The sequence length is shown on the abscissa; the conditional probability (in percentages) is given on the ordinate. Sequence length 1 represents the base rate (BR) / percentage of frequency of negative communicative behavior for both groups: 25% of all communicative behavior in the asthmatic group and 20% in the control group is negative. Sequence length 2 shows that the conditional probability that partner B will respond negatively to a negative statement of partner A is 42% for the asthma group. The probability that partner A will again respond negatively to partner B has increased to 47% at sequence length 3. The pattern of negative escalation continues up to sequence length 7, with a maximum probability of 68% of a negative response. Probability of negative reciprocity is still 63% at sequence length 8. Only then does the sequence end. In contrast, controls show only a short negative escalation pattern. The probability of negative responding declines as early as after sequence length 3, and the negative reciprocity ends by sequence length 4.

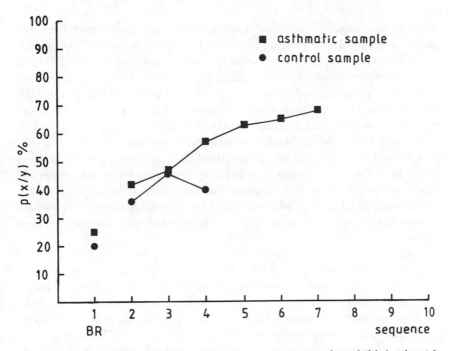

Figure 1.   Escalation of negative communication in mother-child dyads with asthmatic versus control children.

Separate analyses of mother-initiated and child-initiated sequences of negative communicative exchange document that long and escalating sequences of negative interaction occur in the asthmatic pairs regardless of whether mother or child initiates the sequence. The sequential pattern suggests that both mothers and asthmatic children contribute to the negative escalation. The analysis of the dominance patterns revealed that the asthmatic children and their mothers control each other to the same extent. This does not imply, however, that they contribute to the characteristic pattern of interaction in the same way. No statements can, therefore, be made on the basis of these analyses concerning which type of mother's negative communicative behavior is reciprocated by which type of child's behavior and vice versa. The findings of correlational analyses reveal that mother's criticism was highly correlated with justification on the part of the asthmatic child, and the child's disagreement was highly correlated with disagreement of the mother. No significant differences were found between the more and the less communicative asthmatic children with respect to HR or FEV_1 changes from the beginning to the end of the problem discussion.

Study 2
Father-child interaction with asthmatic children appears to have been neglected. The aim of the following study was to help overcome this gap in addition to measuring the verbal as well as nonverbal expressions of emotion (Winter
et al., 1990). Asthmatic and control children, aged 6 to 13 years, and their respective fathers participated in the study. As in the previous study, the father and
the child were asked to discuss a mutual problem. Again, recordings were taken
throughout the discussion and the interactions were coded according to the KPI
which integrates verbal and nonverbal behavioral aspects. The asthmatic children showed more negative communicative behavior in interaction with their
fathers than did their controls. At the same time, their fathers also expressed
more negative communicative behavior than the fathers of the control children.
In addition, the asthmatic children showed less positive communicative behavior than their controls. A trend in the same direction was observed for their
fathers.

Summary and Discussion
Although some discrepancies were found with respect to the children's communicative expressiveness while interacting with their mothers versus their fathers,
no significant overall deficit was found in their readiness to verbally and nonverbally express their emotions. Futhermore, no deficit was found in the expression
of negative emotion. On the contrary, in interactions with the fathers there were
indications that the asthmatic children verbally express more negative emotion
than their controls. In interactions with their mothers, it was found that the
asthmatic children contributed more than their controls to negative escalations.

Discussion

This review shows that emotional expressiveness as it relates to childhood asthma is a very complex issue. The question remains: Are there deficits in the expression of emotions in asthmatic children? The findings presented showed no
consistent pattern of deficits in the emotional expression of asthmatic children
as compared with controls. There was no global or generalized deficit covering
any categories of emotions, situations or communication channels (verbal and
nonverbal). There was also no global and generalized deficit pertaining to the
expression of the categories of "negative" emotions over situations and communication channels. This suggests that the alexithymia concept is not tenable: If
any consistent deficit should exist in the facial expression of emotion, it is likely
to be highly context specific. Even when the demand characteristics in the situations were only slightly changed, the deficits in the asthmatic children's expressiveness that had been previously found twice, were not again observed. If there
is a context dependent deficit, the crucial variable(s) will still have to be identi-

fied. The same holds true for the identification of a specific deficit in the expression of aggression/anger, which has been postulated by some authors as evoking a fear of separation from the object of love.

Besides varying the situations in which the children's behavior is observed, it may be advantageous to vary the means of analyses. The previous analyses compared group means of child behavior over situations that have been regarded as static rather than interactional. To identify potential deficits in the expression of emotions, it would be important to look at the sequential patterns in which expressions of emotions are exchanged between interacting individuals. Detailed information may, for instance, be obtained by observing which expressive behavior of the child is followed by what expressive behavior of the mother and vice versa. The respective analyses are in fact under way. As a preliminary step, transition-frequencies were computed indicating how often – after the beginning and after the end of the expression of a specific category of emotion by one interaction partner – a certain type of emotion was expressed by the other partner within one second's time. The transition frequencies per mother-child dyad were totalled over each group and entered into matrices. Since detailed statistical evaluations are still lacking, the following examples are solely aimed at illustrating what kind of information may be obtained by such analyses: Within the asthmatic group, fewer children expressed anger immediately after their mother had done so than in the control sample. Interestingly, analyses of variance did not show significant between-group differences in the children's expression of anger. According to the transition frequency counts, more of the asthmatic children answered with nonspecific facial expressions to smiles from their mothers, whereas analyses of variance again revealed no significant differences between groups with respect to the children's nonspecific facial movements (Florin, 1988). It seems premature to interpret these findings. The examples were meant only to illustrate that microanalyses of interactional behavior may lead substantially to more differentiated and more concrete descriptions of abnormal patterns in the expressions of emotions, than simple comparisons of means that do not take into account the sequence of events.

There are also no apparent shortcomings in the verbal expression of emotions in asthmatic children. On the contrary, more negative verbal communicative behavior of the asthmatics was observed in the child-father interactions. Moreover, in the child-mother interactions, the asthmatics contributed more than their controls to long and escalating sequences of negative communication. These findings do not fit into the definition of alexithymia in its narrowest sense, namely that there is an inability of psychosomatic patients to verbally express their feelings.

It should not be overlooked, however, that the conditions under which the children were observed were not designed to evoke very strong or deep emotions. It needs to be clarified whether deficits in the expression of emotions would be apparent if the child was asked to talk about a personally traumatic event, for instance an event that is closely associated with feelings of shame and guilt. As Pennebaker et al. (1987, 1988a,b) have pointed out, it may be that these traumatic events and their accompaning feelings are held back over long periods of time. It may be that this holding back of emotional expression may result in the phenomena described as alexithymia, particularly in situations where the patients are reminded of the traumatic events. It is probable that initial interviews given by psychotherapists with psychosomatic patients will touch on emotions associated with memories of extremely stressful or traumatic experiences. Interestingly, it was during such initial interviews that alexithymia was first observed in psychosomatic patients.

Considering the psychophysiological findings, no consistent relationship was found between heart rate and respiration measures. When these physiological measures were then related to emotional expressiveness, once again no consistent pattern emerged. The first mentioned finding indicates that sympathetic arousal, as reflected in heart rate acceleration, does not necessarily increase bronchodilation. This observation is in line with the observations by Hahn and Clark (1967) who noted that sympathetic activity is sometimes increased in situations where bronchoconstriction is observed. These conflicting results may indicate that asthmatics have a disorder of adrenergic function. It is possible that asthmatics do not adequately respond to circulating catecholamines or sympathetic stimulation which may result in bronchoconstriction (Szentivanyi, 1968; in Steptoe, 1984). Another explanation would be that adrenergic responses are impaired at the level of initial output, rather than at receptor sites (Mathé & Knapp, 1971). No firm conclusions on the relationship of heart rate and respiration measures can be drawn, however, from the findings reported since there are some shortcomings with the respiration measures used in the studies reviewed. First, the PEFR as well as the FEV_1 demand an effort from the side of the child. The reliability of these measures is, therefore, largely dependent upon the child's motivation to cooperate. Secondly, these measures may, in and of themselves, precipitate a mild bronchoconstriction by stimulation of epithelial receptors in the airways. Thirdly, the measures are discontinuous and, therefore, cannot depict the fluctuations in pulmonary function throughout the experimental study. To closer examine the relationship between heart rate and curtailments in pulmonary function, it should be considered in further studies whether microanalyses could be performed on the basis of continuous and simultaneous monitoring of both heart rate and airways obstruction. It would then be possible to investigate the temporal relationship between cardiac and respiratory reactivity. This goal is, nonetheless, difficult to achieve. At present, whole body plethysmography is acknowledged as the device that provides the most accurate and at the same time continuous measurements of pulmonary function. Unfortunately, this device also has its disadvantages, particularly with psychological studies: The child has to be confined in an airtight box. This makes interactional research impossible. Investigations of the relationship between the expression of emotions and physiological measures may also benefit from analysing the data on a more precise temporal basis.

There are various aspects that should be considered in future research. The studies reviewed had the advantage of dealing with a fairly homogenous population, namely with asthmatic children between the ages of 6 and 13. Possibly, this population may have been too heterogenous. Recent findings suggest, for example, that a fairly large subgroup of children suffering from atopic disorders also display specific behavioral patterns (Roth et al., 1990). It may, therefore, be advantageous to assess IgE levels in order to distinguish subgroups of asthmatic children which may differ with respect to their expressions of emotions and/or their psychophysiological patterns.

The improved methodology could eventually lead to a better understanding of the psychobiological mechanisms involved in childhood asthma. This would, no doubt, have a great influence on the development of effective behaviorally oriented intervention methods.

References

Alexander, F. (1950). *Psychosomatic medicine*. New York: Norton.

Auffermann, G. (1987). *Mimischer Emotionsausdruck bei Kindern mit Bronchialasthma*. Diploma thesis. Marburg (Germany): Philipps University, Dept. of Psychology.

Bestmann-Seidel, B. (1985). *Emotionaler Ausdruck und subjektives Erleben bei Kindern mit Asthmabronchiale*. Diploma thesis. Marburg (Germany): Philipps University, Dept. of Psychology.

Boushey, H.A. (1981). Neural mechanisms in asthma. In H. Weiner, M.A. Hofer & A.J. Stunkard (Eds.), *Brain, behavior and bodily disease*. New York: Raven.

Boushey, H.A., Holtzmann, M.J., Sheller, J.R., & Nadel, J.A. (1980). Bronchial hyperreactivity. *American Review of Respiratory Disorders, 121*, 389-413.

Ekman, P., & Friesen, W.V. (1978). *Facial Action Coding System*. Palo Alto, CA: Consulting Psychologists Press.

Emde, H. (1986). *Emotionaler Ausdruck und physiologische Parameter bei Kindern mit Asthmabronchiale*. Diploma thesis. Marburg (Germany): Philipps University, Dept. of Psychology.

Florin, I. (1988). *Emotionsausdruck. Bericht an die Deutsche Forschungsgemeinschaft*. Marburg: Philipps University, Dept. of Psychology.

Florin, I., Freudenberg, G., & Hollaender, J. (1985). Facial expressions of emotional and physiologic reactions in children with bronchial asthma. *Psychosomatic Medicine, 47*, 383-392.

Ford, M.M. (1969). Aetiology of asthma: a review of 11,551 cases (1958-1968). *Medical Journal of Australia, 1*, 628-631.

Gerhards, F. (1988). *Emotionsausdruck und emotionales Erleben bei psychosomatisch Kranken. Eine Kritik des Alexithymiekonzepts.* Opladen: Westdeutscher Verlag.

Hahlweg, K., Reisner, L., Kohli, G., Vollmer, M., Schindler, L., & Revenstorf, D. (1984). Development and validity of a new system to analyse interpersonal communication. In K. Hahlweg et al. (Eds.), *Understanding major mental disorder: The contribution of family interaction research.* New York: Family Process Press.

Hahlweg, K., Goldstein, M.J., Nuechterlein, K.H., Magana, A.B., Mintz, J., Doane, J.A., Miklowitz, D.I., & Snyder, K. (1989). Expressed emotion and patient-relative interaction in families of recent onset schizophrenics. *Journal of Consulting and Clinical Psychology, 57,* 11-18.

Hahn, W.W., & Clark, J.A. (1967). Psychophysiological reactivity of asthmatic children. *Psychosomatic Medicine, 29,* 526-536.

Hermanns, J., Florin, I., Dietrich, M., Rieger, C., & Hahlweg, K. (1989a). Maternal criticism, mother-child interaction, and bronchial asthma. *Journal of Psychosomatic Research, 33,* 469-476.

Hermanns, J., Florin, I., Dietrich, M., Lugt-Tappeser, H., Rieger, C., & Roth, W. (1989b). Negative mother-child communication and bronchial asthma. *The German Journal of Psychology, 13,* 285-292.

Hollaender, J., & Florin, I. (1983). Expressed emotion and airway conductance in children with bronchial asthma. *Journal of Psychosomatic Research, 27,* 307-311.

Holman, C.W., & Muschenheim, C. (1972). *Bronchopulmonary diseases and related disorders.* Vol. 2. New York: Harper & Row.

Izard, C.E. (1979). *The Maximally Discriminative Facial Movement Coding System.* University of Delaware, Newark: Instructional Resources Center.

Kamarck, T.W., Manuck, S.B., & Jennings, J.R. (1990). Social support reduces cardiovvascular reactivity in psychological challenge: A laboratory model. *Psychosomatic Medicine, 52,* 42-58.

Kiecolt-Glaser, J.K., Garner, W., Speicher, C.E., Penn, G.M., Holliday, J., & Glaser, R. (1984). Psychosocial modifiers of immunocompetence in medical students. *Psychosomatic Medicine, 46,* 7-14.

Kraepelin, S. (1954). The frequency of bronchial asthma in Swedish school children. *Acta Paediatrica Scandinavia, 43,* 149-157.

Levy, S.M., Heberman, R.B., Whiteside, T., Sazo, K., Lee, J., & Kirkwood, J. (1990). Perceived social support and tumor estrogen/progesterone receptor status as predictors of natural killer cell activity in breast cancer patients. *Psychosomatic Medicine, 52,* 73-85.

Linden-Holtum, U. (1986). *Mimischer Emotionsausdruck und physiologische Reaktionen bei Kindern mit Asthma bronchiale.* Diploma thesis. Marburg (Germany): Philipps University, Dept. of Psychology.

Marx, D., Zöfel, C., Linden, U., Bönner, H., Franzen, U., & Florin, I. (1986). Expression of emotion in asthmatic children and their mothers. *Journal of Psychosomatic Research, 30*, 609-616.

Mathé, A.A., & Knapp, P.M. (1971). Emotional and adrenal reaction to stress in bronchial asthma. *Psychosomatic Medicine, 33*, 323-340.

McFadden, E.R., Luparello, T., Lyons, H.A., & Bleeker, F. (1969). The mechanism of action of suggestion in the induction of acute asthma attacks. *Psychosomatic Medicine, 31*, 134-143.

McFadden, E.R., Jr. (1980). Asthma; pathophysiology. *Seminars in Respiratory Medicine, 1*, 297-303.

Nemiah, J.C., Freyberger, H., & Sifneos, P.E. (1976). Alexithymia: A view of the psychosomatic process. In O.W. Hill (Ed.). *Modern trends in psychosomatic medicine.* Vol 3, London: Butterworths.

Nemiah, J.C., Sifneos, P.E. & Apfel-Savitz, R. (1977). A comparison of the oxygen consumption of normal and alexithymic subjects in response to affect-provoking thoughts. *Psychotherapy and Psychosomatics 28*, 167-171.

Pennebaker, J.W., Hughes, C.F., & O'Heeron, R.C. (1987). The psychophysiology of confession: Linking inhibitory and psychosomatic processes. *Journal of Personality and Social Psychology, 52*, 781-793.

Pennebaker, J.W., Kiecolt-Glaser, J.K. & Glaser, R. (1988a). Disclosure of traumas and immune function: health implications for psychotherapy. *Journal of Consulting and Clinical Psychology, 56*, 239-245.

Pennebaker, J.W., & Susman, J.R. (1988b). Disclosure of traumas and psychosomatic processes. *Social Science in Medicine, 26*, 327-332.

Revenstorf, D., Schindler, L., Hahlweg, K., & Kunert, H. (1984). Application of time-series analysis in marital therapy. In K. Hahlweg & N.S. Jacobson (Eds.), *Marital interaction: Analysis and modification.* New York: Guilford Press.

Richter, R., & Dahme, B. (1982). Bronchial asthma in adults: There is little evidence for the effectiveness of behavioral therapy and relaxation. *Journal of Psychosomatic Research, 26*, 533-540.

Roth, N., Beyreiß, J., Hoffman, B., & Schlottke, P. (1990). A biobehavioral approach to the coincidence of atopic and behavioral disorders in children. In: International Society of Behavioral Medicine (Ed.), *Proceedings of the First International Congress of Behavioral Medicine.* Uppsala (Sweden): Reprocentralen HSC.

Sifneos, P.E. (1973). The prevalence of "alexithymic" characteristics in psychosomatic patients. *Psychotherapy and Psychosomatics, 22*, 255-262.

Steptoe, A. (1984). Psychological aspects of bronchial asthma. In S. Rachman (ed.), *Contributions to medical psychology,* Vol 3, pp. 7-30, New York: Pergamon.

Straker, N., & Tamerin J. (1974). Aggression and childhood asthma: A study in a natural setting. *Journal of Psychosomatic Research, 18*, 131-135.

Tal, A., & Miklich, D.R. (1976). Emotionally induced decreases in pulmonary flow rates in asthmatic children. *Psychosomatic Medicine, 38*, 191-200.

Weiner, H. (1977). *Psychobiology and human disease.* New York: Elsevier, p. 252.

Winter, H., Schöbinger, R., Florin, I., Lindemann, H. (1990). Father-child interaction and childhood asthma. In European Association of Behavioural Therapy (Ed.), *Proceedings of the XXth Conference of the European Association of Behavioural Therapy. Paris.*

Zöfel, C. (1986). *Mimische Emotionsäußerung und physiologische Reaktionen bei Kindern mit Asthmabronchiale in einer Interaktionssituation mit ihren Müttern.* Diploma thesis. Marburg (Germany): Philipps University, Dept. of Psychology.

Acknowledgements: This review was supported by the Stiftung Volkswagenwerk. Support for part of the experimental studies was provided by the Deutsche Forschungsgemeinschaft.

Cardiovascular Reactivity and Emotional Control

Helmuth P. Huber and Margit Gramer

Emotions have long been known to be associated with cardiovascular changes. For example, we feel our hearts beating when we are afraid, or hear the blood rushing in our ears when angry. Furthermore, we may blush with embarrassment, or blanch with fear. Generally, it appears to be fairly well established that cardiovascular changes covary with different emotions. However, till now there is no empirical evidence that bears directly on the issue of causality. Obviously, only demonstrating concomitance between behavioral states and cardiovascular changes is incomplete because it leaves out the mechanisms by which feelings (the conscious side of emotions), overt behavioral acts (i.e., active vs. passive coping, facial or postural expressions), and expressive somatic and visceral processes interact. In other words, to contribute to the issue of cardiovascular reactivity and emotional control, it has to be shown that influences on the cardiovascular system can be evoked by manipulating environmental conditions implicating specific emotional states.

A Brief Historical Overview: Major Directions in Research on Emotions

The notion of a relationship between cardiovascular activity and emotional states should be examined within the context of theories of emotion. In the course of a one-hundred-year history of theory and research on emotion, the major topics have been the issues of peripheral versus central processes in the generation of emotions, and of specific physiological states versus general arousal as the substrate of different emotions.

While Lange (1885; translated in Dunlap, 1922) assumed that bodily changes (in particular, vasomotor processes in visceral-glandular organs) can be identified with emotions, James (1884) held that feelings are produced by *afferent feedback* from visceral-glandular and voluntary-striate muscle responses to external stimulation. James' feedback theory implies that different emotional states are characterized by different bodily response patterns. The notion of emotional control by peripheral visceral and somatic changes following the perception of a stimulus object plays an important role in modern research on emotions as well (Ekman, 1989; Ekman, Levinson, & Friesen, 1983; Fehr & Stern, 1970; Izard, 1971, 1977).

In line with the theory of discrete emotions via feedback from discrete expressions, Izard (1971) postulated nine discrete fundamental emotions: Interest, enjoyment, surprise, distress, disgust, anger, shame, fear and contempt. Furthermore, he assumed that each emotion consists of three interrelated components, namely, neural activity, striate muscle or facial-postural activity, and subjective experience. The emotional system is supposed to be related to two auxiliary systems: the brain stem reticular system, and the glandular-visceral system. If an emotion reaches substantial intensity, all physiological systems are involved to some extent. Two of the more important ones are the cardiovascular and the respiratory system. Izard argued that in the case of the fundamental emotions the underlying neural activity follows innate structures and pathways. Efferent discharges innervate the striate muscles involved in the facial-postural patterning of a given emotion. Subjective experience is viewed as generated by feedback from the emotion-specific patterning in the striate muscles (primarily facial, secondarily postural and locomotor) to the associative areas of the brain. The *Maximally Discriminative Facial Movement Coding System* (Izard, 1979) provides an objective description of the nine fundamental emotional expressions posited by Izard's theory of differential emotions.

The communication of emotions is central to early social experience, and there is no doubt about the communicative impact of facial expressions. The neurological and psychological mechanisms for producing facial expressions were examined in an excellent review by Rinn (1984).

The hypothesis that feedback from peripheral changes may account for the specifity of different emotions was rejected by Cannon (1927). He claimed that the particular quality of emotional experiences is due to specific patterns of activity in thalamic neurones. The "centralistic" perspective of Cannon's thalamic theory was extended by Papez (1937). He proposed a detailed neural circuit as the neurophysiological substrate of emotions which is referred to as the "Papez circle". MacLean (1949) viewed the structures of the limbic lobe as "visceral brain".

A kind of intermediate position between the "peripheralistic" and "centralistic" view was taken by Schachter and Singer (1962). This approach came to be known as the "two-factor" or "cognitive-arousal" theory of emotion. According to this theoretical position, the occurrence of an emotional state is the result of the interaction between two components: physiological arousal (which is conceptualized as emotionally non-specific), and cognition about the arousing situation. In other words, if physiological arousal (usually sympathetic arousal) of sufficient intensity is present, the particular quality of the experienced emotional state is determined by exclusively cognitive processes. As to everyday emotional experiences, Nisbett and Schachter (1966) stated: "In nature, of course, cognitive or situational factors trigger physiological processes, and the triggering stimulus usually imposes the label we attach to our feelings" (p. 228). For the case of unexplained arousal, it is assumed that emerging "evaluative needs" would act on an individual "to understand and label his bodily feelings"

(Schachter & Singer, 1962, p. 381). A critical examination of the cognitive-arousal theory and its attributional extensions from both a conceptual and an empirical point of view was attempted by Reisenzein (1983).

At present, the "biological" nature of emotion has been widely recognized. Panksepp (1989) stated: "Had the visceral/emotional nervous system been known at the turn of the century, the James-Lange theory may never have been proposed. Rather, the prevailing view may have been that affective states can be instigated by various sensory and perceptual inputs to subcortical emotive circuits, including those arising from certain higher brain processes (explaining how cognitions come to evoke affective experiences)" (pp. 6-7). In his recent summary concerning the neurobiological nature of brainstem systems for the elaboration of primary emotions, Panksepp saw adequate evidence for the existence of five emotive command circuits of the visceral brain which were referred to as (1) the foraging-expectancy-curiosity-investigatory system, (2) the anger-rage circuit, (3) the anxiety-fear circuit, (4) the separation-distress-sorrow-anguish-panic network, and (5) the social-play circuitry. It is likely that emotionality emerging from these command circuits is being modulated by feedback from peripheral autonomic and somatic changes.

Measurement and Experimental Paradigms

Generally, reactivity scores are conceived as change scores. The measurement models, or rather, the specific indicand-indicator relationship underlying some commonly used methods for scoring physiological reactivity, have recently been made explicit by Stemmler (1987). For scoring cardiovascular reactivity, three types of change scores have been widely employed: First, unweighted difference scores (usually obtained by substracting a base value from a reaction value); second, difference scores with weighted base values (e.g., the *Autonomic Lability Score* suggested by Lacey, 1956; or adjustment of reaction level by means of analysis of covariance using baseline level as covariate); third, percentage scores (defined as the difference between reaction and base value divided by the base value). Stemmler pointed out that different scoring methods account for different fractions of interindividual and intraindividual variance. Therefore, scoring methods must be carefully selected with respect to a particular research question.

Cardiovascular reactivity is usually assessed by measuring cardiac output (CO), blood pressure (BP), and blood flow (BF) in various vascular beds (cutaneous and in skeletal muscles). CO is a function of heart rate (HR) and stroke volume (SV), which may be calculated as $CO = SV \times HR$. In conjunction with a more or less constant SV, CO is primarily controlled by HR. The SV is mainly triggered by venous return (filling pressure of the ventricles) and myocardial contractility (Obrist, 1981). The filling pressure of the ventricles is governed by active and passive changes in venous compliance, especially of the splanchnic capacitance vessels (Shepherd, 1990). Myocardial contractility is also referred to as the "inotropic activity" of the heart.

Evaluation of CO is necessary if the systemic vascular resistance (R) is to be assessed. R may be obtained from R = MAP/CO, where MAP is the mean arterial pressure. MAP is defined as the integral of the pressure curve of the entire cardiac cycle divided by the interbeat interval (1/HR). Most of the studies, however, resort to a rule of thumb according to which MAP results from MAP = DBP + (SBP – DBP)/3, where SBP is the systolic, and DBP is the diastolic blood pressure. Vascular resistance in a limb (e.g., in the forearm) can be calculated as R(forearm) = MAP/FBF, where FBF is the forearm blood flow. A non-invasive estimate of changes in FBF is provided by the technique of venous-occlusion plethysmography. As to cutaneous blood flow, relatively inexpensive methods are available for indirect measurement of relative changes. One of these techniques is photoelectric plethysmography. A comprehensive description of the physiological bases of cardiovascular measures utilized in psychophysiology was given by Larsen, Schneiderman, and DeCarlo Pasin (1986).

Our basic assumption is that cardiovascular responses result from many interacting causes and controlling systems. However, it would be misguiding to attempt a comprehensive and detailed review. Rather, the purpose of this article is to delineate some selected findings pertinent to the cardiovascular psychophysiology of emotions. Accordingly, this review centers around some findings from experimental paradigms that suggest the mechanisms by which emotional states and cardiovascular responses may interact.

Four research paradigms may be readily identified: (1) Evaluation of myocardial and peripheral vascular responses during emotional and physical stress, (2) generalization from laboratory to non-laboratory settings and ambulatory monitoring of HR and BP during daily activities, (3) analyses of actual cardiovascular responses and self-reported bodily changes associated with experimentally induced target emotions, and (4) investigation of individual difference variables.

Myocardial and Peripheral Vascular Responses during Emotional and Physical Stress

Exercise and the Emotional Pressure Response

There is accumulating evidence that changes in CO and other aspects of cardiovascular function can be evoked by exercise (e.g., graded work load on the bicycle ergometer), and also by a variety of psychologically stressful tasks such as mental arithmetic, unsignaled shock avoidance, anagrams, or challenging videogames (cf., Allen & Crowell, 1989; Allen, Obrist, Sherwood, & Crowell, 1987; Brod, 1963; Carroll & Roy, 1989; Ewart et al., 1986; Hijzen & Slangen,

1985; Obrist et al., 1974). Because the exercise response represents the metabolically appropriate manner in which the cardiovascular system adjusts to increased energy requirements, it provides a necessary background to understanding the mechanisms underlying the interaction between emotionally stressful events and cardiovascular responses. Therefore, studies designed to examine cardiovascular reactivity during emotional stress, should always include an exercise task to provide a measure of the normal CO-oxygen uptake relationship.

According to Obrist (1981), the critical features of the exercise response appear to be an increase in CO, and a relocation of BF to the active skeletal musculature and the heart. For increasing the flow to the active muscles, CO is aided by an elevation of SBP. Furthermore, BF in the splanchnic and renal circulation is decreased. The increase in CO has a significant neurogenic component. Dependent on intrinsic vascular autoregulation, vascular resistance in the working muscles is found to be decreased. Thus, DBP is held either constant or is even decreased. Because SV changes only minimally above resting levels, increases in CO during exercise result largely from increases in HR. So the conclusion may be drawn that a pronounced cardiac acceleration in the presence of relatively constant or even decreased DBP indicates a considerably speeded arterial-venous runoff. From a metabolical point of view, cutaneous BF seems to be of minor importance. Initially, cutaneous BF decreases during exercise due to neurogenic processes. However, as exercise continues, this decrease is reversed.

Brod (1963, 1982) claimed that cardiovascular changes during emotional stress are similar to those occurring under medium or high workloads. However, the point is that the hemodynamic changes during exercise are appropriate with respect to the immediate metabolic demands. By contrast, with the "emotional pressure response" the observed increase in CO and the ensuing overperfusion of the tissues are in excess of the current metabolic requirements. The hypothesis of metabolic inappropriateness is supported by Brod's (1982) findings that during both a challenging mental arithmetic task and exercise, FBF increased, but the arterial-venous blood oxygen content difference from the vasculature of the forearm muscles decreased during mental arithmetic and increased during exercise. Studies using pharmacological blockades identified beta-adrenergic reactivity as a major mediator of the metabolically excessive responses during emotional stress (Langer et al., 1985; Obrist et al., 1974; Sherwood, Allen, Obrist, & Langer, 1986). Obrist (1981) suggested that such inappropriate cardiovascular adjustments may be involved in the etiology of cardiovascular disorders (particularly, essential hypertension).

Reports of HR decreasing in anticipation of aversive stimuli, during sensory intake and unsignaled reaction time tasks, led to the concept of "cardio-somatic relationship" (Obrist, 1981). That is to say, in the case of passive coping there is a covariation between HR and somatomotor activity. These effects were proposed "... to reflect a common central nervous system mechanism integrating somatic-motor and cardiovascular events, such as occurs during exercise" (Obrist, Light, Langer, & Koepke, 1986, p. 633). Referring to a central command theory, physical and emotional stress were often supposed to exert similar effects on the cardiovascular system (Smith, Rushmer & Lasher, 1960). However, in the presence of recent results, the hypothesis that the emotional pressure response is similar to an exercise-like response cannot be maintained any longer. Even if there are directionally similar effects, vascular responses during emotional stress may be dependent on different mechanisms (Langer et al., 1985).

Myocardial and Vascular Mechanisms

The notion of the emotional pressure response is a construct with multiple dimensions. It follows the well established principle of "situational stereotypy" (Lacey, 1967), which postulates that tasks with different behavioral demands evoke different response patterns. For instance, Allen, Obrist, Sherwood, and Crowell (1987) found quite different hemodynamic patterns in 25 healthy male students during reaction time, mental arithmetic, and cold pressor tasks. Increase in CO during the reaction time task was due to a modest increase in HR with augmented SV, whereas increases in CO during mental arithmetic and cold pressor tasks were due to substantial HR increases accompanied by a decrease in SV. With respect to the mediating neurogenic mechanisms, Allen et al. argued that the finding of decreased total peripheral resistance as well as the insignificant increase in DBP during the reaction time task is indicative of beta-adrenergically mediated vasodilation. Furthermore, as suggested by the levels of SBP and especially DBP, the influence of beta-adrenergic activation during mental arithmetic seemed to be relatively small, so that alpha-adrenergic vasoconstrictive effects may have been allowed to operate. Finally, the overall increase in total peripheral resistance observed during the cold pressor test suggests that alpha-adrenergic vasoconstriction is the most important autonomic factor triggering the hemodynamic response to this task.

In a more recent study in 51 male college students, Allen and Crowell (1989) used respiratory sinus arrhythmia as a non-invasive index of parasympathetic nervous system activity on heart, in addition to measures reflecting primarily sympathetic nervous system activity. The findings confirmed the results of previous research on different autonomic response patterns to qualitatively different emotional stressors. Moreover, the results revealed significant differences between the levels of respiratory sinus arrhythmia during reaction time, mental arithmetic, and cold pressure tasks, indicating the greatest vagal withdrawal during mental arithmetic. These findings are in line with the results presented by Steptoe and Sawada (1989). They examined the baroreceptor cardiac reflex sensitivity (expressed as change in interbeat interval in ms per mmHg change in SBP) in 24 female nurses during psychological stress and relaxation. It was shown that baroreflex sensitivity was reduced significantly during mental arithmetic (mean 14.2 ms per mmHg), but not during the cold pressor test (mean 17.4 ms per mmHg). Compared to the task levels, relaxation was associated with an increase in baroreflex sensitivity from 17.1 to 19.8 ms per mmHg. Interestingly, Lehrer, Groveman, Randolph, Miller, and Pollack (1989) found a pattern of poor physiological modulation for task performance (on a logical memory and a paced arithmetic test) in patients with closed head injuries.

Evidence that electrocardiographic (ECG) response patterns during emotional and physical stress are qualitatively different ones, was presented by Hijzen and Slangen (1985). Different degrees of emotional stress were elicited in a field situation in which 58 male normotensive subjects were watching the last five rounds of a European soccer competition on TV. Exercise ECG (recorded during work load on a bicycle ergometer) and emotional stress ECG were compared at equal HR levels. In comparison with the emotional stress condition, during exercise the ST segment was more depressed, T-wave amplitudes were larger, and QT and PQ intervals were significantly shorter. These results confirm the hypothesis that the left sympathetic cardiac nerves are dominant during physical stress, while the right cardiac nerves dominate during emotional stress. The relationship of emotional stress to the duration of the QT interval was also examined by Huang, Ebey, and Wolf (1989). In accordance with the results of Hijzen and Slangen, the QT interval was found to be lengthened during feelings of hopelessness and dejection. However, discussions of frustrating and anxiety-producing events in the lives of the subjects were associated with shortening of QT. Unfortunately, no exercise control was included in this study.

The majority of studies in this area are concerned with *acute* cardiovascular reactivity to laboratory-induced psychological stress (Krantz & Manuck, 1984). To our knowledge, there is only one psychophysiological study which addressed the issue of exposure to *prolonged* psychological challenge, using a task with minimal energy requirements. Carroll and Roy (1989) examined cardiovascular reactivity in 18 normotensive adults prior to, during, and after a mental arithmetic task of 16-minute duration. HR showed a marked elevation during the first 4 min of mental arithmetic followed by a gradual decrease to pre-task values. A similar picture emerged from T-wave amplitude responses. By contrast, BP displayed a more or less sustained increase, with DBP showing a more pronounced pattern of sustained elevation than SBP. Digital blood volume pulse exhibited a similar sustained response.

Carrol and Roy discussed two explanations which could account for these results. First, in the course of prolonged emotional stress, alpha-adrenergic effects on the vasculature may become predominant over beta-adrenergic effects on the heart; second, initially increased CO may trigger intrinsically mediated autoregulation of vascular resistance because of metabolically inappropriate tissue perfusion. In other words, to return blood flow to appropriate levels, the arterioles begin to constrict. With either effect (neurogenic or intrinsic), the reduced venous return of blood to the heart acts to reduce CO. However, the price to be paid for increased peripheral resistance is elevated BP (particularly, increased DBP).

It is an intriguing research perspective that the hemodynamic changes observed during long-term exposure to emotional stress may mirror the shifting hemodynamic patterns in the early stages of essential hypertension as proposed by Obrist's (1981) and Obrist et al.'s (1986) hemodynamic model. Apparently, these speculations are in accordance with findings reported by Ewart, Harris, Zeger, and Russel (1986) who investigated changes in HR and BP during a challenging videogame in 38 normotensive adolescents with and 39 subjects without parental history of hypertension. It was found that a persistently diminished pulse pressure (SBP minus DBP) was the cardiovascular response that most reliably characterized normotensive adolescents with familial hypertension. These pulse pressure differences were highly reproducible over a 14-month follow-up period. Certainly, further investigation is required to determine whether repeatedly increased peripheral resistance due to autoregulatory processes ensuing from prolonged emotional stress may finally result in structural changes such as hypertrophic narrowing in the resistive vessels (Folkow, 1977). In particular, BP reactivity in children appears to be a potentially important field of research that has been understudied as yet (Sallis, Dimsdale, & Caine, 1988).

Generalization from Laboratory to Non-Laboratory Settings and Ambulatory Monitoring of HR and BP during Daily Activities

One of the major questions is whether cardiovascular responses to laboratory-induced stress are predictive of cardiovascular responses to stresses of normal daily living at home and at work. A second question to be dealt with is concerned with the covariation of particular emotional states (i.e., happiness, anxiety, or anger) and BP during daily activities. The availability of non-invasive ambulatory HR and BP monitoring devices provides the means to explore the relationship between cardiovascular reactivity to emotional stress in laboratory and natural environments.

Generalizations from Laboratory to Non-Laboratory Settings

McKinney et al. (1985) determined the test-retest reliability of 11 cardiovascular variables during a resting baseline and three common stress tasks such as videogame, multiple-choice reaction time task and cold pressure test. Sixty healthy males underwent the testing twice, approximately 3 months apart. The test-retest coefficients ranged from 0.32 to 0.82. As expected, for the majority of comparisons absolute levels were found to show greater coefficients of test-retest reliability than change scores (defined as difference between task and baseline levels). There was also some evidence for concurrent validity in that BP readings taken during the stress tasks were more highly correlated with ambulatory BP readings at home and at work than casual office pressures. Without exception, SBP values were more highly correlated than DBP values. Similarily, Frederikson, Blumenthal, Evans, Sherwood, and Light (1989) reported that SBP levels recorded during mental arithmetic revealed a positive association with ambulatory levels recorded during work. Change scores, however, failed to show any association with ambulatory BP levels.

In another study on 119 black and white females and males, Ironson et al. (1989) found that baseline levels of SBP and DBP turned out to be the strongest predictors of ambulatory SBP and DBP at home and at work. Baseline BP accounted for as much as 36-59% of the variance in ambulatory BP. By contrast, task reactivity added little predictive information. It accounted for less than 7% beyond the variance accounted for by the baseline. The issue of using baseline levels which are defined as "pretask levels" (that is to say, resting states that anticipate exposure to experimental procedures), has been addressed by Obrist (1981) and Obrist et al. (1986).

In a thoroughly designed multi-method laboratory-field study in 58 male students, Fahrenberg, Foerster, Schneider, Müller, and Myrtek (1986) investigated the predictability of individual differences in a field setting from laboratory measures. The generalizability study revealed that the coefficients of laboratory-field correlations, if squared, indicate only a small percentage of common variance. Hence, to increase the "practical relevance" in investigations of psychophysiological responses during emotionally activating and physically challenging tasks, it was suggested that studies of this type should directly assess individual differences in the criterion situations themselves. These conclusions are in accordance with the findings reported by Van Egeren and Sparrow (1989).

HR and BP during Daily Activities

There are only few studies designed to investigate the relationship between BP and emotional states in individuals during customary activities in familiar environments. In a study presented by Southard, Eisler, and Skidmore (1988), 49 primarily normotensive subjects (30 males and 19 females) were instructed to record their BP and mood state every 2 hours over a period of 2 days. Adjective checklists describing mood states and perceptions of environment were completed just prior to BP measurements. BP and HR recordings utilized a semi-automated device. Within-subjects analyses revealed that holding anger in was associated with elevated SBP, while expressing anger outwardly was related to increased HR. Moreover, perceptions of the environment as hostile and demanding were associated with both high SBP and high DBP. The Type A mood cluster, containing the anxious/tense, active, aggressive, assertive, hard-driving, and self-confident adjectives, discriminated between high and low SBP as well as between high and low HR readings. Also distinguishing between high and low SBP readings was the negative mood cluster, including the worried, depressed, time-pressure, hostile/angry, and anxious/tense adjectives. The positive mood cluster, consisting of the interested, energetic, and patient adjectives, was associated with increased HR, but not with elevated BP.

A similar study was carried out by Stephens, Crowther, Koss, and Bolen (1988). BP was recorded every 15 minutes over a 24-hour period, using a fully automated ambulatory BP monitor. Subjects were instructed to keep a Daily Activities Diary, where all behavioral data were entered at each cuff inflation. The diary contained 15 activity categories (e.g., shopping, housework, eating, phone talk, social behavior, reading/writing, passive recreation, sleeping) and three levels of social involvement (alone, uninvolved, and involved). The sample included 21 normotensives, 20 borderline hypertensives, and 20 sustained essential hypertensives. ANOVAs comparing these groups on mean BP readings for each activity and social involvement category indicated that in the case of significant group differences the two hypertensive groups consistently showed higher BP readings than the normotensive group. However, only few differences emerged between the borderline and the sustained essential hypertensive groups. Interestingly, for three activities (i.e., doing housework, preparing meals, and driving or riding a car) no differences were found among the groups for both SBP and DBP readings. Four activities (participation in meetings at work, walking, shopping, and sleeping) evoked significant group differences on SBP, whereas no differences were found for DBP. The opposite pattern emerged for grooming. It is important to note that comparisons for medicated and unmedicated subjects revealed no significant differences.

James et al. (1986) examined differences in BP associated with self-reported emotional states in 90 borderline hypertensives during 24-hour ambulatory BP monitoring. Again, the automatic timer was preset to 15-minute intervals. Subjects were instructed to record their degree of experienced happiness, anger, or anxiety on a scale from one to ten prior to the BP recording. Subjects were also asked to record their activities, postures, and situations (e.g., at home or at work). Analyses of standardized SBP and DBP readings revealed that emotional states are the most statistically significant source of variation. Multiple comparisons indicated that both SBP and DBP during reported anger and anxiety are significantly higher than during reported happiness. In addition, anxiety-associated pressures are significantly higher outside the home than at home. Moreover, BP readings varied with the experienced intensity of emotional arousal during happiness and anxiety. Specifically, ANCOVA results showed that as the degree of happiness increases, SBP decreases, and that as anxiety intensity increases, DBP increases. Reported anger intensity was not associated with either SBP and DBP. The emotional effects were also related to the variability in BP over the day such that the greater the variability, the greater the average emotional effects on BP.

From studies on ambulatory monitoring of BP and HR during daily activities in familiar environments at home and at work, the following conclusions may be drawn: First, there is a significant contribution of emotional states to the variations of BP and HR, an effect that appears to be largely independent of posture and location of subjects during measurement; second, in accordance with laboratory findings concerning responses to emotional stress, perceptions of the environment as demanding or even hostile are consistently associated with elevated SBP and DBP; third, different emotions tend to evoke different cardiovascular response patterns; fourth, the emotional impact on BP is also dependent on the variability of BP over the day; and fifth, differences in BP elevations between normotensives, borderline hypertensives, and sustained essential hypertensives cannot be fully understood without taking into account the respective patterns of behavior.

Analyses of Actual Cardiovascular Responses and Self-Reported Bodily Changes Associated with Experimentally Induced Target Emotions

Presumably, the first to demonstrate that laboratory-induced target emotions are accompanied by specific changes in the patterning of respiration, pulse rate, and pulse volume amplitude were pioneers such as Alechsieff, Gent, Meumann and Zoneff, and Wundt. The findings of this early research on physiological specificity of emotions are well documented in Wundt's 3-volume work *Grundzüge der physiologischen Psychologie* (Foundations of Physiological Psychology, Vol. II, 1910, pp.301-316; Vol. III, 1911, pp. 191-212). In the second half of our century, Ax's (1953) experiment on the physiological differentiation between anger and fear is a landmark in cardiovascular psychophysiology of emotions. Ax suggested that the fear pattern resembles the action produced by injection of epinephrine (E), while the anger pattern resembles the changes evoked by both E and NE (norepinephrine). E has been conceived as an emergency stimulant which acts to cause significant increases in CO, HR, and SBP, no pronounced effects on DBP, and a decrease in peripheral resistance; NE is assumed to produce no change or a moderate increase in CO, but a significant rise in SBP, DBP, HR, and peripheral resistance (cf. Buss, 1961).

Actual Cardiovascular Responses

Following Ax (1953), experimental work focused on the question of physiological differentiability of anger and fear (e.g., Frankenhäuser, 1978, 1984; Funkenstein, King, & Drolette, 1954, 1957; Schachter, 1957). Results from studies of physiological reactions and catecholamine excretion during states of anger and fear have been reviewed by Wagner (1989). He held that there is sufficient evidence for a clear differentiation between anger and fear in terms of their cardiovascular patterns.

Gatchel and Barnes (1989) surmised that the prominence of theories advocating general arousal patterns (e.g., Schachter & Singer, 1962; Selye, 1976) slowed the research for specific physiological response patterns associated with distinct emotions. However, recent research efforts have focused again on the issue of physiological specificity of emotions.

One of the most widely cited studies dealing with emotion-specific activity in the autonomic nervous system was presented by Ekman, Levenson, and Friesen (1983). They examined a sample of six target emotions: fear, anger, surprise, disgust, sadness, and happiness. In order to minimize contamination of emotions by frustration or embarassment, twelve professional actors and four scientists who studied the face served as subjects. The target emotions were induced by two types of tasks, that is "directed facial action" and "relived emotion". The directed facial action task included six trials; subjects were precisely told which muscles to contract, without being asked to produce an emotional expression. The facial expressions were to be held for 10 seconds. The relived emotion task resembled imagery tasks; subjects were asked to experience each of the six emotions by reliving past emotional experiences for 30 seconds. Autonomic data were evaluated only when the intensity of the experienced emotion reached at least the midpoint on a scale from 0 to 8.

Multivariate analyses of change scores for the two tasks revealed that the elicited emotions were associated with different autonomic response patterns, which were not due to somatic changes: First, in the directed facial action task, anger, fear and sadness were differentiated from happiness, disgust and surprise by higher HR, and anger differed from fear and sadness by increased skin temperature; second, in the relived emotion task, sadness was differentiated from fear, anger and disgust by larger decreases in skin resistance; third, across both tasks, HR accelerated more during anger and fear than during happiness, and finger temperatures were higher during anger than during happiness. Ekman et al. proposed that "it was contracting the facial muscles into the universal emotion signals" (p.1210) which evoked emotion-specific autonomic activity. Research methods and new results providing evidence of universals in facial expressions of emotion have been reviewed by Ekman (1989).

The traditional notion of stimulus specificity includes emotion specificity (Engel, 1972). Therefore, the situational context of emotion induction is usually considered as part of the definition of the stimulus. By contrast, Stemmler (1989) suggested distinguishing between situational response specificity and physiological emotion specificity. He discussed three specificity models which assume different degrees of influence from emotional stimuli on physiological reactivity. First, the model of *"emotion nonspecifity"* implies that physiological responses are not an integral part of emotion and that specific emotion profiles do not exist; however, the existence of specific context profiles is not precluded. Second, the model of *"context-deviation specifity of emotion"* proposes that emotion modifies the influences of situational context variables on physiological reactivity. Third, the model of *"absolute emotion specifity"* claims that different emotional states are necessarily associated with different response patterns which can be clearly discriminated from any situational context specifity. These models have not been adequately considered in previous studies of emotion specifity.

Consistent with the multitrait-multimethod concept for validation of constructs, Stemmler (1989) employed a convergent and a discriminant validation approach. Forty-two female medical students served as subjects. Fear and anger were evoked in both a real-life and an affective imagery context. Happiness was induced by announcement of an unexpected monetary extra bonus, but there was no happiness imagery. The dependent measures included self-reports of emotional experience, EMG, body movements, HR, respiration rate, skin temperature, pulse volume amplitude, pulse transit time (or more precisely, R wave to pulse wave interval), and electrodermal activity (skin conductance reactivity and skin conductance level). Unfortunately, no BP readings were taken. Reactivity was defined in terms of centered difference scores which were subjected to a McCall normalizing transformation. Multivariate comparisons among the reactivity profiles revealed discriminant validity for fear and anger in the real-life context, whereas during imagery no differences were found at all. Compared to anger, real-life induction of fear resulted in lower skin conductance levels, a marked decrease in finger pulse volume amplitude, and in lower head temperature. Furthermore, there was no evidence for convergent validity in either situational context. Obviously, no empirical support was found for the absolute emotion specifity model. With respect to real-life induction of fear and anger, however, the data are consistent with the model of context-deviation specifity of emotion.

Waters, Bernard, and Buco (1989) raised the intriguing question of whether self-report of peripheral somatic and autonomic nervous system responses to emotion-provoking imagery could predict individuals' patterns of physiological responses to the same imagery. Like Stemmler's (1989) model of context-deviation specifity of emotion, Water's approach to test the validity of self-reported patterns of physiological responses during particular emotional states is based on Lang's (1979) bio-informational theory of emotional imagery. That is to say, emotional responses are considered to "occur in stimulus contexts, which define the function of these behavioral transactions. Thus, stimulus information defines the direction of approach and avoidance and is as pertinent to emotional cognition as is the response code" (Lang, 1984, p. 195).

Self-Reported Bodily Changes

Self-reports of peripheral physiological responses to emotion-provoking stimuli can be assessed via the "Autonomic Nervous System Response Inventory" (ANSRI) developed by Waters, Cohen, Bernard, Buco, and Dreger (1984). It comprises 51 items, each one representing a peripheral physiological response (e.g., "Breathing became rapid") which is supposed to occur during emotional states such as fear, anger, sadness, joy, or during physical activity. Subjects are instructed to rate each item as being present on a scale form 1 to 5. The target emotions were initially reconstructed from memory and then imaged. The ANSRI consists of 12 physiological scales (P scales) covering different functions (e.g., P 1 = Cardiac, P 2 = Cardiovascular, P 3 = Skin, P 7 = Respiration, P 12 = Thermoregulation).

In an experiment conducted by Waters et al. (1989), the same target emotion used to evoke arousal for the ANSRI self-report was also used to elicit arousal 2 weeks later during recording of BP, vasomotor response, HR, respiration rate, EMG (forehead and forearm), skin resistance level, and skin temperature. Fifty-two undergraduate volunteers participated in the study. A first step of statistical analysis was designed to examine if imagery periods evoked substantial physiological reactivity. A MANOVA performed for each imagery condition on all physiological measures revealed significant differences between the measures taken during baseline and subsequent imagery periods. In a second step, the ANSRI P scales for a given target emotion (e.g., fear) were entered as predictors of each physiological measure recorded during imagery of that emotion. Stepwise multiple regression analyses showed that the ANSRI P scales were able to reliably predict physiological responses during imagery of fear, anger, sadness, and joy. As expected, the measures which can be predicted vary from emotion to emotion. However, cardiovascular, respiration and electrodermal measures were predicted best. P scales 2 (Cardiovascular), 3 (Skin), 11 (Eyes), 4 (Sudomotor), 6 (Muscle Tension), 7 (Respiration), and 1 (Cardiac) turned out to be the most powerful predictors (in that order). So the ANSRI appears to be a valid instrument for measuring cardiovascular responses to emotion-evoking situations. This is not to say, of course, that self-reported patterns of peripheral bodily responses can replace direct physiological measurement in the search for emotion-specific autonomic and somatic activity. However, Waters et al. (1989) were able to demonstrate that emotions can be differentiated on the basis of perceived bodily changes.

The study of Dalkvist and Rollenhagen (1989a) was also concerned with self-reported reactions in emotions. However, the subjects were required to report on memorized rather than on immediately perceived reactions. Sixty undergraduate students (31 males and 29 females) were given a booklet containing one sheet with scales for 23 emotions (e.g., anxiety, happiness, anger, relief, hope, disappointment, sadness, fear, pride, shame). Each of the 23 emotions was to be rated with respect to 21 different bodily reactions (e.g., face temperature, lump in the throat, respiration rate, pulse rate, tension of jaw muscles, hand temperature, perspiration, pulse, temporary shiver). Correlations among the mean physiological variables were factor analyzed.

It was found that the bodily reactions associated with 23 emotions can be described along four dimensions. The first factor may be interpreted as a general arousal dimension covering both ergotropic and trophotropic responses. It is mainly characterized by responses occuring during exercise under high work load. Factor scores indicate that anxiety, anger, and fear are located at the ergotropic end of the continuum, whereas relief, sadness and sentimentality are at the trophotropic end. The second factor is essentially unipolar. It comprises both parasympathetic activity (e.g., wateriness in the eyes, a lump in the throat, pressure on the chest) and facial muscle reactions (orientation of eyebrows and orientation of the corners of the mouth). Far the highest factor score applies to sadness. The third factor appears to represent a combined pattern of adrenergic and parasympathetic reactions. It has been referred to as specific arousal. The negative pole is defined by decreased temperature in the hands and the face, and also by an urge to urinate and agitation in the stomach, whereas the positive pole may be described in terms of increased temperature in the hands and the face, and increased salivary secretion. Factor scores reveal that the negative pole is closely related to fear, helplessness and anxiety. On the other hand, the positive pole is strongly associated with anger. Finally, the fourth dimension is represented by the symptoms of goose pimples and temporary shiver which are important for increasing or perserving body heat. High positive factor scores were found for fear, aesthetic experience, lust, sadness and sentimentality. It is difficult to recognize a common psychological property in these emotions.

The findings of Dalkvist and Rollenhagen (1989a) are largely consistent with results obtained from measuring actual physiological responses during laboratory-induced emotions. Furthermore, the data support the hypothesis that different emotions may be characterized by different patterns of self-reported bodily changes.

In another study, Dalkvist and Rollenhagen (1989b) attempted a structural description of three aspects of emotions, namely global feeling, perceived bodily reactions and the cognitive content. Like self-reported bodily changes, the feeling data could be described in terms of four dimensions (i.e., hedonic tone, potency, excitement, and positive relatedness) as well. Moreover, the feeling dimensions exhibited a rather strong correlation with the four physiological factors (i.e., general arousal, sadness reactions, specific arousal, and goose pimples and shiver). The most remarkable correlations were between general arousal and excitement ($r = 0.72$), sadness reactions (comprising parasympathetic and facial muscle activity) and hedonic tone ($r = -0.83$), specific arousal and potency ($r = 0.58$), and goose pimples and shiver and positive relatedness ($r = 0.53$). Among the six cognitive factors (i.e., general evaluation, absence of positive value, other responsible, future, object-self agency, and goal-orientation), only the dimension of general arousal turned out to be strongly related to the factors of the feeling and physiological domains. The most impressive correlations were between general evaluation and hedonic tone (r = 0.89), and general evaluation and sadness reactions (r = -.71).

The results presented by Dalkvist and Rollenhagen (1989a,b) have important implications for emotion theory. Consequently, they bear also on the issue of cardiovascular reactivity and emotional control. First, with respect to the fairly good match of the feeling domain with the structure of memorized bodily changes during emotional states, it may be concluded that perceived bodily reactions contribute to emotional experience. Second, arousal in emotion appears to be essentially two-dimensional: there are two arousal dimensions in the feeling domain (i.e., excitement and potency), and two arousal dimensions in the domain of perceived bodily reactions (i.e., general arousal and specific arousal). These findings are clearly inconsistent with theories advocating general arousal patterns. Third, the influence of cognitive appraisal on feelings and perceived bodily changes, as indexed by the correlations between the general evaluation factor and both the hedonic tone and sadness reactions, appears to be confined to a few dimensions within the feeling and physiological domains.

Investigation of Individual Difference Variables

A large body of well founded data indicates that there are wide individual differences in autonomic nervous system responses to emotional stress (Engel & Bickford, 1961; Fahrenberg, 1986; Krantz & Manuck, 1984; Lacey, Bateman, & Van Lehn, 1953; Obrist et al., 1986). Recent literature also documents the influence of certain demographic characteristics such as age, sex, racial or ethnic origin on cardiovascular reactivity.

Age, Sex, and Ethnicity

Age and sex are important determinants of cardiovascular adjustments during emotional stress. Gintner, Hollandsworth, and Intrieri (1986) found an age-related decrease in HR during active coping in a sample of 60 normotensive male volunteers with ages between 15-55 years. Matthews and Stoney (1988) examined the influence of sex and age on BP and HR reactivity in 125 women, 93 men, 121 girls, and 96 boys. Again, adults displayed smaller HR responses than did children. The inverse relationship between age and HR reactivity could be due to an age-dependent attenuation of beta-adrenergic influences on the myocardium. Moreover, Matthews and Stoney found that adult males exhibited larger SBP and DBP responses to all stressors than adult females. Compared to SBP, no sex differences were obtained for DBP among children. The results of a meta-analysis carried out by Stoney, Davis, and Matthews (1987) on studies from 1965-1986 revealed higher resting HR and HR reactivity in females, whereas males showed higher SBP levels and increased SBP reactivity. There is also some evidence that BP reactivity may depend on the menstrual cycle phase. Hastrup and Light (1984) found sex differences when readings were taken during the follicular phase, whereas no differences were observed during the luteal phase. However, these findings are not consistent with the results reported by Stoney, Langer, and Gelling (1986).

Studies of psychosocial factors and cardiovascular diseases suggest that psychosocial resources provide a protective function against elevated BP. Dressler, Dos Santos, and Viteri (1986) observed highest mean BP in mixed race and black Brazilians who had low psychosocial resources; by contrast, Afro-Brazilians with high psychosocial resources showed lower BP readings than white Brazilians. Research on black-white differences in stressor-induced cardiovascular and neurohumoral responses indicate increased BP reactivity in Blacks (Anderson, Lane, Muranaka, Williams, & Houseworth, 1988). Similarily, Tischenkel et al. (1989) reported that Blacks displayed higher DBP responses during the cold pressor test than did Whites. The apparent differential vasoconstriction in Blacks and Whites has been discussed in terms of differences in alpha-adrenergic influences. As to black-white differences in HR reactivity, inconsistent results are reported (Anderson et al., 1988; McNeilly & Zeichner, 1989).

Several studies suggest a genetic contribution to individual differences in cardiovascular reactivity. Normotensive offspring of parents with essential hypertension were found to exhibit exaggerated HR and/or BP reactivity (Ditto, 1986; Hastrup, Kraemer, Hotchkiss, & Johnson, 1986; Manuck, Proietti, Rader, & Polefrone, 1985; Musante, Treiber, Strong, & Levy, 1990). Some additional support comes from twin studies. Smith et al. (1987) examined possible genetic influence on cardiovascular reactivity to laboratory-induced stress in 82 monozygotic (MZ) and 88 dizygotic (DZ) adult male twin pairs. Estimates of heritability for SBP and DBP reactivity were marginally significant, whereas analyses of HR reactivity did not reveal a heritable component. It may be concluded that there are at least some genetic influences in BP reactivity to emotional stress. The importance of non-genetic and extrafamilial determinants was clearly demonstrated by Matthews et al. (1988). They tested the extent of parent-offspring and sibling resemblances in BP and HR responses during challenging tasks in 142 families. Results showed a pronounced lack of siblings' resemblances. Furthermore, parents and offspring shared no similarities, except in SBP responses to isometric handgrip exercise.

Apart from investigating demographic and genetic influences, there is a large body of literature pertaining to the role of anger and hostility in cardiovascular reactivity and the development of cardiovascular disorders (Diamond, 1982; Harrell, 1980; Krantz & Manuck, 1984; Mann, 1986). Research on the emotional complex of anger and hostility was instigated more than 50 years ago by Alexander's (1939) proposal that chronic inhibition of rage may lead to a chronic elevation of BP. He described hypertensives as persons who are unable to express their anger because of competing tendencies toward passive, dependent and anxious behavior. Subsequent studies mainly dealt with three questions: First, the relationship between hostility as a trait and cardiovascular reactivity; second, anger expression and cardiovascular reactivity; and third, assertiveness and cardiovascular reactivity.

Hostility and Cardiovascular Reactivity

Hostility assessed by the Cook-Medley Hostility (Ho) Scale (Cook & Medley, 1954) has been proposed to predict the development of coronary heart disease (CHD). This hypothesis was tested in a 33-year follow-up study of 1,399 male university students by Hearn, Murray, and Luepker (1989). Contrary to expectation, however higher Ho scores were not predictive of CHD morbidity or CHD mortality.

Using another hostility measure, Koskenvuo et al. (1988) investigated the association between hostility and ischemic heart disease (IHD) during a 3-year follow-up in 3,750 Finnish men aged 40-59 years. It was found that hostility did not predict IHD among healthy men, but extreme hostility turned out to be a strong determinant of coronary attack in men with previous IHD and hypertension. Obviously, hostility is not a proven risk factor in all populations. It also remains unclear how hostility asserts its influence on the disease process. One possible pathway through which hostility could contribute to CHD is enhanced SNS-mediated reactivity. That is to say, it is assumed that highly hostile persons spend most of their time in a heightened arousal state. Nevertheless, studies exposing high and low hostile subjects to traditional laboratory stressors were unable to demonstrate differences in cardiovascular reactivity. Only more socially oriented tasks stimulating a high level of interpersonal conflict (e.g., anagram task with harassment), or situations involving social interaction (e.g., role-play or discussion task) were shown to evoke larger SBP and DBP responses in subjects with high hostility compared to low hostile controls (Smith & Allred, 1989; Suarez & Williams, 1989; Weidner, Friend, Ficarrotto, & Mendell, 1989). Thus the *interaction* between situational characteristics and hostility appears to determine the level of cardiovascular arousal.

Anger Expression and Cardiovascular Reactivity

Indirect experimental evidence for the importance of anger expression in cardiovascular processes comes from the work of Hokanson and Burgess (1962a,b) and Hokanson, Burgess, and Cohen (1963). In the line of these studies, Huber, Hauke, and Gramer (1988) examined the relationship between frustration and cardiovascular arousal (BP and HR). Frustration was induced by modifying the standard instruction of a concentration performance test. Half of the 112 male and 112 female subjects underwent either a frustrating or non-frustrating experience. Under the non-frustrating control condition there were only minor changes in cardiovascular arousal. In frustrated subjects, however, a substantial increase in SBP, DBP, and HR was found. Additionally, the results indicated that frustrated subjects who were given an opportunity to physically or verbally aggress against the frustrator, exhibited significant reduction in cardiovascular arousal. Elevations in BP and HR following the frustration manipulations can be considered as a sympathetic alarm reaction. The decrease of arousal subsequent to the expression of aggression in frustrated subjects was discussed in terms of the catharsis hypothesis.

In research that directly tries to establish a link between anger expression and cardiovascular reactivity, individuals are typically classified as "anger in" (suppression of anger) and "anger out" (expression of anger) by means of self-report scales (Spielberger et al., 1985). This distinction was introduced by Funkenstein, King, and Drolette (1954). Methodologically, research follows several directions. The dominant strategy has been to look for a predicted BP difference between anger in and anger out subjects in various racial and stress area groups. Harburg et al. (1973) found that anger was generally related to higher SBP and DBP in black and white subjects. Using Harburg's Anger In/Anger Out scale, Dimsdale et al. (1986) studied 572 men and women who participated in a BP screening program. There were interesting race and sex differences in this sample. After controlling for age and social class, the relationship between suppressed anger and SBP remained significant for white men, exhibited a trend in black men, and was not significant for women. Across all analyses, DBD was not associated with suppressed anger.

Cottington, Matthews, Talbott, and Kuller (1986) examined the modifying affects of suppressed anger on the relationships between job stress and hypertension. Suppressed anger was assessed by the *Multidimensional Anger Inventory* developed by Siegel (1985). Prevalence of hypertension (defined as DBP $\geq$ 90 mmHg) was highest among men who suppress their anger *and* reported more job stress (indexed by job future ambiguity, dissatisfaction with coworkers, and dissatisfaction with promotions). Conversely, a more "reflective" coping style which bypasses anger and focuses on problem solving, appears to be associated with lower levels of DBP and lower evidence of hypertension than a coping style focusing around "resentment" implying both anger in and anger out (Harburg, Blakelook, & Roeper, 1979).

It was critically noted by Goldstein, Edelberg, Meier, and Davis (1988) that Cottington et al. (1986) used a version of Siegel's Anger-In scale which included only items that assess the prolongation of the feeling of anger. This scale was labeled "Anger-In/Brood" by Siegel. Hence, it does not seem to be conceptually equivalent to the notion of suppressing the expression of anger. In Goldstein's study, 29 normotensive and 16 hypertensive subjects rated on analog scales the anger they experienced at home and at work (Experienced Anger). Furthermore, they rated the likelihood that others would be aware of their anger (Expressed Anger). Across the whole group, statistical analyses revealed an inverse relationship between expressed Anger and both SBP and DBP, but not between HR and Expressed Anger. No significant association was found between Experienced Anger and cardiovascular reactivity.

There is also some support for the hypothesis that expressing anger outwardly may be related to heightened SBP and DBP (Siegel, 1984). In summary, it may be concluded that merely being exposed to a stressful situation is not sufficient to produce sustained elevated BP. However, there is a substantial lack of knowledge regarding the mode and direction of anger expression.

Assertiveness and Cardiovascular Reactivity

Another direction of research in this field is more experimentally oriented. It focuses on interactive behavior and its concomitant cardiovascular reactivity of normotensive and hypertensive subjects when exposed to interpersonal conflict situations. The general assumption underlying this paradigm is that conflicts regarding anger expression are related to deficits in assertiveness.

Keane et al. (1982) assessed the performance of three groups of 12 subjects each (i.e., hypertensives, normotensive medical outpatients, and normotensive controls) in role-played scenes requiring negative assertion (e.g., expressing criticism) and positive assertion (e.g., expressing appreciation). It was found that hypertensives were less assertive than their normotensive controls. However, the normotensive medical outpatients responded equally unassertive in the same role-played scenes. So unassertiveness does not seem to be unique to hypertensive individuals. Furthermore, BP and HR were higher during negative than during positive scenes. Yet, there were no significant between-group differences in cardiovascular reactivity. Similar results were reported by Delamater et al. (1989).

Morrison, Bellack, and Manuck (1985) suggested that considering subgroups of cardiovascular response clusters could help to clarify the question whether hypertensives are different in their social interactions from normotensive persons. The authors identified two types of response patterns among their hypertensives: One group with increased pulse pressure due to large SBP elevations, and an another group displaying low pulse pressure associated with substantial DBP reactions. With respect to overall assertiveness, subjects of the first group were more assertive than those of the second group, but equal to normotensives. Moreover, they were also rated more aggressive than normotensives. Subjects of the second group appeared to be lower in assertiveness than did normotensive controls.

At present, there is no clear answer to the question whether hypertensives are less assertive than normotensive individuals. Facing the heterogeneity of hypertensives with respect to cardiovascular reactivity, controlled naturalistic studies of interpersonal interactions are needed, including different hypertensive response types.

Summary and Conclusions

As pointed out at the beginning of this review, the issue of cardiovascular reactivity and emotional control has to be discussed within the context of theories of emotion. The question whether emotions emerge from central brain processes, or alternatively, from peripheral autonomic and somatic changes appears to be inappropriate in the presence of modern psychobiological research. Rather, one may hold that emotional states can be instigated by inputs to certain subcortical command circuits, including information from cortical processes and feedback from peripheral changes as well.

There seems to be no doubt about the existence of discrete fundamental emotions such as enjoyment, disgust, anger or fear. However, a consistent picture of differences in cardiovascular and other physiological measures has been demonstrated only for fear and anger. Attempts to differentiate among other emotions have yielded much less consistent findings. The partial failure to show physiological specificity for a wide range of emotions may be due to difficulties in evoking different and relatively pure emotions. Using affective imagery of memorized life scenes rather than external laboratory stimuli as a means of producing emotions, did not turn out to be a real alternative. Presumably, the only way to elicit pure and authentic emotions of sufficient intensity is to use experimental conditions approaching real-life situations as close as possible.

Obviously, the notion that cardiovascular arousal is essentially unidimensional is not consistent with the results of recent research efforts focusing on the search for physiological specificity of emotions. The principle of stimulus-specific response patterns has been widely accepted. However, research on emotion specificity has been based largely on the concept of absolute emotion specificity, neglecting the modifying influences of the situational context variables. Stemmler's (1989) model of context-deviation specificity of emotion opens a promising perspective for further studies of physiological specificity of emotions.

Cardiovascular reactivity is usually defined in terms of change scores. Unfortunately, treating a difference score as though it were a single score has serious pitfalls. Some persisting dilemmas in the measurement of change (e.g., the over-correction – under-correction dilemma, the unreliability-invalidity dilemma, or the physicalism-subjectivism dilemma) were discussed by Bereiter (1963).

A considerable number of inconsistencies between studies of cardiovascular reactivity may be due to large errors of measurement associated with change scores. Furthermore, Stemmler (1987) demonstrated that the different reactivity scores (such as the unweighted difference between task and baseline level, Lacey's Autonomic Lability Score, percentage scores, or normalized differences) account for different proportions of the interindividual and intraindividual variance.

The issue raised by individual differences in cardiovascular reactivity resulting from the choice of the reference level was addressed by Obrist (1981). He found that using a pretask baseline instead of a relaxation baseline as a standard of comparison acted to underestimate HR and BP reactivity in some subjects. Consequently, the reference level as well as the method for scoring reactivity needs careful selecting with regard to the given research objectives.

Available data suggest that there is a close relationship between experimentally induced emotional states and cardiovascular reactivity. Yet, before using cardiovascular responses to index emotional states, further studies are needed to deepen our understanding of the mechanisms underlying individual differences in cardiovascular and neuroendocrine reactivity. Different cardiovascular response patterns associated with different behavioral requirements such as active vs. passive coping need not necessarily reflect differences in emotional states.

Certain psychological traits (e.g., hostility) have been discusssed as possible mediators of cardiovascular reactivity, and in the long run as predictors of cardiovascular diseases. However, results from epidemiological and experimental research bearing on this issue are not convincing. Moreover, it will not suffice to view CHD or essential hypertension as associated with certain traits such as the inability to express hostility, without ascertaining the triggering mechanisms. Further research is needed to elucidate the interaction between environmental events and the individual's propensity to react.

References

Alexander, F. (1939). Emotional factors in essential hypertension: Presentation of a tentative hypothesis. *Psychosomatic Medicine, 1*, 173-179.

Allen, M.T. & Crowell, M.D. (1989). Patterns of autonomic response during laboratory stressors. *Psychophysiology, 26*, 603-614.

Allen, M.T., Obrist, P.A., Sherwood, A., & Crowell, M.D. (1987). Evaluation of myocardial and peripheral vascular responses during reaction time, mental arithmetic, and cold pressor tasks. *Psychophysiology, 24*, 648-656.

Anderson, N.B., Lane, J.D., Muranaka, M., Williams, R.B., Jr., & Houseworth, S.J. (1988). Racial differences in blood pressure and forearm vascular responses to the cold face stimulus. *Pychosomatic Medicine, 50*, 57-63.

Ax, A.F. (1953). The physiological differentiation between fear and anger in humans. *Psychosomatic Medicine, 14*, 433-442.

Bereiter, C. (1963). Some persisting dilemmas in the measurement of change. In C.W. Harris (Ed.), *Problems of measuring change* (pp. 3-20). Madison: University of Wisconsin Press.

Brod, J. (1963). Hemodynamic basis of acute pressor reactions and hypertension. *British Heart Journal, 25*, 227-245.

Brod, J. (1982). Emotionelle pressorische Reaktionen und etablierter Hochdruck beim Menschen. In D. Vaitl (Ed.), *Essentielle Hypertonie. Psychologisch-medizinische Aspekte* (pp. 25-61). Berlin: Springer-Verlag.

Buss, A.H. (1961). *The psychology of aggression*. New York: Wiley.

Cannon, W.B. (1927). The James-Lange theory of emotions: A critical examination and an alternative theory. *American Journal of Psychology, 39,* 106-124.

Carroll, D., & Roy, M.P. (1989). Cardiovascular activity during prolonged mental arithmetic challenge: shifts in the haemodynamic control of blood pressure? *Journal of Physiology, 3,* 403-408.

Cook, W.W., & Medley, D.M. (1954). Proposed hostility and pharisaic-virtue scales for the MMPI. *Journal of Applied Psychology, 38,* 414-418.

Cottington, E.M., Matthews, K.A., Talbott, E., & Kuller, L.H. (1986). Occupational stress, suppressed anger, and hypertension. *Psychosomatic Medicine, 48,* 249-260.

Dalkvist, J., & Rollenhagen, C. (1989a). *The structure of perceived bodily reactions in emotions.* Reports from the Department of Psychology, University of Stockholm, No. 705.

Dalkvist, J., & Rollenhagen, C. (1989b). *Three aspects of emotion awareness: feeling, perceived bodily reaction and cognition.* Reports from the Department of Psychology, University of Stockholm, No. 709.

Delamater, A.M., Taylor, C.B., Schneider, J., Allen, R., Chesney, M.A., & Agras, W.S. (1989). Interpersonal behavior and cardiovascular reactivity in pharmacologically-treated hypertensives. *Journal of Psychosomatic Research, 33,* 335-345.

Diamond, E.L. (1982). The role of anger and hostility in essential hypertension and coronary heart disease. *Psychological Bulletin, 92,* 410-433.

Dimsdale, J.E., Pierce, C., Schoenfeld, D., Brown, A., Zusman, R. & Graham, R. (1986). Suppressed anger and blood pressure: The effects of race, sex, social class, obesity, and age. *Psychosomatic Medicine, 48,* 430-436.

Ditto, B. (1986). Parental history of essential hypertension, active coping, and cardiovascular reactivity. *Psychophysiology, 23,* 62-70.

Dressler, W.W., Dos Santos, J.E., & Viteri, F.E. (1986). Blood pressure, ethnicity, and psychosocial resources. *Psychosomatic Medicine, 48,* 509-519.

Ekman, P. (1989). The argument and evidence about universals in facial expressions of emotion. In H. Wagner & A. Manstead (Eds.), *Handbook of social psychophysiology* (pp. 143-164). Wiley: Chichester.

Ekman, P., Levenson, R.W., & Friesen, W.V. (1983). Autonomic nervous system activity distinguishes among emotions. *Science, 221,* 1208-1210.

Engel, B.T. (1972). Response specifity. In N.S. Greenfield & R.A. Sternbach (Eds.), *Handbook of psychophysiology* (pp. 571-576). New York: Holt, Rinehart and Winston.

Engel, B.T., & Bickford, A.F. (1961). Response specifity: Stimulus response and individual-response specifity in essential hypertensives. *Archives of General Psychiatry, 5,* 478-489.

Ewart, C.K., Harris, W.L., Zeger, S., & Russel, G.A. (1986). Diminished pulse pressure under mental stress characterized normotensive adolescents with parental high blood pressure. *Psychosomatic Medicine, 48,* 489-501.

Fahrenberg, J. (1986). Psychophysiological individuality: a pattern analytic approach to personality research and psychosomatic medicine. *Advances in Behaviour Research and Therapy, 8,* 43-100.

Fahrenberg, J., Foerster, F., Schneider, H.-J., Müller, W., & Myrtek, M. (1986). Predictability of individual differences in activation processes in a field setting based on laboratory measures. *Psychophysiology, 23,* 323-333.

Fehr, F.S., & Stern, J.A. (1970). Peripheral physiological variables and emotion: The James-Lange theory revisited. *Psychological Bulletin, 74,* 411-424.

Folkow, B. (1977). Role of vascular factor in hypertension. *Contributions to Nephrology, 8,* 81-94.

Frankenhäuser, M. (1978). *Psychoneuroendocrine sex differences in adaptation to the psychosocial environment.* New York: Academic Press.

Frankenhäuser, M. (1984). Psychoneuroendocrine approaches to the study of stressful person-environment transactions. In H.Selye (Ed.), *Selye's guide to stress research* (pp. 46-70). New York: Van Nostrand Reinhold.

Frederikson, M., Blumenthal, J.A., Evans, D.D., Sherwood, A., & Light, K.C. (1989). Cardiovascular responses in the laboratory and in the natural environment: Is blood pressure reactivity to laboratory-induced mental stress related to ambulatory blood pressure during everyday life? *Journal of Psychosomatic Research, 33,* 753-762.

Funkenstein, D.H., King, S.H., & Drolette, M.E. (1954). The direction of anger during a laboratory stress-inducing situation. *Psychosomatic Medicine, 16,* 404-413.

Funkenstein, D.H., King, S.H., & Drolette, M.E. (1957). *Mastery of stress.* Cambridge, Ma: Harvard University Press.

Gatchel, R.J., & Barnes, D. (1989). Physiological self-control and emotion. In H. Wagner & A. Manstead (Eds.), *Handbook of social psychophysiology* (pp. 121-142). Chichester: New York.

Gintner, G.G., Hollandsworth, J.G., & Intrieri, R.C. (1986). Age differences in cardiovascular reactivity under active coping conditions. *Psychophysiology, 23,* 113-120.

Goldstein, H.S., Edelberg, R., Meier, C.F., & Davis, L. (1988). Relationship of resting blood pressure and heart rate to experienced anger and expressed anger. *Psychosomatic Medicine, 50,* 321-329.

Harburg, E., Blakelook, E.H., & Roeper, P.J. (1979). Resentful and reflective coping with arbitrary authority and blood pressure: Detroit. *Psychosomatic Medicine, 41,* 189-202.

Harburg, E., Erfurt, J.C., Hauenstein, L.S., Chape, C., Schull, W.J., & Schork, M.A. (1973). Socio-ecological stress, suppressed hostility, skin color, and black-white male blood pressure: Detroit. *Psychosomatic Medicine, 35,* 276-296.

Harrell, J.B. (1980). Psychological factors and hypertension: A status report. *Psychological Bulletin, 87,* 482-501.

Hastrup, J.L., Kraemer, D.L., Hotchkiss, A.P., & Johnson, C.A. (1986). Cardiovascular responsivity to stress: Family patterns and the effects of instructions. *Journal of Psychosomatic Research, 30*, 233-241.

Hastrup, J.L., & Light, K.C. (1984). Sex differences in cardiovascular stress responses: Modulation as a function of menstrual cycle phases. *Journal of Psychosomatic Research, 28*, 475-483.

Hearn, M., Murray, D.M., & Luepker, R.V. (1989). Hostility, coronary heart disease, and total mortality: A 33-year follow-up study of university students. *Journal of Behavioral Medicine, 12*, 105-121.

Hijzen, T.H., & Slangen, J.L. (1985). The electrocardiogram during emotional and physical stress. *International Journal of Psychophysiology, 2*, 273-279.

Hokanson, J.E., & Burgess, M. (1962a). The effects of three types of aggression on vascular processes. *Journal of Abnormal and Social Psychology, 64*, 446-449.

Hokanson, J.E., & Burgess, M. (1962b). The effects of status, type of frustration, and aggression on vascular processes. *Journal of Abnormal and Social Psychology, 65*, 232-237.

Hokanson, J.E., & Burgess, M., & Cohen, M.F. (1963). Effects of displaced aggression on systolic blood pressure. *Journal of Abnormal and Social Psychology, 67*, 214-218.

Huang, M.H., Ebey, J., & Wolf, S. (1989). Responses of the QT interval of the electrocardiogram during emotional stress. *Psychosomatic Medicine, 51*, 419-427.

Huber, H.P., Hauke, D., & Gramer, M. (1988). Frustrationsbedingter Blutdruckanstieg und dessen Abbau durch aggressive Reaktionen. *Zeitschrift für experimentelle und angewandte Psychologie, 35*, 427-440.

Ironson, G.H., Gellman, M.D., Spitzer, S.B., Llabre, M.M., DeCarlo Pasin, R., Weidler, D.J., & Schneiderman, N. (1989). Predicting home and work blood pressure measurements from resting baselines and laboratory reactivity in black and white Americans. *Psychophysiology, 26*, 174-184.

Izard, C.E. (1971). *The face of emotion.* New York: Appleton-Century Crofts.

Izard, C.E. (1977). *Human emotions.* New York: Plenum Press.

Izard, C.E. (1979). *The Maximally Discrimination Facial Movement Coding System (Max).* Newark: Instructional Resources Center, University of Delaware.

James, G.D., Yee, L.S., Harshfield, G.A., Blank, S.G., & Pickering, T.G. (1986). The influence of happiness, anger, and anxiety on the blood pressure of borderline hypertensives. *Psychosomatic Medicine, 48*, 502-508.

James, W. (1884). What is an emotion? *Mind, 9*, 188-205.

Keane, T.M., Martin, J.E., Berler, E.S., Wooten, L.S., Fleece, E.L., & Williams, J.G. (1982). Are hypertensives less assertive? A controlled evaluation. *Journal of Consulting and Clinical Psychology, 50*, 499-508.

Koskenvuo, M., Kaprio, J., Rose, R.J., Kesäniemi, A., Sarna, S., Heikkilä, K., & Langinvainio, H. (1988). Hostility as a risk factor for mortality and ischemic heart disease in men. *Psychosomatic Medicine, 50*, 330-340.

Krantz, D.S., & Manuck, S.B. (1984). Acute psychophysiologic reactivity and risk of cardiovascular disease: A review and methodologic critique. *Psychological Bulletin, 96*, 435-464.

Lacey, J.I. (1956). The evaluation of autonomic responses: toward a general solution. *Annals of the New York Academy of Sciences, 67*, 123-164.

Lacey, J.I. (1967). Somatic response patterning and stress: Some revisions of activation theory. In M.H. Appley & R. Trumble (Eds.), *Psychological stress: Issues in research* (pp. 14-42). New York: Appleton-Century-Crofts.

Lacey, J.I., Bateman, D.E., & Van Lehn, R. (1953). Autonomic response specifity: An experimental study. *Psychosomatic Medicine, 15*, 8-21.

Lang, P.J. (1979). A bio-informational theory of emotional imagery. *Psychophysiology, 16*, 495-512.

Lang, P.J. (1984). Cognition in emotion: concept and action. In C.E. Izard, J. Kagan & R.B. Zajonc (Eds.), *Emotions, cognitions, and behavior* (pp. 192-226). Cambridge: Cambridge University Press.

Lange, C. (1885). *The emotions.* Denmark (Original reference unavailable). Translated by H.Kurella. Leipzig: Theodor Thomas, 1887; retranslated by Istar A. Haupt for K. Dunlap (Ed.), The emotions. Baltimore: Williams & Wilkins, (1922).

Langer, A.W., McCubbin, J.A., Stoney, C.M., Hutcheson, J.S., Charlton, J.D., & Obrist, P.A. (1985). Cardiopulmonary adjustments during exercise and an aversive reaction time task: Effects of beta-adrenoceptor blockade. *Psychophysiology, 22*, 59-68.

Larsen, P.B., Schneiderman, N., & DeCarlo Pasin, R. (1986). Physiological bases of cardiovascular psychophysiology. In M.G.H. Coles, E. Donchin & S.W. Porges (Eds.), *Psychophysiology: Systems, processes, and applications* (pp. 122-165). Amsterdam: Elsevier.

Lehrer, P.M., Groveman, A., Randolph, C., Miller, M.H., & Pollack, I. (1989). Physiological response patterns to cognitive testing in adults with closed head injuries. *Psychophysiology, 26*, 668-675.

MacLean, P.D. (1949). Psychosomatic disease and the "visceral brain": Recent developments bearing on the Papez theory of emotion. *Psychosomatic Medicine, 11*, 338-353.

Mann, A.H. (1986). The psychological aspects of essential hypertension. *Journal of Psychosomatic Research, 30*, 527-541.

Manuck, S.B., Proietti, J.M., Rader, S.J., & Polefrone, J.M. (1985). Parental hypertension, affect and cardiovascular response to cognitive challenge. *Psychosomatic Medicine, 47*, 189-200.

Matthews, K.A., Manuck, S.B., Stoney, C.M., Rakaczky, C.J., McCann, B.S., Saab, P.G., Woodall, K.L., Block, D.R., Visintainer, P.F., & Engebretson, T.O. (1988). Familial aggregation of blood pressure and heart rate responses during behavioral stress. *Psychosomatic Medicine, 50*, 341-352.

Matthews, K.A., & Stoney, C.M. (1988). Influences of sex and age on cardiovascular responses during stress. *Psychosomatic Medicine, 50,* 46-56.

McKinney, M.E., Miner, M.H., Rüddel, H., McIlvain, H.E., Witte, H., Buell, J.C., Eliot, R.S., & Grant, L.B. (1985). The standardized mental stress test protocol: Test-retest reliability and comparison with ambulatory blood pressure monitoring. *Psychophysiology, 22,* 453-463.

McNeilly, M., & Zeichner, A. (1989). Neuropeptide and cardiovascular responses to intravenous catheterization in normotensive and hypertensive Blacks and Whites. *Health Psychology, 8,* 487-501.

Morrison, R.L., Bellack, A.S., & Manuck, S.B. (1985). Role of social competence in borderline essential hypertension. *Journal of Consulting and Clinical Psychology, 53,* 248-255.

Musante, L., Treiber, F.A., Strong, W.B., & Levy, M. (1990). Family history of hypertension and cardiovascular reactivity to forehead cold stimulation in black male children. *Journal of Psychosomatic Research, 34,* 111-116.

Nisbett, R.E., & Schachter, S. (1966). Cognitive manipulation of pain. *Journal of Experimental Social Psychology, 2,* 227-236.

Obrist, P.A. (1981). *Cardiovascular psychophysiology: A Perspective.* New York: Plenum Press.

Obrist, P.A., Lawler, J.E., Howard, J.L., Smithson, K.W., Martin, P.L., & Manning, J. (1974). Sympathetic influences on cardiac rate and contractility during acute stress in humans. *Psychophysiology, 11,* 405-427.

Obrist, P.A., Light, K.C., Langer, A.W., & Koepke, J.P. (1986). Psychosomatics. In M.G.H. Coles, E. Donchin & S.W. Porges (Eds.), *Psychophysiology: Systems, processes, and applications* (pp. 626-645). Amsterdam: Elsevier.

Panksepp, J. (1989). The neurobiology of emotions: Of animal brains and human feelings. In H. Wagner & A. Manstead (Eds.), *Handbook of social psychophysiology* (pp. 5-26).

Papez, J.W. (1937). A proposed mechanism of emotion. *Archives of Neurological Psychiatry, 38,* 725-743.

Reisenzein, R. (1983). The Schachter theory of emotion: Two decades later. *Psychological Bulletin, 94,* 239-264.

Rinn, W.E. (1984). The neuropsychology of facial expression: A review of the neurological and psychological mechanisms for producing facial expressions. *Psychological Bulletin, 95,* 52-77.

Sallis, J.F., Dimsdale, J.E., & Caine, C. (1988). Blood pressure reactivity in children. *Journal of Psychosomatic Research, 32,* 1-12.

Schachter, J. (1957). Pain, fear, and anger in hypertensives and normotensives: a psychophysiological study. *Psychosomatic Medicine, 19,* 17-29.

Schachter, S. & Singer, J.E. (1962). Cognitive, social, and physiological determinants of emotional state. *Psychological Review, 69,* 379-399.

Selye, H. (1976). *The stress of life.* New York: Mc Graw-Hill.

Shepherd, J.T. (1990). Heart failure: Role of cardiovascular reflexes. *Cardioscience, 1,* 7-12.

Sherwood, A., Allen, M.T., Obrist, P.A., & Langer, A.W. (1986). Evaluation of beta-adrenergic influences on cardiovascular and metabolic adjustments to physical and psychological stress. *Psychophysiology, 23*, 89-104.

Siegel, J.M. (1984). Anger and cardiovascular risk in adolescents. *Health Psychology, 3*, 293-313.

Siegel, J.M. (1985). The measurement of anger as a multidimensional construct. In M.A. Chesney & R.H. Rosenman (Eds.), *Anger and hostility in cardiovascular and behavioral disorders* (pp. 59-82). Washington: Hemisphere.

Smith, O.A.,Jr., Rushmer, R.F., & Lasher, E.P., (1960). Similarity of cardiovascular responses to exercise and to diencephalon stimulation. *American Journal of Physiology, 198*, 1130-1142.

Smith, T.W., & Allred, K.D. (1989). Blood-pressure responses during social interaction in high- and low-cynically hostile males. *Journal of Behavioral Medicine, 12*, 135-143.

Smith, T.W., Turner, C.W., Ford, M.H., Hunt, S.C., Barlow, G.K., Stults, B.M., & Williams, R.R. (1987). Blood pressure reactivity in adult male twins. *Health Psychology, 6*, 209-220.

Southard, D.R., Eisler, R.M., & Skidmore, J.R. (1988). Covariation of mood and blood pressure during daily activities. *Journal of Behavioral Medicine, 11*, 537-551.

Spielberger, C.D., Johnson, E.H., Russell, S.F., Crane, R.J., Jacobs, G.A., & Worden, T.J. (1985). The experience and expression of anger: Construction and validation of an anger expression scale. In M.A. Chesney & R.H. Rosenman (Eds.), *Anger and hostility in cardiovascular and behavioral disorders* (pp. 5-30). Washington: Hemisphere.

Stemmler, G. (1987). Implicit measurement models in methods for scoring physiological reactivity. *Journal of Physiology, 1*, 113-125.

Stemmler, G. (1989). The autonomic differentiation of emotions revisited: Convergent and discriminant validation. *Psychophysiology, 26*, 617-632.

Stephens, M.A.P., Crowther, J.H., Koss, P.G., & Bolen, K. (1988). Effects of daily activities and social behavior on blood pressure elevation. *Journal of Behavioral Medicine, 11*, 553-563.

Steptoe, A., & Sawada, Y. (1989). Assessment of baroreceptor reflex function during mental stress and relaxation. *Psychophysiology, 26*, 140-147.

Stoney, C.M., Davis, M.C., & Matthews, K.A. (1987). Sex differences in physiological responses to stress and in coronary heart disease: A causal link? *Psychophysiology, 24*, 127-131.

Stoney, C.M., Langer, A.W., & Gelling, P.D. (1986). The effects of menstrual cycle phase on cardiovascular and pulmonary responses to behavioral stress. *Psychophysiology, 23*, 393-402.

Suarez, E.C., & Williams, R.B. (1989). Situational determinants of cardiovascular and emotional reactivity in high and low hostile men. *Psychosomatic Medicine, 51*, 404-418.

Tischenkel, N.J., Saab, P.G., Schneiderman, N., Nelesen, R.A., DeCarlo Pasin, R., Goldstein, D.A., Spitzer, S.B., Woo-Ming, R., & Weidler, D.J. (1989). Cardiovascular and neurohumoral responses to behavioral challenge as a function of race and sex. *Health Psychology, 8,* 503-524.

Van Egeren, L.F., & Sparrow, A.W. (1989). Laboratory stress testing to assess real-life cardiovascular reactivity. *Psychosomatic Medicine, 51,* 1-9.

Wagner, H. (1989). The peripheral physiological differentiation of emotions. In H. Wagner & A. Manstead (Eds.), *Handbook of social psychophysiology* (pp. 77-98). Chichester: Wiley.

Waters, W.F., Bernard, B.A., & Buco, S.M. (1989). The autonomic nervous system response inventory (ANSRI): Prediction of psychophysiological response. *Journal of Psychosomatic Research, 33,* 347-361.

Waters, W.F., Cohen, R.A., Bernard, B.A., Buco, S.M., & Dreger, R.M. (1984). An Autonomic, Nervous System Response Inventory (ANSRI): scaling, reliability, and cross-validation. *Journal of Behavioral Medicine, 7,* 315-341.

Weidner, G., Friend, R., Ficarrotto, T.J., & Mendell, N.R. (1989). Hostility and cardiovascular reactivity to stress in women and men. *Psychosomatic Medicine, 51,* 36-45.

Wundt, W. (1910). *Grundzüge der physiologischen Psychologie.* (Vol. II, 6th edition). Leipzig: Engelmann.

Wundt, W. (1911). *Grundzüge der physiologischen Psychologie.* (Vol. III, 6th edition). Leipzig: Engelmann.

Behavioral and Emotional Inhibition in Head Pain

HARALD C. TRAUE AND ALISON MICHAEL

The concept of headache patients being emotionally inhibited has a long medical tradition. A foremost extensive personality description based on clinically orientated observations originated with Wolff (1937). According to his studies, headache and migraine patients in particular are ambitious, efficiency orientated, perfectionistic, obsessive, neat, conscientious, rigid, and suppress their aggressiveness as well. They are characterised by "a quality of studied poise, most often accompanied with tense facial expression with furrowed forehead, contractions between the eye brows, etc." (p. 905).

However, the idea of inhibited aggressiveness as a feature of migraine patients is distinctly much older, dating back to the late Middle Ages. Later, in a document from 1734, patients were said to be "ira, imprimis tacita et supressa" (when in a rage, they are particularily calm and restrained) (cited from Jonckheere, 1971). Ever since Georg Engel described the "pain-prone patient" in the *American Journal of Medicine* (1959), the hypothesis of suppressed anger and aggression as the personality characteristic for headache patients has been like a red thread extending through the pain literature. This interpretation has not gone unchallenged though: It has recently been strongly contested on empirical grounds (Kröner-Herwig, 1990; Roy, 1985).

This paper therefore addresses the role of behavioral inhibition and increased physiological reactivity as a part of maladaptation and the interaction between an individual and his or her social environment. Although reduced expressiveness and heightened bodily reactions may be adaptive when faced with a social stress situation, in the long run these behaviors can take a harmful toll on the organism. "The risk of being given an opportunity to develop adaptability to acute challenges is that the adaptations may not serve long range goals very well" (B.T. Engel, 1986, p. 472).

To begin with, findings on suppressed aggressiveness as a personality attribute should be analysed critically. Then findings about observed emotional behavior should be reported on. It is of course true also that suppressed aggression must not be sought in a selfportrait, but demonstrated as deficiencies in expressive behavior. Subsequently, the question should be addressed as to whether inhibition of expression is connected with pathophysiological mechanisms of headaches. Finally, we will discuss whether expressive behavior is related to stress and coping and will also clarify whether inhibited emotional expressiveness affects the social support system, to the extent that factors acting as stress buffers are impaired.

Inhibition and Emotion

Recent conceptualizations view emotions as a process of appraisal of transactions with the environment (Lazarus, 1966). Emotions are believed to be comprised of a variety of components: cognitive interpretation of intero- and exteroreceptive stimuli, physiological pattern of arousal, motoric mobilization, and affective expressions. These different components are mediated by the central nervous system as a result of the interaction between the individual and the social and physical environment. The emotion can be considered as a response to environmental stimuli or as an act to control the environment (Traue, 1989a).

Brady (1975) made a basic distinction between emotional events that occur "inside" and "outside" the skin. Thus cognitive experiential and most of the physiological processes that are within the skin are covert events, while verbal and motor behavior are overt events. Expressive motor behavior in emotion has two important functions: firstly, as a communicative function, it facilitates regulation of person-environment transactions; and secondly, the feedback function of behavioral expression controls the internal (intraindividual) regulation of emotion. Active responding may influence the experienced stress indirectly through the attenuation of the stressful agent controlling the environment, or directly through self-regulation. Thus, expressive behavior is simultaneously part of emotional processes and a coping response. Suppression of aggression and anger, or more generally stated: inhibition of emotional expressiveness is a part of emotional behavior overall.

Emotional Inhibition as a Personality Construct

The personality descriptions of headache sufferers in clinical reports and case studies involve a large number of psychometric analyses. Time and again they showed elevated scores for neuroticism, anxiety, depression and hysteria. Some studies would have profitted from dealing psychometrically with deficits in the perception and expression of anger. These empirical findings would have confirmed the clinical picture of the headache personality, provided that these features were specific for headache sufferers. In fact, however, a differentiation between headache patients and other psychosomatic patients is not possible (Henryk-Gutt, & Rees, 1973). Just as unsuccessful has been the search for a specific personality profile for the various headache syndromes (Kröner, 1982).

We will now review the frequently cited psychometric studies on the hypothesized relationship between anger and aggression. One often mentioned paper was published by Ross and McNaughton (1945). The authors themselves concluded that through their study using projective techniques the role of ambition, perfectionism, and social conformity could be proved. It may well be worth considering the possibility, however, that their investigation regarding the supression of anger was not valid. Despite our critical analysis, we find the paper frequently quoted as proof of the suppression of anger hypothesis.

Another paper frequently cited came from Bihldorf and coworkers (1971). here the explicit hypothesis of anger suppression was explained as being characteristic of migraine patients in comparision to other headache sufferers. However, through a critical review and a statistical re-analysis of the original data, Gerhard (in press) demonstrated that the migraine patients examined only made two significant statements out of 41 items, that is: "when I express my anger, I am afraid that something will happen to me" and "if more people expressed their anger when they felt it, there would be less trouble in the world." When one takes into account the likelihood of an alpha-error, then this finding, too, is still not a clear confirmation of the anger suppression hypothesis. Nevertheless, this paper is also often cited as support.

In a more recent study by Huber and coworkers (1982), 50 headache patients, 45 otherwise psychosomatically ill patients, and 45 healthy women, were examined with the *FPI (Freiburger Persönlichkeitsinventar,* a widely used German personality inventory). Both the aggressiveness and the social dominance scales served to operationalize anger expression. At first there was an insignificantly small difference between the groups, and this fact alone undermines the suppression of anger hypothesis. In addition, the items for the scales have very little in common with the specific expression of anger. Moreover, a questionnaire whose items were very carefully directed at the question of suppressed anxiety and anger, and whose contents were also specifically orientated towards daily life events, was not able to give support for the hypothesis (Schnarch & Hunter, 1979). The psychometric examination of headaches does not therefore address the specific personality attributes from which therapeutic inferences could be suggested.

From our psychometric point of view, the suppression of anger (aggression or anxiety) hypothesis has not been substantiated; on the contrary we feel that the psychometric studies under consideration here (and other studies not mentioned), inadequately tackled the complexities in question. Subjective scales record mental attitudes more easily than self-observations, and as a result one's own suppressed behavior does not automatically reflect an attitude towards anger expression. In addition, the need to conform to others, which has been claimed to be frequent in some headache sufferers, might be reflected in subjective statements and misconceptions which might well skew the results.

According to some researchers and clinicians, headache patients may be prone to a general suppression of emotions – "bottling up their feelings" – or else be less able to recognize their emotions than pain-free individuals, thus fulfilling the definition of an alexithymia (e.g., Dalsgaard-Nielsen, 1965). If this is the case, then these patients could scarcely report repressed anger, anxiety and aggression, as they would not be experiencing these emotions as strongly as other people do. Further scrutiny of the hypothesis must therefore focus on the observed behavior of patients, or rather attend to the question of impaired self-perception of emotions.

Behavioral Inhibition and Stress

As a rule, clinical observations of patients fail to comply with strict criteria. Nevertheless it is still striking to note where the published clinical observations vary from psychometric findings. One reason for this could be the lack of observations on healthy subjects by clinicians – an error which is avoided in psychometric studies with control groups. Perhaps another reason why the published results vary so much is that clinical observations are simultaneously extraneous observations of overt behavior, while the test data always refer to subjective descriptions. A further possibility may potentially derive from the methods used for data collection. Clinical observations are obtained under interactive conditions, such as during clinical interviews in which the clinician relies on the contents of statements as well as externally observable behavior, e.g. facial expression, communicative behavior, tone of voice, etc. This has two consequences for empirical analysis. Firstly, the situational context must generate emotional expressiveness – which is certainly not the case in a test situation – and secondly, emotional behavior must be observed or quantified in another manner than by means of questionnaire data.

In the 40's, Reich (reprinted 1969) already emphasized the situational dependence of the development of repressed expressiveness in headache patients. As a biologically oriented psychodynamic clinician, he considered the socially punishing environmental conditions as the cause of active emotional restraint: "Our patients report without exception on childhood periods in their life, when they learned by means of physiological activity to suppress their feelings of anger, anxiety and love" (p. 258).

In this respect the studies from Scholz and colleagues (Grothgar & Scholz, 1987; Scholz, 1985) are particularly suitable for examining the inhibition of the anger expression hypothesis. Migraine patients (n=24), pain patients (n=24) and healthy controls (n=24), were allocated either to an anger or a control condition. The anger condition was depicted as a competitive task in which the subjects had to solve very difficult anagrams. Anger was experimentally generated by a confederate of the experimenter, who consistently solved the tasks more quickly and mentioned this fact. The tasks were easier in the control condition and subjects were always allowed to win. The patients' and controls' behavior was video-recorded and, subsequently, facial expression, gestures, and verbal anger expression were evaluated with the help of a category system. A list of adjectives which the subjects were required to fill out demonstrated that the anger-provoking situations in fact had had the desired effect. All subjects in the anger-provoking condition were angrier and more annoyed than those in the control condition. Interestingly, the migraine patients marked even more words for anger than the two control groups. Therefore migraine patients must have developed more anger and irritation under the anger-provoking condition, while exhibiting less corresponding overt expression.

This experimental finding is supported by Gerhards' study (in press). Gerhards carried out standardized interviews concerning anger- and anxiety-induced situations which the subjects had to actively envisage. Migraine patients and matched controls were interviewed. The subjects whose inner excitement or strain was elicited as a result of the interview, evidenced raised scores on a specially devised scale. The emotional content of the interview was subjected to a quantitative content analysis. As in the former study by Scholz, migraine patients reported more inner arousal than controls (p=.06). Content analysis for migraine patients resulted in significantly fewer verbal anger phrases (p=0.03), yet no differences in the anxiety utterances. Thus the investigation offers further support for repressed anger in migraine patients. However, this is still not a question of alexithymic behavior, as migraine patients reported much more excitement than controls. Moreover, the suppressed emotion was specifically for anger in the interview material of migraine sufferers, while other emotions of similiar dimension were verbalized by both migraine and controls.

Muscular activity has different functions as covert or as overt behavior. Emotional and communicative expression of behavior is associated among other things with motor activity, which is a quality of emotional expressiveness and a component of complex behavioral processes and is also subject to classic and operant conditioning (Englis et al., 1982). As the head and neck musculature is of undeniable importance in the origin and maintenence of tension headaches – under the assumption that this musculature is a main source for this type of pain – motor behavior, and in particular expressive behavior in headache sufferers, is of significance. It is conceivable that under unfavorable circumstances expressive behavior for mainly negative emotions like anger and aggressiveness is punished socially and thus justifiably avoided, with such avoidance behavior or inhibition being very adaptable in the short term, helping to modify a socially stressful situation. Simultaneously, though, a reduction of emotional expressiveness is conditioned by the learning mechanism of negative reinforcement.

In order to examine the inhibited expressiveness hypothesis for tension headache, an experiment with a social stressor as a triggering condition for inhibited expression was performed by Traue and coworkers (1985): The study compared nonverbal expressiveness in a symptom-free state, during a situational stressor in tension headache and non-headache controls. Subjects were individuals with a history of tension headache or with no such history. For the headache group, the mean reported duration of a headache problem was 1.9 years, that is, this was a group of headache patients without a long (and thereby problematic) pain history.

The following experimental phases were then presented: (1) Relaxation: During this period the assistant guided the subjects through a series of Jacobson progressive relaxation and breathing exercises designed to relax the head and upper body musculature. (2) TAT-Anticipation: Subjects were presented with a picture from the *Thematic Apperception Test* (TAT) and were instructed by the assistant that after a 1 min. preparation interval, they would be required to tell a "good" story about the picture. (3) TAT-Story: During this phase the subject delivered his or her TAT-Story while overt behavior was monitored on video. Then followed a phase of (4) critique: When the subjects finished the story, the assistant told them that in a standardized text "a good short story should arouse your curiosity about something"; that "the story should move along fast enough to keep your interest alive to the end" and so forth. Then the subject was required to react to the assistant's critique: (5) Response. The subject was then debriefed and dismissed.

Video monitoring was performed using two video cameras: one positioned in front of the subject to afford a clear record of all facial and upper body movement and the other positioned for procedural monitoring above and behind the subject. Procedural monitoring was necessary because precise timing of recording was dependent on the somewhat unpredictable nature of the interaction between subject and assistant.

For behavioral rating, three raters, naive to the experimental hypotheses, were trained to rate the video recording using tapes from a pilot study. Tapes were divided into four components, corresponding to the four experimental phases: TAT-Anticipation, TAT-Story, Critique and Response. Each tape was viewed twice without sound and rated first for Head and Hand Gestures and then a second time for facial behavior in terms of Tension, Activity and Expressiveness.

For the head and hand ratings, movements were defined as any uninterrupted physical adjustment of head or hands. A simple count of independent head and hand movements was made within each component. For facial ratings, during their second viewing of the tape raters were instructed to focus only on the face. Facial ratings were made along a 7-point scale for each of three dimensions: (a) Tension – the perceived tenseness or relaxation embodied in the face, (b) Activity – the degree of facial communicative movement independent of affect, and, (c) Expressiveness – the "affective forcefulness" evident in the subject's face. Tension and Expressiveness ratings were obtained from each of the four experimental phases while Activity judgments were made only for the phases when the subject was actively conversing (TAT-Story and Response to Critique).

Concerning the nonverbal behavior of the tension headache patients, the analysis of ratings was based on the arithmetic mean of the independent raters' judgments on each behavior index within each session phase. Inspection of the group values indicated that the headache group displayed less head and hand movement during each experimental phase. Analysis of these differences with two-tailed Mann-Whitney U-tests indicated that statistically significant group differences in head movement were restricted to the TAT-Anticipation phase (p= .04).

The results of the analysis for Expressiveness, Tension and Activity ratings, again using the Mann-Whitney U-tests, revealed that the headache subjects displayed significantly higher levels of facial tension (p= .03). Comparison of group expressiveness ratings indicated that, overall, the headache group was significantly less expressive (p= .04). Facial activity ratings were consistent with the expressiveness findings; the headache group exhibited less facial activity although differences were statistically significant only in the Response phase (p= .02). For the expressiveness and tension measures, group differences were found across the majority of within-session phases. During the TAT-Story phase however, no group differences emerged regardless of measure.

This investigation confirms the claim that tension headache patients are less expressive overall compared with pain-free controls, communicate less, and show fewer communicative movements of the head and arms. In contrast to the experiment on migraine patients, the emotional behavior of patients and subjects was not qualitatively evaluated, so that no statements as to specific suppression of anger or aggressiveness are possible.

Inhibition and Bodily Reactions Under Stress

Inhibition and Psychosomatics

Numerous studies have shown that people with repressed or deficient emotional expressiveness are more physiologically active under social stress than expressive individuals – showing evidence of an inverse relationship between expressiveness and arousal (Traue, 1986; see also Traue & Pennebaker's chapter in this volume). Under the well-established assumption that elevated activity in a particular physiological system may increase a person's vulnerability for developing a psychosomatic disorder in that system, factors that contribute to physiological reactivity are important to the understanding of the etiology and maintenance of such disorders. Nevertheless the empirical data from the above reports were collected through very different methods, and as a suppressed or deficient expression of emotion can be operationalized in many ways, a uniform concept of this inverse relationship is scarcely possible.

Individuals who appear inhibited in either verbal or motor responses towards emotional stimuli have been labelled "internalized" (Buck, 1979), "alexithymic" (Nemiah, 1977), or "repressed" (Byrne, 1961). There are numerous empirical findings for the internalized and repressed constructs which describe a negative relationship between autonomic activity and inhibition of emotions, while no such investigations exist for the alexithymic characterization. Anderson (1981) examined the relationship between the verbal expression of affect and stress in relation to physiological responses in a variety of psychosomatic disorders: Patients who suffered from tension and migraine headaches, rheumatoid arthritis, or hypertension were compared to normals. During mental and physical stress and relaxation periods, records were made of heart rate, body temperature, EDA, systolic and diastolic blood pressure, along with an EMG measurement from the forehead and forearm. Subjective data in the form of stress ratings were raised on strain experienced during the experiment, as were general comments on daily and life stresses. All physiological parameters except for diastolic blood pressure presented with significant rises in association with stress. The average physiological scores were then correlated with subjective stress ratings. Uniting the physiological parameters into a total value of activity, a relationship was found between arousal and subjective stress rating of r = -.11 for controls, -.10 for BP patients, -.28 for headaches, and r = -.06 for rheumatoid arthritis patients. This generally negative relationship held also for the correlation between everyday stress, life strains and the physiological measures. This means that in this study, particularly for headache patients (that is, for migraine and tension headache patients) a significantly negative relationship could be demonstrated between physiological arousal and subjective appraisals of stress. However the inhibition of expression construct is only very indirectly operationalized in this paper, since it is exclusively based on subjective comments about stress that could only be elevated as such, and by no means on the actual expressive behavior of patients and subjects.

Inhibition, Physiological Reactivity and Headache

In the above reported studies by Scholz (1985) and Grothgar and Scholz (1987), such physiological reactions of the patients and subjects as pulse rate, and diastolic and systolic pressure were elevated during a socially stressful condition. The choice of physiological parameters was made in accordance with Funkenstein and coworkers (1954), as the physiological reactions of the emotion of anger were held to be the most appropriate for describing anger. It turned out that during the anger provoking condition, the physiological parameters of the migraine patients were the most varied. Migraines reacted more with vasodilation while controls showed more vasoconstriction. Simultaneously, migraines described themselves as being quite emotionally irritated, yet revealed less overt expression of anger. The authors summarized their results as meaning that "… at least on a cognitive level migraine patients are able to detect anger. They do not differ from other pain patients with respect to their evaluation of a repressive psychosocial situation which has a distinct character of achievement and goal attainment. Despite this, certain idiosyncratic coping processes in migraine patients concerning behavioral and psychophysiological aspects can be determined. The physiological effects on migraine patients of the anger pro-voking conditions are rather like the anger-in pattern…which consists of an increase in heart rate and systolic blood pressure and a decrease in dyastolic blood pressure" (p. 209). Although no relationship had been found in this study between physiological and emotional expressiveness measures, it demonstrates that a specific physiological arousal occurs concurrently with the experience of a reduction in openly expressed anger. This pattern is specific to migraine patients and cannot be observed in controls.

While physiological reactions of the vascular system of the head are taken as the physiological basis of migraine disturbance, muscular reactions play an im-portant role in tension headache. Through his descriptions of pain patients, Reich (reprinted 1969) had already developed his "muscular armouring" theory (the somatization of the psychological repression mechanisms), in connection with inhibited expressiveness. He thought that "tension and cramps of muscle are the bodily realization of suppression and both are the basis for the mainten-ance of disorders" (p. 260). The headache patient represents a clinical example of this description of a person who, in his own opinion, is wrongly told off in front of colleagues, restrains his impulse to put up a struggle and instead "puts on a poker face." Further clinical exploration would certainly find that this patient's expression of anger and rage, with a corresponding facial expression, had been objected to by the parents.

In such instances of operant conditioning by social punishment, increased and prolonged muscle tension thrives on two sources: the original impulse to act remains intact because it is not fulfilled; and in addition, this demands mus-cle work to resist the impulsive urge to act. As an etiological factor in various myogenic pain disorders, e.g. muscle contraction headache, critical muscular activity may be classified as: a dysfunctional increase, a prolonged recovery fol-lowing stressful events, a heightened tension in relief situations and a prolonged duration of the stressor. An individual develops myogenic pain in a particular muscular system when the muscle activity increases to a critical point within a certain period of time (Bischoff & Traue, 1983). In the previously mentioned experiment on stress, muscle activity of the left and right frontalis as well as the trapezius muscle was recorded and placed in relation to expressiveness. The EMG values were higher in the forehead and neck regions for tension headaches than for the pain-free controls in the social stress situation. As the investigation dealt with pain-free intervals, it is not concerned with the pain as a reason for the elevated tension values. However these values must be considered as a specif-ic response by tension headache patients to social stress.

As previously illustrated, patients in the same social stress situation are less expressive with their head and hands when participating in communicative events. They are characterized by their restrained expressiveness. In order to verify the global relationship between expressiveness and muscle tension, correlations have been found between behavioral expression and EMG scores and vice versa. The correlation between facial expressiveness, head and hand movements, and EMG values are, however, consistently negative but still significant. The expressiveness scales which did most strongly discriminate between the experimental groups, had highly negative correlations with EMG activity. It was also demonstrated that persons with the least movement and expression simultaneously displayed the greatest muscle tension in stressful social situations. Significantly less movement was also measured in Bischoff and Sauermann's study (1985), during and after a mental stressor with tension headache patients. However, no EMG measures were done, so that it cannot be claimed that this is a result of an inverse relationship between muscle tension and expressive movements.

The negative relationship between expressiveness and muscle tension can be theoretically explained in terms of learning theory: with increased straining of head muscles, facial expression is suppressed so as to avoid facing up to the unpleasant consequences of self expression of anger or annoyance or so as to limit the duration of social stress and thus avoid an active and stressful dispute that would otherwise in fact help to resolve a difficult social situation (Bischoff & Traue, 1983).

The pathophysiological connection is not so easy to account for in the relation between physiological activity and reduced expression in migraines. It is conceivable, however, that a neurophysiological association exists between inhibition and physiological response of the vascular system by way of a third common construct such as was developed by Gray (1976): the behavioral inhibition system (BIS). Alternatively, inhibited expression, thus suppression of feelings, might itself be viewed as an active process which operates as a stressor in the individual (Pennebaker, 1985). When stress situations are frequent and inhibition is habitual, then a patient's sensitive physiological system becomes the weak link and symptoms in the form of headache can develop or be maintained. At the present status of research here, a decision cannot be given for one of the two hypothetical assumptions.

Social Psychology of Behavioral Inhibition

Behavioral Inhibition and Coping

Previous chapters have shown that reduced expressiveness is related to physiological parameters which are also related to pain processes. In this way for example, inhibiton can thus influence physiological reactions under stress so that dysfunctional muscle activity is likely. Deriving from this psychobiological connection, inhibition has further consequences for the regulation of emotions and social behavior.

Firstly, people normally react to emotion-releasing stimuli, and such reactive expression is realized through facial muscle activity and movements with reafferent neuronal signals in the CNS, which contributes to the individual's emotional experience. In fact, however, subjective emotional experience does not depend exclusively on this nervous input as claimed in the facial feedback hypothesis (Buck, 1980), but feedback does contribute positively to sensitivity towards the physiological aspects of emotion. If this sensitivity is disrupted, an individual will not adequately perceive increased muscle tension or other ANS reactions caused by stress, and consequently does not initiate healthy relaxing behavior. Bischoff and Sauermann (1989) were able to demonstrate, in a signal detection design, that the hypothesis of deficient perception of muscle tension holds for tension headaches. These patients were less reliably able to judge the extent of their muscle strain than controls.

Secondly, when the expressive components of emotional reactions are systematically repressed, then the individual "unlearns" an accurate assessment of stressful circumstances. This learning mechanism occurs since the estimated load of a stress situation is not only dependent on external features of the situation but on the subjective experience of stress-conditioned reactions as well. In the course of time, when an inhibited person takes bodily reactions into account when evaluating a situation, his or her judgement will be impaired when the original physiological correlates of mainly negative emotions are confused and subsequently superimposed by tense muscle states. In fact people with chronic headaches and with tension headaches are inclined to underestimate situational stress (Knapp, 1983 a,b; Schlote, 1989). If one also considers muscle activity as part of a more general pattern of human motor activity in emotional processes, it is evident that muscle tension may be controlled by learning mechanisms. Classical or operant conditioning of motor behavior may lead to hyperactivity in a particular muscle system. Expressive behavior is prone to become punished under certain conditions of socialisation starting with an individual history of increased tension and reduced expressiveness.

Thirdly, inhibited expressiveness under socially stressful encounters can be interpreted as a deficit in coping behavior. Such a deficit during social stress hampers the affected person's ability to actively influence a stressful environment, for example by confronting the social stressor directly. These so-called social or natural stressors are encountered at work, or with family or peer group members; they relate to interpersonal problems and are integrated into one's life style; and they tend to exert their influence over long time periods ranging from hours, weeks, or even months. Also, stressors like one's boss or partner frequently have no reason to change their own behavior. As a result, one's social control mechanism is affected in the area of human relations.

Lastly, such inhibited expressiveness in social relations also exerts an influence on social relations and therefore on the social support network. Along with the ability to cope, a stable social system is both useful and helpful in mastering the strains of stress. For that reason the social support system is also considered as a stress buffer. Behavioral deficits in communicative and emotional areas can only adversely affect the relations between an individual and his immediate environment, thus also impairing the social network.

Behavioral Inhibition and Social Support

Cobb (1976) defined social support as individual beliefs of being valued, cared for, loved, and belonging to a network of communication and mutual obligation. A person can only develop this impression when he or she in fact has communicative expressive abilities, and the willingness to communicate. It is important to point out that expression of emotion and affect fulfill very essential communicative roles. Emotional expression is especially important for dealing with the persons to whom one relates most closely in a social circle; it helps to indicate for them which circumstances upset, strain, or please the person concerned. The social environment can assist the individual to avoid stress and to prevent it occurring again in the future; and in situations where harmful influences of life events and daily hassles cannot be prevented, the social environment can support a victim of such circumstances and ensure counterbalancing experiences. Therefore emotional openness and communicativeness are vital when setting up a protective social support system (Florin, 1985).

In clinical interviews, patients frequently mentioned anxieties in the social domain as basic stressors or triggers for headaches. Naturally, marriage relationships belong to this domain, especially partnership conflicts for persons living together. Several studies show that there is a connection between disturbed marital relationships and a lack of nonverbal communication. Thus, married couples with positive self-assessments of their relationship had the most nonverbal behavioral activity in a role play. They demonstrated, by way of example, a good deal of eye contact, touched frequently, often showed a position with open extremities. Another study illustrated through comparison between contented and discontented couples that the contented couples showed significantly more positive facial expressions during a conversation than the discontented ones did. In addition, the discontented married couples were not as well able to encode or decode the ambiguous content in analytic communications with the help of the partner's nonverbal signs (for a review see Traue, 1989b).

With the help of social support scales questions can be put about whether a person feels loved, believes that someone cares about him or her, can count on help, feels valued, and so on. As long as the manner in which a person expresses internal cognitions and feelings has an influence on the establishment of a social support system, such types of behavior must also be related to these reactions in the social environment, with the possible result being that a person can assume that he or she is cared for or would receive help in an emergency, etc.

Some social-psychological studies confirm that helping behavior is as highly rated by other persons as actual social support, because, for example, the possibilty of receiving help from other people always involves social support (Willis, 1987). But, helpfulness towards a person is strongly dependent on nonverbal signs from this person. Thus helpfulness diminishes with increasing interpersonal distance. Eye contact has a similar effect as interpersonal distance: one looks continuously at a passersby when asking for help. Positive reactions are then more likely than with very brief eye contact. Nonverbal expression in dyadic situations also influences the mutual readiness of the individual to share personal experiences and talk about oneself (thus developing self-disclosure).

Independent of the particular headache type, the social psychological hypothesis of a positive relationship was tested between overt expressiveness and subjective report of social support indicators (Traue, 1991). We rated and coded several behavioral variables from interview data material of a group of chronic headache sufferers with varying diagnoses and a mean pain duration of 18 years. The patients were referred to our outpatient pain clinic by other clinics and G.P. Offices. They underwent several headache diagnostic procedures. A semi-structured behavioral analytic interview as part of the diagnostic procedure was used as the data basis of this study. Since a complete analysis of the interview regarding nonverbal codings and ratings would have been unduly largescale and costly, two related parts to each interview were chosen. One dealt with a neutral theme, behavior in recreation, and the other a socially prohibited one, behavior in sexuality. The interview sequences were all three minutes long. A control group of 25 subjects was selected, and matched for age and gender with the clinical sample. Expressiveness was operationalized with the help of several nonverbal behavioral and rating scales chosen according to Friedman and co-workers' (1985) studies on CHD risk factors.

In order to operationalize social support scales we used the subscales Social Status and Social Activity, derived from a German biographical inventory for the diagnosis of disturbed behavior (BIV, *Biographisches Inventar für Verhaltensstörungen*). In addition, the Extraversion subscale of this test and a Depression scale were used as control variables. The dimension of Parental Upbringing Behavior was also employed as the life history of socialization plays a decisive role in developing an expressive behavioral style. In order to test the relationship between social support and nonverbal expressiveness, correlations were calculated between the subjective support scales and the nonverbal behavioral data. First we used averaged values from leisure time and sexuality topics in the correlations; however, these correlation coefficients were rather small; very few significant relationships were evidenced in the correlation table. Indeed correlations of the expressiveness variables were in the expected direction though mostly just short of the significance level. Examination of the correlation matrix, which was separated into the leisure and sexuality topics used in the clinical interviews, revealed that in most cases the relationships were evident within the prohibited topic rather than in the non-prohibited one. This means that probably more critical behavior is provoked under the former than the latter theme.

To take into consideration situational differences in expression, intraindividual differences between expressiveness scores were calculated and tested for with a dependent T-test for random samples. Results showed that expressiveness tended to diminish on the sexual topic. However, there was significantly more head shaking during the prohibited theme in comparison with the recreational theme. During the 3 minutes of the interview sequences, subjects spoke 15.6 seconds less during the sexual topic than in the recreational one. As there was a difference in expression during both interview themes, the intraindividual differences between sexuality and leisure time themes were now correlated with the subjective social support scales. The intraindividual differences can naturally be either negative or positive. When a difference score is positive, it means that the corresponding behavior appears to a lesser extent during the recreational theme than in the sexuality theme.

Table 1:   Correlations between nonverbal behavior difference-scores (intraindividual differences between behavior in sexuality topic and leisure topic from initial interviews) and social support scales, depression and extraversion (df=34, *=P<.05, **=P<.01).

BIV-Scales

difference-scores tabu-leisure theme	social status	parental upbringing	social activating	depression	extraversion
head shaking	-.51 **	-.03	-.36 *	-.31 *	.04
head movements (total)	-.39 *	-.22	-.1	-.25	-.21
expressiveness	-.03	-.29	-.29	-.19	.08
tension	.11	.17	.48 **	.32 *	-.09
nervousness	-.19	.39 *	.05	.22	-.08
nervous mouth movements	.23	-.09	.09	.32 *	.03
spreech frequency	.16	-.06	.11	.09	-.46 **
speech duration	-.32 *	.01	-.33 *	-.28	-.01
eye contact	-.15	-.15	-.54 **	-.12	.00
smiling frequency	.01	-.31 *	-.38 *	.03	-.15

The correlation matrix (see Table 1) can be interpreted in the following way: the less expressive individuals were during the socially prohibited topic, the more difficulty they had in assessing their own situation in the social environment, and in addition, the more depressive they described themselves. Quite the opposite is the relationship between the rated appraisals of tension and nervousness: The more tense the patients were judged by independent raters during the sexuality theme compared to the leisure theme, the more depressive they were depicted and less able to participate in social activities. The poor ratings of Parental Upringing correlate above all and on a particularly high level with the observed nonverbal nervousness of the subjects. A positive relationship was evidenced through smiling activities. There is a very strong relationship between social activity and tension as well as eye contact and smiling frequency. According to Yarczower and coworkers' (1979) studies, under decisive socialization conditions, social inhibitions already develop during the first years of life with strong familial relationships. Izard formulated it thus: "... as the individual moves into later childhood, peers and parents begin to discourage the ready display of strong emotions on the face" (1971, p. 192). This is in accordance with the observed correlation between parental upringing scale and reduced expressiveness ratings in our investigation.

It was somewhat surprising to find a significant correlation between parental upringing and smiling. On the one hand, smiling is interpretated as a positive expression of friendliness; on the other it can well be a behavioral strategy for deception: "A casual smile may serve to mask an uneasiness that may accompany the deception" (Riggio & Friedman, 1983, p. 901). That a number of our subjects interpreted smiling as a strategy for masking other emotions is also suggested in our results showing that smiling and tension were equally loaded in the factor analysis of nonverbal variables, and negatively correlated with expressiveness (Traue, 1989b). Moreover, this particular finding also points to the problem of operationalizing expressive deficits. Deficient or inhibited expression must not necessarily be associated with an impairment of the whole expression, but as another disguise in the form of yet another expression.

Likewise, it must be noted critically that social support scales only weakly correlate with the average nonverbal behavior of patients. Significant correlations resulted only from the difference values between sexual and leisure themes. Here the correlations clearly highlight a problematic view of the social support system, as expressive behavior was repressed during the sexuality theme compared with the recreational one. In other words, the patients speak less, maintain less eye contact, make fewer hand movements, demonstrate less head shaking and less facial expression, but leave one with a tense and nervous impression. Therefore here it is the intraindividual differences which are correlated with the social support scales and not simply expressiveness. Therefore again the specific role of situational factors of the critical behavior is implicated.

Conclusions

Theory of Emotion and Inhibition

This chapter has demonstrated that inhibition of expression has a twofold meaning for the origin and maintenance of headaches. On the one hand, inhibition functions to the benefit of the individual, and is accompanied by increased physiological activity. On the other hand inhibited expressiveness is an overt display in the social environment of deficits in emotions and communication. This double problem fits contemporary emotional concepts. The question of the specific role of motor mechanisms in emotional processes and inhibition is broadly discussed in Leventhal's perception-motor theory of emotional processes (Leventhal & Mosbach, 1983). According to this theory, there are three simultaneous levels of emotional processes: the expressive motor level, the scematic level and the conceptual level. According to Leventhal and Mosbach, emotional behavior is directed on the conceptual level by rules on how to handle emotional episodes and on arbitrary reactions to emotional releasing stimuli. It is decisive, however, that the three levels of mastering the emotional processing mutually coincide, so that spontaneous motor reactions of arbitrary motor reactions can be superimposed or concealed and vice versa.

Accordingly, two paradoxical effects can occur through experiments on the arbitrary control over automatic expressive movements: The arbitrary suppression of spontaneous expression of feelings leads to an intensified experience of these feelings and an increased physiological response. Conversely, the arbitrary copying of a spontaneous expression can imply a weakening of emotional experience and a reduction of the physiological processes which participate in it (the so-called Leventhal Effect). This theory also explicitly describes a mechanism which assumes that the inhibition of affect leads to a rise in intense feeling and, associated with that, to increased motor activity (tensed-up muscles). Besides this, Leventhal's theory also explains the suppression of expressive motor behavior as an active process with concomitant stress induced through the effort and strain of suppressing the emotional impulse. This is in aggreement with Pennebaker (1985) who understood the inhibition of feelings as active stress, with self-disclosure therefore allowing for a release of these stressors and thus leading to an improvement of health.

An explicit social-psychological and psychophysiological theory forms the basis of the illness model of Temoshok (1983). According to this model the development of illness in the direction of psychic or psychosomatic disturbances depends on three dimensions: severity of stressors, coping style and coping abilities. Whether a person under stressful conditions with a given lack in coping abilities then develops a mental or psychosomatic disorder, depends on whether he or she tends to internalize or externalize in coping. Internalizing is thus understood as "the representation of aspects of the environment in the organism as perceptions" and an externalizing coping style denotes the "manifestation in the environment of some aspects of an organism's informational state and terms or as an expression of a thought or an emotion" (p. 217). This theory is concerned with internalizing and in particular externalizing as coping styles, and purports to describe finally whether a psychopathological or a psychosomatic disturbance will arise.

Moreover, in this multidimensional illness theory, the stress concept is intergrated with the coping concept. "It is hypothesized that for situations of chronic stress, the nature of the expressed symptom is a function of three factors: coping style (internalizing or externalizing), severity of the stressor (slight or extreme), and coping abilities (including intelligence, education, flexibility, experience, psychological and physical health, social support, money and so forth). These three factors are thought to determine the transformational level at which stressful information can be accommodated" (p. 221).

The findings on the headache syndrome fit well into this illness concept: on the one hand headache patients are depicted as inhibited in their expressiveness. Therefore they fulfill the features of internalization and so accordingly they externalize their emotions and needs insufficiently in the form of actions and expressions in their social environment. Their impulsiveness and inner emotions remain activated together with their underlying motor and autonomic correlates, which may manifest themselves in the long term as a pain syndrome. In addition, an impairment of the social support system corresponds with inhibited expression, and thus with the internalized coping style; as a result, patients are more susceptable to being stressed.

Inhibition, Headache and Clinical Procedures

1. Diagnosis: Empirical studies have reported on the differences between headaches' and controls' expressive behavior and have been performed with various methods relying on external observations. Self-observational data, which are mostly obtained through questionnaires and psychometric investigations, generally yield little data for objectively recording the individual differences of emotional processing. Although there are admitted advantages to using questionnaires and personality inventories, and though their reliability and validity are known, the same advantages may be cancelled out because of the irrelevance of the findings. Unfortunately no clinically useful instruments are available for the observations and measurement of nonverbal behavior (Traue, 1989b). Those methods which were used in empirical studies were developed and employed for research purposes. Moreover, the rating of expressive behavior requires norms for diagnostic purposes, in which individual data could be located in relation to their divergence from a norm data sample. Such norms are very rarely available, as is generally the case with clinically used methods. A further problem is the situational dependence of expressive behavior which has been sufficiently veri-

fied by the experimental data. Nonverbal behavioral measures for diagnostic purposes should also be measured in standardized socially stressful situations (e.g. role plays). The aim of clinical research must be to develop clinically applicable procedures as well as coding and rating scales for the assessment of the expressive behavior.

2. Therapy: This survey shows that restrained expressiveness is an important factor in the development and maintenance of headaches. Therefore therapeutic interventions should focus on this behavioral deficit. The patient could profit from becoming able to directly influence stressful situations by improving his or her expressive ability skills when confronted with social stress. The development of such therapeutic strategies can be used successfully as interventions against psychosomatic disorders that are already present. Elements of a therapy can encourage expressiveness, for example "Concordance Therapy" (Gerber et al., 1989).

3. Prevention: The data on the role of socialization for suppressed expressive behavior (see also Traue & Pennebaker as well as Asendorpf in this volume) yield some useful aspects for the primary prevention of headaches; the correlations described here between reduced expressiveness and problematic parental upbringing do so also. Preventative strategies should influence childrearing styles which inhibit spontaneous expression, and this is especially the case as headaches are the most frequently mentioned physical symptom by school children between the ages 10 and 14 (Wehner et al., 1992). Thus it is necessary to regard inhibited expressiveness as a risk factor which can, however, be altered through timely primary prevention (Traue & Kraus, 1988).

References

Anderson, C.D. (1981). Expression of affect and physiological response in psychosomatic patients. *Journal of Psychosomatic Research, 25*, 143-149.

Bihldorf, J.P., King, S.H., & Parnes, L.R. (1971). Psychological factors in headache. *Headache, 11*, 177-127.

Bischoff, C., & Sauermann, G. (1989). Perception of muscle tension and myogenic headache: a signal detection analysis. In: C. Bischoff, H.C. Traue, & H. Zenz (Eds.), *Clinical perspectives on headache and low back pain* (pp. 93-111). Lewiston, New York, Toronto: Hogrefe & Huber Publishers.

Bischoff, C., & Sauermann, G. (1985). Nichtinstrumentelles motorisches Verhalten von Personen mit und ohne Spannungskopfschmerz während und nach kognitiver Belastung. In: H.U. Wittchen, & J.C. Brengelmann (Eds.), *Experimentelle Befunde der psychologischen Therapieforschung bei akuten und chronischen Schmerzzuständen* (pp. 66-90). Berlin, Heidelberg, New York: Springer.

Bischoff, C., & Traue, H.C. (1983). Myogenic headache. In: K.A. Holroyd, B. Schlote, & H. Zenz (Eds.), *Perspectives in research on headache*. Lewiston, New York, Toronto: Hogrefe & Huber Publishers.

Brady, J.P. (1975). Towards a behavioral biology of emotion. In L. Levi (Ed), *Emotions: Their parameters and measurement*. New York: Raven Press.

Buck, R. (1979). Individual differences in nonverbal sending accuracy and electrodermal responding: The externalizing /internalizing dimension. In R. Rosenthal (Ed.), *Skill in nonverbal communication* (pp. 140-170). Cambridge, Mass.: Oelgeschlager, Gunn & Hain.

Buck, R. (1984). *The communication of emotion*. New York: Guilford.

Byrne, D. (1961). The repression sensitization scale: Rationale, reliability and validity. *Journal of Personality, 29*, 334-349.

Cobb, S.(1976). Social support as a moderation of life stress. *Psychosomatic Medicine, 38*, 300-314.

Dalsgaard-Nielsen, T. (1965). Migraine and heredity. *Acta Neurologica Scandinavica, 41*, 287-300.

Engel, B.T. (1986). Psychosomatic medicine, behavioral medicine, just plain medicine. *Psychosomatic Medicine, 48*, 466-478.

Engel, G. (1959). "Psychogenic" pain and the pain prone patient. *American Journal of Medicine, 26*, 899-918.

Englis, B.G., Vaughn, K.B., & Lanzetta, J.T. (1982). Conditioning of counterempathetic emotional responses. *Journal of Experimental Social Psychology, 18*, 375-391.

Florin, I. (1985). Bewältigungsverhalten und Krankheit. In: H.D. Basler, & I. Florin (Ed.), *Klinische Psychologie und körperliche Krankheit* (pp. 126-145). Stuttgart: Kohlhammer.

Friedman, H.S., Hall, J.A., & Harris, M.J. (1985). Type A behavior, nonverbal expressive style and health. *Journal of Personality and Social Psychology, 48 (5)*, 1299-1315.

Funkenstein, D.H., King, S.H., & Drolette, M.E., (1954). The direction of anger during a laboratory stress inducing situation. *Psychosomatic Medicine, 16*, 405-413.

Gerber, W.D., Miltner, W., Birbaumer, N & Haag, G. (1989). *Konkordanztherapie*. München: Röttger Verlag.

Gerhards, F. (in press). Ärgerausdruckshemmung bei Migränekranken. *Zeitschrift für Klinische Psychologie*.

Gray, J.A. (1976). The behavioral inhibition system: A possible substrate for anxiety. In: M.P. Feldman & A.M. Brodhurst (Eds.), *Theoretical and experimental base of behavior modification* (pp. 96-110). New York: Wiley.

Grothgar, B., & Scholz, O.B. (1987). On specific behavior of migraine patients in an anger provoking situation. *Headache, 27*, 206-210.

Henryk-Gutt, R., & Rees, W.L. (1973). Psychological aspects of migraine. *Journal of Psychosomatic Research 17*, 141-153.

Hollaender, J., & Florin, I.(1983). Expressed emotion and airway conductance in children with bronchial asthma. *Journal of Psychosomatic Research, 27 (4)*, 307-311.

Huber, H.P. Herper, R., & Huber, D. (1982). Migräne und Persönlichkeit: Eine psychometrische Studie. In Huber, H.P. (Hrsg.), *Migräne* (pp. 96-110). München: Urban & Schwarzenberg.

Jonkheere, P. (1971). The chronic headache patient: A psychodynamic study of 30 cases compared with cardiovascular patients. *Psychotherapy & Psychosomatics, 19*, 53-61.

Izard, C.E. (1971). *The face of emotion*. New York: Appleton Century Crofts.

Knapp, T.W. (1983a). *Migräne 1: Symptomatologie und Ätiologie*. Weinheim: Beltz.

Knapp, T.W. (1983b). *Migräne 2: Psychologische Therapie*. Weinheim: Beltz.

Kröner, B. (1982). Untersuchungen zur Persönlichkeitsstruktur von Patienten mit unterschiedlichen Kopfschmerzsyndromen. *Diagnostica, 28*, 168-184.

Kröner-Herwig, B. (1990). Die Schmerzpersönlichkeit: Eine Fiktion. In H.D. Basler, C. Franz, B. Kröner-Herwig, H.P. Rehfisch, & H. Seemann (Eds), *Psychologische Schmerztherapie* (pp. 353-390). Heidelberg: Springer Verlag.

Lazarus, R.S. (1966). *Psychological stress and coping process*. New York: McGraw Hill.

Leventhal, H., & Mosbach, P.A. (1983). The perceptual-motor theory of emotion. In J.T. Cacioppo, R.E. Petty, & D. Shapiro (Eds.), *Social psychophysiology*. New York: Guilford Press.

Nemiah, J.C. (1977). Alexithymia: Theoretical considerations. *Psychotherapy and Psychosomatics, 28*, 199-206.

Pennebaker, J.W. (1985). Traumatic experience and psychosomatic disease: Exploring the roles of behavioral inhibition, obsession and confiding. *Canadian Psychology, 26 (2)*, 82-94.

Reich, W. (1969, reprint). *Die Funktion des Orgasmus*. Köln: Kiepenheuer & Witsch.

Riggio, R.E., & Friedman, H.S. (1983). Individual differences and cues to deception. *Journal of Personality and Social Psychology, 45*, 899-915.

Ross, W.D., & McNaughton, F.L. (1945). Objective personality studies in migraine by means of the Rorschach method. *Psychosomatic Medicine, 7*, 73-79.

Roy, R. (1985). Engel's painprone patient, 25 years thereafter. *Psychotherapy and Psychosomatics, 43*, 126-135.

Schlote, B. (1989). Longterm registration of muscle tension among office workers suffering from headache. In C. Bischoff, H.C. Traue, & H. Zenz (Eds.), *Clinical perspectives on headache and low back pain* (pp. 46-63). Lewiston, New York, Toronto: Hogrefe & Huber Publishers.

Schnarch, D.M., & Hunter, J.E. (1979). Personality differences between randomly selected migrainous and non migrainous people. *Psychotherapy: Theory, research and practice, 16*, 297-309.

Scholz, O.B. (1985). Persönlichkeitspsychologische Besonderheiten bei Migränepatienten. *Psycho, 11*, 286-299.

Temoshok, L. (1983). Emotion, adaptation, and disease: A multidimensional theory. In L. Temoshok, C. v. Dyke, & L.S. Zegans (Eds.), *Emotions in health and illness* (pp. 29-44). New York: Grune & Stratton.

Traue, H.C., Gottwald, A., Henderson, P.R. & Bakal, D.A. (1985). Nonverbal expressivity and EMG activity in tension headache sufferers and controls. *Journal of Psychosomatic Research, 29*, 375-381.

Traue, H.C. (1986). Über die Inhibition von Ausdruck als Komponente psychosomatischer Störungen. *Zeitschrift für Psychosomatische Medizin und Psychoanalyse, 32*, 349-360.

Traue, H.C., & Kraus, W. (1988). Ausdruckshemmung als Risikofaktor: Eine verhaltensmedizinische Analyse. *Praxis der klinischen Verhaltensmedizin und Rehabilitation, 2*, 89-95.

Traue, H.C. (1989a). Behavioral inhibition in stress disorders and myogenic pain. In C. Bischoff, H.C. Traue, & H. Zenz (Eds.), *Clinical perspectives on headache and low back pain*. Lewiston, New York, Toronto: Hogrefe & Huber Publishers.

Traue, H.C. (1989b). *Gefühlsausdruck, Hemmung und Muskelspannung unter sozialem Streß: Verhaltensmedizin myogener Kopfschmerzen*. Göttingen: Verlag für Psychologie.

Traue, H.C. (1991). Gehemmte Expressivität, Arousal und soziale Unterstützung. In J. Haisch, & H.-P. Zeitler (Ed.), *Gesundheitspsychologie. Zur Sozialpsychologie der Prävention und Krankheitsbewältigung* (pp. 345-360). Heidelberg: Asanger.

Wehner, C., Zenz, H. & Hrabal, V. (1992). Das Beschwerdebild körperlicher Beeinträchtigung während der Pubertät. In H. Zenz, V. Hrabal & P. Marschall (Eds.), Entwicklungsdruck und Erziehungslast. Göttingen: Verlag für Psychologie, Hogrefe.

Willis, T.A. (1987). Help seeking as a coping mechanism. In C.R. Snyder, & C.E. Ford (Eds), *Coping with negative life events* (pp. 19-50). New York, London: Plenum Press.

Wolff, H.G. (1937). Personality features and reactions of subject with migraine. *Archives of Neurology and Psychiatry, 37*, 895-921.

Yarczower, M., Kilbride, J.E. & Hill, L.A. (1979). Imitation and inhibition of facial expression. *Developmental Psychology, 15*, 453-454.

Acknowledgements: This review was written with the help of grants from the German Research Foundation (DFG).

Emotions and Health Outcomes: Some Theoretical and Methodological Considerations

Lydia Temoshok

While the role of emotion in the etiology and progression of various illnesses and medical conditions has been frequently evoked, it has not been systematically investigated. The psychosomatic and behavioral medicine literature is dotted with reports of associations between particular emotional and health phenomena, but rarely are these discussed as part of the larger theoretical picture. In many instances, the concept of emotion is merged, confused, or simply assumed to be symonymous with the equally murkey concept of "stress".

Almost a decade ago, I posed a theory of emotion, adaptation, and disease (Temoshok, 1983), in which physical as well as mental disorders were seen as manifestations of emotional phenomena expressed as a function of coping style, severity of stressors, and coping abilities/resources. My purpose in this chapter, however, is not to revisit this model with a comprehensive revision or updated review of emotions in health and illness. Instead, I will use this occasion to introduce some theoretical and methodological issues that I believe are particularly pertinent for discussion as research in this arena moves toward the next century. The health outcomes I will use as my illustrations are from the literature on psychosocial oncology and psychoneuroimmunology, because these are the areas with which I am most familiar.

Some Theoretical Considerations

Figure 1 presents various options for describing explicit or implicit hypotheses concerning the links between "independent" variables, mediating mechanisms, and "outcome" variables. The independent, mediating, or outcome variables in this model may be either biomedical or psychosocial.

Most studies in the biomedical arena are concerned solely with the top line of relationships: understanding links between biomedical independent variables and biomedical outcome variables, and/or biomedical mediating mechanisms (A—C, A—B, or A—B—C). Studies in the neurosciences that document neuroanatomical, neuroendocrine, and neurochemical links to the immune system explicitly examine bidirectional pathways of communication between nervous and immune systems, and thus can be characterized as A—B/ B—A (cf. Ader, Felten, & Cohen, 1991). Most of these studies have been conducted using animal models.

248 LYDIA TEMOSHOK

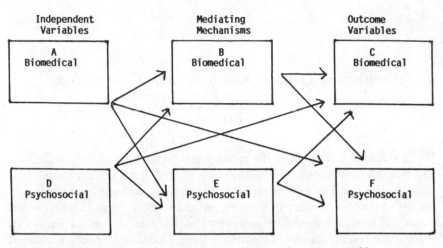

Figure 1:   Combinations of independent, mediating and outcome variables.

When the "mind" is added as an ingredient to the central nervous system, the psychological dimension emerges into the forefront, along with the causal directionality implied in the term "psychoneuroimmunology" (the field is not, for example, called "immunoneuropsychology"). This directionality is implicit in many psychoneuroimmunological studies: psychosocial or "stress" factors (D) produce some change in immunologic measures (B). Few psychoneuroimmunological studies provide links between the three domains of variables (e.g., D—B—C).

Studies in psychosocial oncology concerned with quality of life issues start with the "somatopsychic" hypothesis: that having cancer (A) affects psychosocial outcomes (F). Intervention studies aimed at, for example, reducing symptoms of nausea can be depicted as A—E—C; that is, the biomedical conditions created by chemotherapy treatment of cancer are influenced using psychosocial (behavioral) techniques to produce a "biomedical" outcome-reduction of nausea. Other studies in psychosocial oncology concerned with cancer etiology or progression usually assume, explicitly or implicitly, the "psychosomatic hypothesis" that psychosocial factors (D) affect cancer outcomes (C).

Being able to visualize all the possible combinations of independent, mediating, and outcome variables in Figure 1 allows alternative explanations of findings to emerge. Many studies in the psychosocial oncology and psychoneuroimmunology literature assume implicitly that connections between psychosocial ("independent") or stress factors and health outcomes are mediated by biological – and particularly, immunological – mechanisms.

For example, a recent set of two studies by Fawzy et al. (1990a and b) evaluated the immediate and long-term effects on immune function measures of a 6-week structured psychiatric group intervention for patients with malignant melanoma. The first study (1990a) reported that the intervention enhanced active problem-oriented coping methods and improved mood states. The second study (1990b) found that the intervention was associated with longer-term (6 month) changes in affective state, coping and the Natural Killer (NK) lymphoid cell system, and that affective measures rather than coping measures showed some significant correlations with immune cell changes. In discussing their results, the authors stated: "The coping and affective status of the patients was improved by the intervention, but the links of these changes to immune cell changes are not established and remain a challenge for future work" (p. 734). While this statement seems appropriately conservative and does not over-interpret their findings, there is the explicit hypothesis that the intervention led to immune cell changes, the underlying assumption that such immune cell changes will have an effect on cancer outcome, and the implicit hypothesis that psychiatric intervention will have an effect on cancer outcome mediated by these particular immune cell changes. In other words, while the authors recognized that these studies did not (yet) establish the empirical links between independent, mediating, and outcome variables, their underlying and stated hypotheses have so dominated their design and methods, *that no alternative hypotheses can be tested.*

Let us contrast the Fawzy et al. studies with another recent study which has been widely cited. Spiegel et al. (1989) found that metastatic breast cancer patients randomized to a weekly supportive group intervention lived significantly longer than did controls, by an average of nearly 18 months. This study is unusual in that it started off as an A—E—F design (metastatic breast cancer – psychosocial intervention – psychosocial outcome), but because a 10-year medical follow-up was added, it became a "retro-prospective" A—E—C design (metastatic breast cancer – psychosocial intervention – cancer outcome). Perhaps because the authors did not begin with the psychosomatic hypothesis (indeed, they stated that there was no intention on the part of the therapists or the patients to affect survival time through group participation), they did not explain their results in terms of biomedical mechanisms. Instead, they hypothesized that social support, the opportunity to express feelings, the group's buffer against social isolation, mobilization of resources, and learning behavioral techniques to control pain may have accounted for the differences observed. Only in the very last words of their article did the authors suggest that biomedical mechanisms may play a role: "Future studies of the impact of psychosocial interventions on medical illness might profitably examine variables such as compliance, health habits, diet, and immune and neuroendocrine function" (p. 890).

Of course, neither the Fawzy et al. nor the Spiegel et al. study was intended to examine the sequence of steps by which a psychosocial intervention might influence cancer outcome. It would be important, however, for future studies to be designed so that they are able to test a number of hypotheses about possible mediating mechanisms – both biomedical and psychosocial, as well as their interactions.

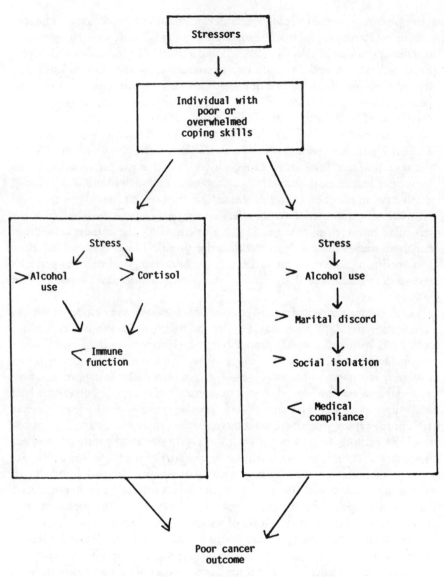

Figure 2:   Negative effects of stressors on health outcomes.

Figure 2 illustrates two alternative pathways by which stressors and psychosocial factors can have a negative effect on health outcomes. On the left hand side of the model is a hypothetical cascade of events that follows from an emphasis on biomedical mechanisms, while the right hand side illustrates a possible chain of psychosocial or behavioral events.

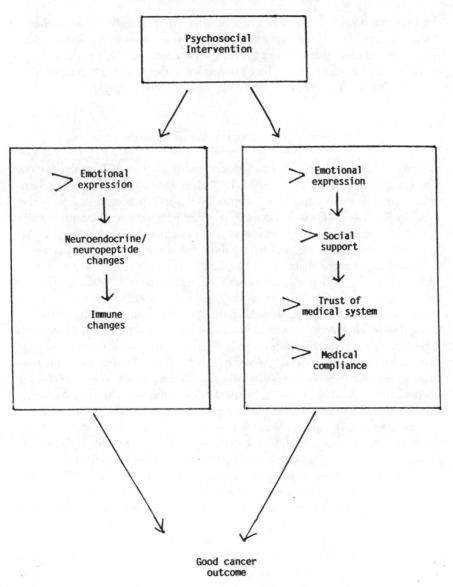

Figure 3:   Positive effects of intervention on health outcomes.

Figure 3 depicts a similar differentiation of mechanisms by which a psychosocial intervention may be linked to good health outcomes via an enhancement of emotional expression. Both sides of the "argument" are plausible, and other chains of events can also be postulated (e.g., emotion in Figure 3 has its effect on the right hand side of the model functioning interpersonally as an *elicitor* of social support; it could also serve intrapersonally as a *motivator* of personal action). I would hope that this is not merely an academic quibble about the contents of what has been a "black box": unless we understand the mechanisms by which an intervention "works," we cannot help it work better.

Some Methodological Considerations

Reviews of outcome studies in psychosocial oncology (Fox & Temoshok, 1988; Gross, 1989; Temoshok, 1987, 1990; Temoshok & Heller, 1984), have reiterated the centrality and importance of emotional non-expressiveness as a psychosocial factor associated with cancer etiology and progression. Conceptual variations on "emotional non-expressiveness" such as emotional "repression" or "inhibition" have been associated with other immunologically-mediated health problems, e.g., Epstein-Barr virus (Esterling et al., 1990), as well as with non-immunologically mediated health problems, e.g., tension headaches (Traue et al., 1985) and general health problems (Pennebaker, 1992).

One of the major methodological challenges in this area is measuring something that is not there (i.e., non-expressiveness). It requires all the insight and ingenuity of a Sherlock Holmes who recognized, in one of his most famous capers, that the fact that the dog *didn't* bark was critical. In the case of the non-barking dog and the non-expressive individual, an analysis of the context is important. It is significant that a dog doesn't bark when approached by a human; it suggests that the human is not a stranger to the dog. Similarly, the context of non-expression is important. Because it is "normal" for most people to express anger, sadness, joy, etc., in different situations, it is noteworthy if there is inappropriate or non-expression of emotion in emotion-laden contexts.

Many studies use self-report measures to assess emotional distress. Because these scales do not include context, a whole dimension of meaning is missed. Further, most self-report measures of emotion have a social desirability bias. It can be argued that for most people admitting that they are very angry is socially undesirable; admitting extreme sadness may imply being out of control – another socially undesirable state. Thus, it is not surprising that the findings of studies that use self-report to measure emotion "contradict" the findings of studies that use other ways to assess emotional expressiveness.

For example, there are apparently contradictory studies which find depression either positively or negatively associated with cancer progression. Greer et al. (1979) found that four out of five breast cancer patients who expressed feelings of helplessness in an interview 3 months after diagnosis had died by the 5-year follow-up, in contrast to only two out of 20 women who expressed either denial or fighting spirit. On the other hand, studies by Derogatis et al. (1979) and Levy (1983) found that 1-year survivors versus non-survivors of metastatic breast cancer reported significantly *lower* levels of depression and other dysphoric moods. Further, Cassileth et al. (1985) found no relationship between a self-report measure of hopelessness and survival or relapse in either the terminally ill group or the group with early stage breast cancer and malignant melanoma. It is my hypothesis that these discrepancies may be attributed to differences in the type of assessment used to measure depression: either independent ratings by two observers of a structured patient interview (Greer et al.) or self-report (Derogatis et al., Levy, Cassileth et al.).

In my own work, there are two studies which have apparently contradictory results. One study (Temoshok, 1985) found that more emotional expressiveness in malignant melanoma patients was significantly correlated with three out of four biologic prognostic indicators: number of lymphocytes at tumor site (positive correlation), thickness of the primary tumor (negative correlation), and mitotic rate of the tumor (negative correlation). A second study (Temoshok, 1988; also briefly described in Temoshok, 1985) found that more emotional distress at time of biopsy of the primary tumor was higher in patients with unfavorable outcome (death, widespread metastases) 3 years later compared to patients with favorable outcome (no evidence of disease), who were matched with the unfavorable outcome group on seven biologic prognostic indicators at the time of biopsy. A logical explanation for these different findings is that in the first study, emotional expressiveness was rated by clinical observers of the videotaped interview, while in the second study, emotional distress was measured by scores on standard self-report scales (Profile of Mood States, Beck Depression Inventory, Taylor Manifest Anxiety Scale, and the Distress Scale from the Minnesota Multiphasic Personality Inventory). One could hypothesize that expressed emotion is a buffer against the pathological effects of stress. Thus, expressing emotion at the very stressful time of biopsy will be associated in the appropriate direction with positive and negative prognostic indicators. On the other hand, for a person who has typically coped with stress by repression, the stress of tumor biopsy and learning one has cancer may overwhelm these repressive defenses. The recognition that one is distressed (manifested by more self-report of distress), may further overwhelm the cancer patient who may now feel out of control in unaccustomed ways. An hypothesis consistent with the literature is that the person who recognizes distress and expresses it does not suffer the same negative physiological consequences as the distressed person who doesn't know how to cope with that distress.

Given these emotional expressiveness measurement conundrums, it makes sense for investigators to consider using combinations of measures, for example, an interview-rated assessment of expressiveness combined with self-report. Other combined or converging measurement strategies will be discussed below.

I would strongly recommend the inclusion of *psychophysiologic* assessment in studies of emotion and health outcomes. Even though skin temperature, skin conductance, heart rate, or respiration are certainly not mediating mechanisms in cancer, it can be argued that by including them, we can examine coping style in a more complex way. For example, we can examine differences between patients whose outward verbal or nonverbal expression of emotion or distress is either congruent or incongruent with indicators of physiologic perturbation. We can examine differences between patients who have a long versus a short return to near-baseline on a certain physiological variable following a psychosocial perturbation. Finally, we can make a more valid cause-effect link between a psychological "event" and a psychophysiological change than with an immunologic change because the former are temporally close to the psychological event.

Kneier and Temoshok (1984) used a *combination* measure of relatively low self-reported perturbation in response to an experimental stressor in conjunction with relatively high physiological arousal (skin conductance) to define a "repressive coping reaction." We found that malignant melanoma patients, matched with cardiovascular disease patients with equivalent physician-rated prognosis, were significantly more "repressive," as well as significantly more "repressive" than non-patient controls.

Another method, using only self-report measures, was inspired by a non-cancer study by Weinberger et al. (1979), who used the Marlowe-Crowne Social Desirability Scale (M-C) in conjunction with the Taylor Manifest Anxiety Scale (MAS) to discriminate four groups: "truly high anxious" (low M-C, high MAS), "truly low anxious" (low M-C, low MAS), "repressors" (high M-C, low MAS), and "defensive high anxious" (high M-C, high MAS). We found that malignant melanoma patients categorized as "defensive high anxious" had the worst prognostic indicators, compared to the other three groups (cf. Temoshok & Fox, 1984). The explanation offered above concerning the added stress of feeling emotionally overwhelmed or out of control would also apply to an understanding of why melanoma patients who were categorized as "defensive high anxious" in this study would have more negative prognostic indicators than those otherwise categorized. In other words, the individual who has a defensive style of repressing negative thoughts (high Marlowe-Crowne) in conjunction with high current anxiety (high Taylor MAS) may bear the full physiological brunt of the physical and psychosocial stressors of a cancer diagnosis.

Concluding Comments

Most of the theoretical and methodological issues raised in this chapter have emerged from thinking about the results of my own studies on malignant melanoma and Human Immunodeficiency Virus, and secondarily, from trying to reconcile my own work with the literature. Thus, my critical stance derives from experience in looking at my own conclusions – and my revisions of these conclusions – as I have been faced with inconsistencies, discrepancies, non-replications, and puzzles. I would hope that one or two of my theoretical or methodological musings on the subject of emotions and health outcomes will touch a familiar chord in colleagues doing similar research, and perhaps strike a new investigator in this challenging field as interesting to test.

References

Ader, R., Felten, D. L., & Cohen, N. (Eds.). (1991). *Psychoneuroimmunology II.* Orlando, FL: Academic Press.

Cassileth, B.R., Lusk, E.J., Miller, D.S., Brown, L.L., & Miller, C. (1985). Psychosocial correlates of survival in advanced maligant disease? *New England Journal of Medicine, 312,* 1551-1555.

Derogatis, L.R., Abeloft, M. D., & Metlisaratos, N. (1979). Psychobiological coping mechanisms and survival time in metastatic breast cancer. *Journal of the American Medical Association, 242,* 1504-1508.

Esterling, B. A., Antoni, M. H., Kumar, M., & Schneiderman, N. (1990). Emotional repression, stress disclosure responses, and Epstein-Barr Capsid Antigen titers. *Psychosomatic Medicine, 52,* 397-410.

Fawzy, F. I., Cousins, N., Fawzy, N. W., Kemeny, M. E., Elashoff, R., & Morton, D. (1990a). A structured psychiatric intervention for cancer patients. I: Changes over time in methods of coping and affective disturbance. *Archives of General Psychiatry, 47,* 720-725.

Fawzy, F. I., Kemeny, M. E., Fawzy, M. W., Elashoff, R., Morton, D., Cousins, N., & Fahey, J. (1990b). A structured psychiatric intervention for cancer patients. II: Changes over time in immunological measures. *Archives of General Psychiatry, 47,* 729-735.

Fox, B.H., & Temoshok, L. (1988). Mind-body and behavior in cancer incidence. *Advances, 5,* 41-56.

Greer, S., Morris, T., & Pettingale, K. W. (1979). Psychological response to breast cancer: Effect on outcome. *Lancet* (October 13), 785-787.

Gross, J. (1989). Emotional expression in cancer onset and progression. *Social Science and Medicine, 28,* 1239-1248.

Kneier, A.W., & Temoshok, L. (1984). Repressive coping reactions in patients with malignant melanoma as compared to cardiovascular disease patients. *Journal of Psychosomatic Research, 28,* 145-155.

Levy, S. (1983). Host differences in neoplastic risk: Behavioral and social contributors to disease. *Health Psychology, 2,* 21-44.

Pennebaker, J. W. (1992). Inhibition as the linchpin of health. In H. S. Friedman (Ed.), *Hostility, health, and coping.* Washington, D.C.: American Psychological Association.

Shekelle, R. B., Raynar, W. J., Ostfield, A. M., Garron, D. C., Bieliauskas, L. A., Liu, S. C., Maliza, C., & Paul, O. (1981). Psychological depression and 17-year risk of death from cancer. *Psychosomatic Medicine, 43,* 117-125.

Spiegel, D., Bloom, J. R., Kraemer, H. C., & Gottheil, E. (1989). Effect of psychosocial treatment on survival of patients with metastatic breast cancer. *Lancet* (October 14), 888-891.

Temoshok, L. (1983). Emotion, adaptation, and disease: A multidimensional theory. In L. Temoshok, C. van Dyke & L. S. Zegans (Eds.), *Emotions in health and illness: Theoretical and research foundations* (pp. 207-233). New York: Grune & Stratton.

Temoshok, L. (1985). Biopsychosocial studies on cutaneous malignant melanoma: Psychosocial factors associated with prognostic indicators, progression, psychophysiology and tumor-host response. *Social Science and Medicine, 20,* 833-840.

Temoshok, L. (1987). Personality, coping style, emotion, and cancer: Toward an integrative model. *Cancer Surveys, 6,* 837-839.

Temoshok, L. (1988). Psychosocial factors related to outcome in cutaneous malignant melanoma: A matched samples design. In: A. Lobo & A. Tres (Eds.), Psicosomática y Cáncer: 6° Symposium Internacional del Grupo Europeo para la Investigación Psicosomática del Cáncer. Madrid: Ministerio de Sanidad y Consumo.

Temoshok, L. (1990). On attempting to articulate the biopsychosocial model: Psychological-psychophysiological homeostasis. In: H.S. Friedman (Ed.), *Personality and disease* (pp. 203-225). New York: John Wiley & Sons.

Temoshok, L., & Fox, B. H. (1984). Coping styles and other psycosocial factors related to medical status and to prognosis in patients with cutaneous malignant melanoma. In B. H. Fox & B. H. Newberry (Eds.), *Impact of psychoendocrine systems in cancer and immunity* (pp. 86-146). Toronto: C. J. Hogrefe.

Temoshok, L., & Heller, B. W. (1984). On comparing apples, oranges, and fruit salad: A methodological overview of medical outcome studies in psychosocial oncology. In C. L. Cooper (Ed.), *Psychosocial stress and cancer.* Chichester: Wiley.

Traue, H. C., Gottwald, A., Henderson, P. R., & Bakal, D. A. (1985). Nonverbal expressiveness and EMG activity in tension headache sufferers and controls. *Journal of Psychosomatic Research, 29,* 375-381.

Weinberger, D.A., Schwartz, G.E., & Davidson, R.J. (1979). Low-anxious, high-anxious, and repressive coping styles: Psychometric patterns and behavioral and physiological responses to stress. *Journal of Abnormal Psychology, 88,* 369-380.

Index

Authors

A

Acherley, W. 29
Achterberg-Lawlis, J. 134, 142
Ader, R. 247, 255
Agras, W. S. 219
Ahrens, S. 25
Ainsworth, M. D. S. 84, 96
Albin, M. 117, 143
Alexander, E. R. 121, 144
Alexander, F. 7, 8, 25, 147, 148, 158, 180, 181, 182, 193, 213, 218
Allaume, R. 57, 77
Allen, M. T. 200, 201, 202, 218, 224
Allen, R. 219
Alley, T. R. 52
Alloway, T. 29
Allred, K. D. 214, 224
Amsterdam, B. K. 85, 96
Anderson, C. D. 47, 51, 151, 158, 233, 243
Anderson, N. B. 213, 218
Angell, M. 32, 51
Anisman, H. 62, 75
Anstadt, T. 177
Antoni, M. H. 42, 55, 110, 113, 255
Apfel-Savitz, R. 195
Appel, M. A. 151, 158, 159
Appley, M. H. 29, 222
Arnold, W.R. 30
Asendorpf, J. B. 16, 17, 22, 23, 26, 80, 81, 82, 85, 87, 88, 89, 90, 91, 93, 95, 96, 102, 243
Attias, J. 55
Auffermann, G. 186, 193
Averill, J. R. 31, 118, 142

Ax, A. F. 207, 218
Axelrod, J. 71, 76

B

Bagby, R. M. 50, 51, 55
Bagley, C. 160
Bakal, D. A. 246, 256
Baker, J. W. 24, 26
Baker, L. 161
Baldessarini, R. J. 64, 71, 76, 79
Bammer, K. 47, 51
Barchas, J. D. 68, 79
Barger, S. D. 105, 114
Barlow, G. K. 224
Barnes, D. 208, 220
Baron, C. 64, 74, 77
Barrett, R. J. 63, 78
Barten, S. 26
Basler, H. D. 245
Bastiaans, J. 53
Bateman, D. E. 212, 222
Baum, A. 41, 51, 113
Beall, S. K . 114, 157, 161
Beidel, D. C. 109, 115
Bellack, A. S. 216, 223
Belle, D. 106, 113
Bereiter, C. 217, 218
Berkowitz, L. 30, 114, 161
Berler, E. S. 221
Bernard, B. A. 209, 210, 225
Berry, M. 25, 26
Berton, K. 44, 55
Bestmann-Seidel, B. 186, 193
Beyrei., J. 195